D1523721

Grim Fairy Tales

Recent Titles in the
Praeger Series in Political Communication
Robert E. Denton, Jr., *General Editor*

Grim Fairy Tales

The Rhetorical Construction of American Welfare Policy

Lisa M. Gring-Pemble

Praeger Series in Political Communication

Westport, Connecticut
London

Library of Congress Cataloging-in-Publication Data

Gring-Pemble, Lisa M.
  Grim fairy tales : the rhetorical construction of American welfare policy / Lisa
M. Gring-Pemble.
      p. cm.—(Praeger series in political communication, ISSN 1062–5623)
    Includes bibliographical references and index.
    ISBN 0–275–97870–2 (alk. paper)
    1. Public welfare—United States. 2. Welfare state. 3. United States—Social
policy. I. Title. II. Series.
HV95.G697   2003
361.6'0973—dc21   2003054720

British Library Cataloguing in Publication Data is available.

Library of Congress Catalog Card Number: 2003054720
ISBN: 0–275–97870–2
ISSN: 1062–5623

First published in 2003

Praeger Publishers, 88 Post Road West, Westport, CT 06881
An imprint of Greenwood Publishing Group, Inc.
www.praeger.com

Printed in the United States of America

The paper used in this book complies with the
Permanent Paper Standard issued by the National
Information Standards Organization (Z39.48–1984).

10 9 8 7 6 5 4 3 2 1

Copyright Acknowledgments

The author and publisher gratefully acknowledge permission to reprint: "Are We
Going to Now Govern by Anecdote?: Rhetorical Constructions of Welfare Recipi-
ents in Congressional Hearings, Debates, and Legislation, 1992–1996" by Lisa M.
Gring-Pemble in *Quarterly Journal of Speech* (November 2001). Used by permis-
sion of the National Communication Association, "Legislating a 'Normal, Classic
Family': the Rhetorical Construction of Families in American Welfare Policy" by
Lisa Gring-Pemble in *Political Communication 20:* 4, http://www.tandf.co.uk.

To Geoffrey, with love

Contents

Series Foreword

Those of us from the discipline of communication studies have long believed that communication is prior to all other fields of inquiry. In several other forums, I have argued that the essence of politics is talk, or human interaction.[1] Such interaction may be formal or informal, verbal or nonverbal, public or private, but it is always persuasive, forcing us consciously or subconsciously to interpret, to evaluate, and to act. Communication is the vehicle for human action.

From this perspective, it is not surprising that Aristotle recognized the natural kinship of politics and communication in his writings *Politics* and *Rhetoric*. In the former, he established that humans are "political beings [who] alone of the animals [are] furnished with the faculty of language."[2] In the latter, he began his systematic analysis of discourse by proclaiming that "rhetorical study, in its strict sense, is concerned with the modes of persuasion."[3] Thus, it was recognized more than 2,300 years ago that politics and communication go hand in hand because they are essential parts of human nature.

In 1981, Dan Nimmo and Keith Sanders proclaimed that political communication was an emerging field.[4] Although its origin, as noted, dates back centuries, a "self-consciously cross-disciplinary" focus began in the late 1950s. Thousands of books and articles later, colleges and universities now offer a variety of graduate and undergraduate course work in the area in such diverse departments as communication, mass communication, journalism, political science, and sociology.[5] In Nimmo and Sanders's early assessment, the "key areas of inquiry" included rhetorical analyses, propaganda analyses, attitude change studies, voting studies, government and the news media, functional and systems analyses, technological changes, media technologies, campaign techniques, and research techniques.[6] In a survey of the state of the field in 1983, the same authors and Lynda Kaid found additional, more specific areas of concern, such as the presidency, political polls, public opinion, debates, and advertising.[7] Since the first study, the authors have also noted a shift away from the rather strict behavioral approach.

A decade later, Dan Nimmo and David Swanson argued that "political communication has developed some identity as a more or less distinct domain of scholarly work."[8] The scope and concerns of the area have further expanded to include critical theories and cultural studies. Although there is no precise definition, method, or disciplinary home of the area of inquiry, its primary domain comprises the role, processes, and effects of communication within the context of politics broadly defined.

In 1985, the editors of *Political Communication Yearbook: 1984* noted that "more things are happening in the study, teaching, and practice of political communication than can be captured within the space limitations of the relatively few publications available."[9] In addition, they argued that the backgrounds of "those involved in the field [are] so varied and pluralist in outlook and approach, ...it [is] a mistake to adhere slavishly to any set format in shaping the content."[10] More recently, Nimmo and Swanson called for "ways of overcoming the unhappy consequences of fragmentation within a framework that respects, encourages, and benefits from diverse scholarly commitments, agendas, and approaches."[11]

In 1988, in agreement with these assessments of the area and with gentle encouragement, Praeger established the Praeger Series in Political Communication, which is open to all qualitative and quantitative methodologies as well as contemporary and historical studies. The key to characterizing the studies in the series is the focus on communication variables or activities within a political context or dimension. As of this writing, more than 80 volumes have been published, and numerous impressive works are forthcoming. Scholars from the disciplines of communication, history, journalism, political science, and sociology have participated in the series.

I am, without shame or modesty, a fan of the series. The joy of serving as its editor is in participating in the dialogue of political communication and in reading the contributors' works. I invite you to join me.

Robert E. Denton, Jr.

NOTES

1. See Robert E. Denton, Jr., *The Symbolic Dimensions of the American Presidency* (Prospect Heights, Ill.: Waveland Press, 1982); Robert E. Denton, Jr., and Gary Woodward, *Political Communication in America* (New York: Praeger, 1985; 2d ed., 1990); Robert E. Denton, Jr., and Dan Hahn, *Presidential Communication* (New York: Praeger, 1986); and Robert E. Denton, Jr., *The Primetime Presidency of Ronald Reagan* (New York: Praeger, 1988).

2. Aristotle, *The Politics of Aristotle,* trans. Ernest Barker (New York: Oxford University Press, 1970), 5.

3. Aristotle, *Rhetoric,* trans. W. Rhys Roberts (New York: The Modern Library, 1954), 22.

4. Dan Nimmo and Keith Sanders, "Introduction: The Emergence of Political Communication as a Field," in *Handbook of Political Communication,* eds. Dan Nimmo and Keith Sanders (Beverly Hills, Calif.: Sage, 1981), 11–36.

5. Ibid., 15.

6. Ibid., 17–27.

7. Keith Sanders, Lynda Kaid, and Dan Nimmo, eds. *Political Communication Yearbook: 1984* (Carbondale: Southern Illinois University Press, 1985), 283–308.

8. Dan Nimmo and David Swanson, "The Field of Political Communication: Beyond the Voter Persuasion Paradigm," in *New Directions in Political Communication,* eds. David Swanson and Dan Nimmo (Beverly Hills, Calif.: Sage, 1990), 8.

9. Sanders, Kaid, and Nimmo, *Political Communication Yearbook: 1984,* xiv.

10. Ibid.

11. Nimmo and Swanson, "The Field of Political Communication," 11.

Preface

From 1992 to 1996, in a series of hearings and debates, congressional representatives and witnesses debated several welfare reform proposals, eventually crafting the controversial 1996 Personal Responsibility and Work Opportunity Reconciliation Act (PRWORA).

Set to expire on October 1, 2002, PRWORA's impending reauthorization prompted considerable congressional discussion. As of the writing of this book, however, PRWORA has not been reauthorized. A series of continuing resolutions has allowed PRWORA to operate beyond the expiration deadline.

Today, many scholars and practitioners have expressed concern over how foreign policy and economic declines will affect welfare reform initiatives. This concern has spawned a multitude of studies to evaluate the effectiveness of recent welfare reforms. How are welfare families faring in an economic downturn? To what extent have the reforms contributed to increased workforce participation, increased earnings, and self-sufficiency on the part of welfare mothers? What effect have the reforms had on teenage pregnancy, marriage, and family formation? These are all important questions worthy of considerable attention.

Nevertheless, one frequently overlooked area of study has been the role of language in shaping policy options, which is the impetus for this book on welfare policy. This book's central goal is to analyze congressional hearings and debates on welfare to understand the role of language in framing welfare policy and contemporary welfare discussions. Through a review of welfare history and a rhetorical analysis of welfare deliberations, this book illustrates the significance of language and ideology in shaping policy outcomes.

Writing this book has been a rewarding challenge. Throughout the course of this project, I have engaged in conversations with a number of scholars and consulted the books, articles, and editorials of many others who work on issues relevant to welfare reform and social policy. I am grateful to all of these individuals who contributed in important ways to the completion of this project. In particular, I want to thank Ron Haskins, former staff director for the Subcommittee on Human Resources of the House Committee on Ways and Means, and David Bradley, executive director for the National Community Action Foundation, both of whom graciously agreed to lengthy interviews. Brookings Institution staff, including Isabel Sawhill and R. Kent Weaver, as well as David L. Featherman, Director of the Institute for Social Research at the University of Michigan, shared relevant research and information. In addition, Cabell S. Brand, founder of Cabell Brand Center on the campus of Roanoke College, was instrumental in connecting me with an important network of scholars and policy makers.

For encouragement and support throughout this project, I am indebted to many colleagues. Special thanks goes to my mentor Martha Solomon Watson (University of Nevada, Las Vegas), Shawn J. Parry-Giles (University of Maryland, College Park), Janette Kenner Muir (George Mason University, New Century College), and Diane M. Blair (California State University, Fresno) for reading and critiquing excerpts from this project. I also wish to thank my colleagues and students at New Century College, George Mason University, for cheerfully collaborating with me in intellectually stimulating learning communities outside the bounds of this project.

For enriching my life and reminding me of what is truly important, I thank my family. I especially wish to thank my parents, David and Susan, for their love, advice and encouragment. It is in honor of my parents, a most extraordinary team, that I write this book. I also want to thank my dear grandfather, Rodney, whose life-long commitment to service and learning is inspiring. My son, Will, brightens my days with his laughter, insatiable curiosity, and amazing sense of wonder for life. Finally, I express my deepest appreciation to my husband and life partner, Geoffrey, to whom this book is dedicated. His constant love, abiding faith, thoughtful intellect, and playful spirit are sources of great joy and comfort.

Part I

The Changing Faces of American Welfare Policy: Historical Roots of Contemporary Welfare Legislation

Chapter 1

Welfare Legislation
Is Symbolic: An Introduction

> What we should attend to...are the discursive practices of policy....
> [T]he important and neglected dimension of welfare policy is sym-
> bolic, and the symbols or interpretations constructed by welfare pol-
> icy discourse are transmitted both by words and arguments about
> policy and by welfare practices. Thus, we cannot understand welfare
> policy and policy science simply as interventions by government to
> alter objective conditions, by manipulating the balance of incentives
> and disincentives attached to work or welfare, for example. Rather,
> policy and policy science are about interpretation.
>
> Frances Fox Piven, 1995, xii

Words and welfare. Stories and public policy. Transcripts from contemporary welfare reform deliberations read like best-selling novels. Woven
throughout the policy transcripts is a compelling narrative, a riveting tale
of heroines like Clarissa Pinkola Estes, a Latina who courageously rose
from the depths of welfare dependence to new heights as a psychoanalyst
with doctoral and postdoctoral degrees (House Committee on Ways and
Means 1995c, 1345). Then there's Jo Sires, a divorced mother of three. After
four years of Aid to Families with Dependent Children (AFDC), this
inventive entrepreneur successfully started her own business, with sales
ranging from $3,000 to $6,000 per month (*Cong. Rec.* 1995, S11761; Senate
Committee on Appropriations 1994b, 37, 38). There are also representatives like Maxine Waters (D-Calif.) and Lynn Woolsey (D-Calif.) whose
current political successes seem to belie their former dependence on public aid.[1] These uplifting stories powerfully reinforce the American dream,
the pull-yourself-up-by-the-bootstraps mentality that assures us that if we
work hard enough and want "it" badly enough, the dream is ours for the
taking.

As with any remarkable tale, however, the stories embedded in policy negotiations also tell of victims and villains. Listen to the tragic story of 17-year-old Ms. Franklin. Living in a windowless shack on the edge of a field with no running water or indoor plumbing, Ms. Franklin was sexually abused by her father for several years before conceiving her first child (House Select Committee on Hunger Domestic Task Force 1992b, 26). There's also Ms. Henderson, an unwed mother of three, who received $723 per month in public assistance. Addicted to crack while pregnant and breastfeeding, she was charged with the murder of her two-month-old infant son, who died from drug-laced breast milk (*Cong. Rec.* 1995, S11778). Gracing the pages of many hearings and debate transcripts is the chilling story of the Chicago Keystone case, in which police officers found 19 children in a filthy, rat-infested, two-room hovel. The four cocaine-addicted mothers of the children squandered their welfare payments to feed their addictions, leaving their children to gnaw on a bone with the family dog (House Committee on Ways and Means 1994a, 521).[2] Like all good fairy tales, these heart-wrenching and painful stories have morals; they warn of the consequences for violating such cherished values as hard work, marriage, and virtuous living.

The stories go even further, as the epigraph to this chapter suggests. The stories structure our collective understanding of both welfare problems and solutions. Through language—anecdotes, metaphors, empirical data—those who testify in the welfare policy deliberations weave a story about welfare. This narrative, in turn, provides policy makers with a framework for interpreting and understanding the complex dynamics of the welfare system. The narrative also offers policy makers evidence to support legislative proposals and policies. Thus, one fundamental guiding assumption of this inquiry is that language plays a significant role in shaping policy outcomes. Indeed, as the following chapters demonstrate, the stories and narratives about welfare recipients, welfare families, and the welfare system exert a powerful influence on both policy proposals and the resulting legislation.

Certainly, other approaches to examining welfare change are both possible and appropriate. For example, scholars have explored the role of public opinion, partisan politics, the press, policy research, and interest groups, among others, in guiding policy decisions. Any of these perspectives "necessarily rests on a simplified model of political life... focusing on what the observer considers the most important causes while paying less attention to others" (Weaver 2000, 23). It is outside the scope of this book to address all of the complex factors that affect welfare policy outcomes. Instead, this book aims to focus on one important and frequently overlooked area of study in the area of welfare reform—the role of language. The role of language in policy formation remains unclear, despite sustained calls to investigate this important relationship.[3]

My purpose in this book is to conduct a case study of a significant piece of legislation, the 1996 Personal Responsibility and Work Opportunity Reconciliation Act, P.L. 104-193 (PRWORA), to contribute to the growing and nascent dialogue on the relationship between rhetoric and public policy.[4] From 1992 to 1996, in a series of hearings and debates, congressional representatives and witnesses deliberated over several welfare reform proposals that eventually culminated in the 1996 act, one of the most controversial social policy reforms in history. The congressional hearings, debates, and subsequent proposals attracted widespread attention from both critics and supporters, initiating heated debates, editorials, opinion polls, protest marches, and policy arguments. *New York Times* reporter Jerry Gray explained in an August 1, 1996, article that many groups, including the U.S. Chamber of Commerce, "hailed the legislation as a reaffirmation of 'America's work ethic.'" "Republican presidential nominee Robert J. Dole praised the bill and said it would be remembered as a Republican victory," reported *Washington Post* correspondent Barbara Vobejda on August 23, 1996. In contrast, reporter Francis X. Clines observed in an August 22, 1996, *New York Times* article that many individuals and groups, such as the nation's Roman Catholic bishops, Children's Defense Fund, National Organization of Women, and Feminist Majority, decried the president's historic signing as a "moment of shame." In an act that "illustrated the deep divisions in the administration over Mr. Clinton's decision to approve the Republican welfare legislation," *New York Times* reporter Alison Mitchell explained in a September 11, 1996, article that several of the Clinton administration's top welfare policy officials—Deputy Assistant Secretary of Human Resources Wendell Primus, Assistant Secretary for Planning and Evaluation Peter Edelman, and Assistant Secretary of Children and Families Mary Jo Bane—resigned in protest over PRWORA's passage. Lauded as "historic welfare legislation… that… rewrites six decades of social policy," and "the most radical overhaul" in welfare policy, the 1996 welfare reform bill officially ended the cash assistance, entitlement-based program, AFDC (Harris and Yang 1996, A1; Vobejda 1996, A1; Weaver 2000, 335–36).

Set to expire on October 1, 2002, PRWORA's impending reauthorization prompted congressional consideration of several proposals. Consistent with the Bush administration's commitment to promoting healthy marriages as a top priority, on May 16, 2002, the House of Representatives passed H.R. 4737, the Personal Responsibility, Work, and Family Act, to encourage marriage [promotion] and responsible fatherhood. Later, on June 26, 2002, the Senate Finance Committee passed a bipartisan reauthorization bill with marriage provisions similar to those in H.R. 4737. This bill never made it to the Senate floor for action, and the expiring 1996 Act was not reauthorized (Parke 2003). A Brookings Institution briefing, from December 11, 2002, explained: "With terrorism and a potential war in Iraq dominating both headlines and politicians' attention, domestic social policy concerns have slipped into the background. Moreover, a worsening federal budget deficit has made it less likely that any costly social policy initiatives can be launched. Congress and the president have not even been able to agree on a reauthorization of the expiring 1996 welfare reform legislation." Currently, many scholars and practitioners have expressed concern over how foreign policy affairs and a troubled economy will affect welfare reform initiatives. If the passage of a GOP bill—H. R., the Personal Responsibility, Work, and Family Act of 2003—by the House on February 13, 2003, is any indication, however, PRWORA will soon be reauthorized in a form similar to the 1996 act, with an even greater emphasis on marriage and work.

This book analyzes the congressional hearings and debates on welfare reform from the 102nd, 103rd, and 104th Congresses to understand how these discursive exchanges shaped PRWORA and how they continue to frame contemporary welfare discussions. Explaining the importance of such an inquiry into the language aspects of welfare reform, political scientist Sanford Schram wrote in his *Words of Welfare:*

[H]ighlighting the ways in which discourse helps construct what is taken to be real, natural, and true creates resources for working toward alternative arrangements.... Welfare policy has therefore not only material consequences in terms of the benefits it supplies. It also has symbolic consequences in reinforcing prevailing understandings of "the poor," "welfare dependency," "dysfunctional families," and so on. In fact, attention to discourse helps show how the symbolic and the material are interrelated. (1995, xxiv)

Indeed, one major goal of this book is to explore the relationship between symbolic talk about welfare and the material consequences of this talk in terms of welfare reform legislation and the lives of welfare recipients.

Because public policies are one powerful vehicle for signaling American values, the hearings and debates surrounding PRWORA provide critics with an appropriate case study to examine the relationship among language, political arguments, and policy formation. Congressional hearings and debates are two important venues for public policy making because they provide a public record of the issues, research, and proposals that ultimately inform legislation (Oleszek 1996, 110–12). In such hearings and debates, the congressional members and participants who testify—public interest groups, policy experts, concerned citizens—articulate their views about a policy issue and together construct a variety of depictions about the problem and potential solutions. Congressional hearings also "suggest something about what sorts of information sources legislators value or at least believe should be provided a forum in which to express their views" (Weaver 2000, 141). The committee report that emerges from these hearings, and that also reflects any amendments to the proposal, becomes the basis for future floor debates in Congress. Thus, in many respects, legislative hearings and debates help frame future policy decisions. Certainly, factors such as partisan politics and negotiations between legislators and special interest groups exert a strong influence on legislative outcomes. Nevertheless, as this study indicates, the link between legislator and witness descriptions of welfare families and corresponding legislation also underscores the significance of language and ideology in shaping policy change.[5]

DEPICTION, NARRATIVE, AND PRESENCE: A FRAMEWORK FOR INQUIRY

Several sets of questions animate this inquiry into how legislators craft public policy and how historical ideologies, narratives, and arguments influence public policy construction.[6] One set of questions facilitates investigation of the historical roots of welfare legislation. How have representations of welfare recipients, welfare providers, and the welfare system evolved throughout American history? How does this historical context frame the hearings and debates over PRWORA and discussions surrounding its subsequent reauthorization? These questions assist in tracing the broad trajectory of welfare reform legislation in American history; they highlight important shifts in public perceptions of welfare, goals of and responsibility for welfare provision, and causes of welfare dependence.

A second set of questions concerns the identification of competing representations (or depictions)[7] of welfare recipients and their families that emerge in the hearings and debates to support various proposals for welfare reform. How do witnesses and legislators depict welfare recipients and their families in the hearings and debates? What arguments and evidence do witnesses and legislators use to warrant these depictions? What values, motives, and assumptions are implicit in these depictions and arguments? These questions assist in acquiring a comprehensive picture of how witnesses and legislators characterize welfare recipients and their families and the roots of the welfare problem.

A third set of questions centers on the role of depictions in social policy making. How do the competing versions of welfare recipients and policy objectives emergent in the hearings and debates play out in enacted legislation? How do the depictions frame the ways legislators can respond in the form of public policies? What are the implications of basing public policy on particular depictions? The objective of this line of inquiry is to assess what this case study of PRWORA can teach about the strengths, weaknesses, values, and pitfalls of the discursive nature of policy making.

A final set of questions interrogates the dynamics of power inherent in the legislative process. How do specific discourse practices and rules in congressional hearings and debates affect the construction of public policy? How does the discourse work to legitimate, privilege, or discount evidence, depictions, and authority? What are the gender, racial, and class implications of the depictions of welfare recipients and their families? These questions seek to unveil the ideological influences in the legislative process by examining how the legislative discourse sustains, challenges, and perpetuates historical values, power relationships, and special interests.

Addressing these questions requires an integrated interdisciplinary approach, drawing on the works of rhetorical theorists, political scientists, feminist scholars, and public policy practitioners. Outlining some of these works provides the methodological and theoretical grounding for the chapters that follow. Specifically, the theories of Michael Osborn, Walter Fisher, and Maurice Charland provide an excellent framework for identifying significant depictions emergent in welfare reform history and contemporary legislative hearings and debates. These works also help assess the influence of the depictions on PRWORA and reauthorization deliberations. Raymie McKerrow's work on critical rhetoric also provides an appropriate theoretical background for uncovering the power dimensions inherent in the legislative process.

Michael Osborn's work on rhetorical depiction seeks to shift the traditional focus of rhetoric from a "study of primarily rational calculations" to one that "emphasizes instead the symbolic moorings of human consciousness." Thus, a focus on depictions "seeks those moments in which audiences encounter significant presentations of reality, and it strives to illuminate the rhetorical implications of such encounters" (1986, 97). The remaining chapters of this book explore "significant presentations of reality" concerning welfare recipients and their attitudes, values, and behaviors as constructed in the hearings and debates. In the end, the chapters demonstrate how these symbolic representations of welfare recipients and their families exert a persuasive force that rivals the traditional rational arguments associated with deliberative hearings.

Defined as "strategic pictures, verbal or nonverbal visualizations that linger in the collective memory of audiences as representative of their subjects," rhetorical depictions perform a vital role in the formation and maintenance of community life, chiefly by embodying accepted cultural values and goals (Osborn, 1986, 79–80). These depictions may assume a variety of forms, including extended anecdotes, metaphors, allegories, and empirical evidence. Taken together, these depictive forms function as brush strokes in painting a vivid portrait of the typical welfare recipient and welfare family. This portrait then serves as the basis for policy formation in the context of a public moral argument.

The lens of depiction complements one of this book's tasks of considering the role of historical context in framing welfare problems and identifying solutions to those welfare problems. Often, "graphic lessons" from the past "lend urgency to present decisions" (93). This book not only attends to depictions of welfare recipients and their families as constructed in the contemporary debate, but it also examines the sociohistorical context of welfare reform in America, from colonial times to the present. As a result, the study illuminates how prevailing characterizations of welfare recipients grounded in historical ideologies and value systems shape resulting legislation.

Another central feature of depictive rhetoric is that depictions imply narratives. Osborn contended that depiction is "more a compression than a reflection. The portrait it offers may express implicitly and simultaneously an assertion concerning the origins of a subject, a prediction of that subject's fate, and the moral stance of the speaker" (79–80). In the context of the welfare reform debate, the depictions of welfare recipients and their families imply welfare narratives. W. Lance Bennett and Murray Edelman made a related point in their study of political narratives: "Just as any narrative is likely to imply a wider set of related stories and an ideology, so a term or a simple reference in any political text may evoke a full-fledged story.... Political communications, then,... are always seedbeds of stories" (1985, 164–165). Similarly, the demographic and character attributes ascribed to welfare recipients in the hearings and debates implicate a more comprehensive story about the past and future behaviors, lifestyles, and aspirations of welfare recipients. Ultimately, these depictions of welfare recipients and their families serve as evidence to support legislative proposals and policies designed to enforce values and desirable behaviors.

In his work on the narrative paradigm, communication theorist Walter Fisher explored how audiences evaluate one form of depictive rhetoric—narratives. The narrative paradigm holds that humans are essentially storytellers who create and communicate stories that form understanding, guide collective reasoning, and shape behavior. "[S]ymbols are created and communicated ultimately as stories meant to give order to human experience and to induce others to dwell in them to establish ways of living in common, in communities in which there is sanction for the story that constitutes one's life" (Fisher 1984, 6). According to Fisher, narration is the dominant mode of human communication and is particularly well suited to evaluating public moral argument such as welfare reform deliberations. "No matter how rigorously a case is argued—scientifically, philosophically, or legally—it will always be a story, an interpretation of some aspect of the world which is historically and culturally grounded and shaped by human personality" (Fisher 1987, 17). Consequently, Fisher believed that the narrative paradigm is the best way to account for how and why people adopt particular stories to create meaning and guide collective action.

In addition to inferring narratives, depictions also imply an ideal audience, or those individuals who would accept the assumptions, values, and narratives embedded in the rhetoric.[8] According to Osborn, "We experience the world either directly or through depictions, and even direct experience can be mediated and predisposed by previous depictions that prepare us for the experience." These "repetitive presentations" draw on deeply seated cultural values that "imply shared evaluative outlooks, which are a necessary condition to mass cooperative action" (1986, 81, 82). As such, depictions are constitutive: They implicate an ideal audience and commit the audience to act in accordance with the narrative logic inherent in the depictions.

Maurice Charland described this process of constitutive rhetoric in greater detail through an analysis of the White Paper and the *Peuple Québécois*. He argued that when individuals recognize themselves as participants in a historical narrative, they become "constituted as a subject in a narrative...constituted with a history, motives, and a *telos*" (1987, 140). Charland explained that constitutive rhetoric acquires this power to frame audience responses because of its ideological nature: "The power of the text is the power of an embodied ideology. The form of an ideological rhetoric is effective because it is within the bodies of those it constitutes as subjects.... Ideology is material because subjects enact their ideology and reconstitute their material world in its image" (143). This passage calls attention to the influence of ideology in decision-making processes. In the case of welfare reform legislation, when legislators and witnesses assent to characterizations of welfare recipients, they also subscribe to the narrative suggested by the depictions. In turn, the logic of the welfare narrative encourages legislators to act consistently with the motives, values, and assumptions embedded in the narrative. Legislator actions are manifested materially in the form of legislation based on the depictions of welfare recipients and their families.

Rhetorical theorist Raymie E. McKerrow (1989) offered a more comprehensive account of how to explore the ideological and power dynamics of discourse in his article "Critical Rhetoric: Theory and Praxis." McKerrow articulated a perspective of critical rhetoric that seeks to understand how discourse creates, sustains, and challenges the social practices that order people's lives. Strongly influenced by Michel Foucault, McKerrow's "Critical Rhetoric" acknowledges that discourse maintains existing power relations through discourse rules and "taken-for-granted" processes that govern who may speak, which topics are appropriate to address, and what counts as authoritative evidence (93).

As is evident in the following chapters, discourse rules surrounding welfare reform hearings and legislation empower dominant social relations in three important ways. First, as demonstrated in chapters 2 and 3, centuries of welfare legislation provide a long history of taken-for-granted discourse that privileges social faith in traditional values. McKerrow explained: "The discourse of power creates and perpetuates the relations, and gives form to the ideology which it projects. Ideology, regardless of its expression, begins with these social relations as integral to its creation.... Power is expressed anonymously, in nondeliberate ways, at a 'deep structure' level and may have its origins in the remoteness of our past (carried forward through a particularizing discursive formation)" (1989, 99). Similarly, this book shows how the historical context surrounding the welfare reform deliberations lends presence to certain values that support existing power relations and structures. Chaim Perelman and L. Olbrechts-Tyteca defined the concept of presence in their comprehensive study of argumentation, *The New Rhetoric: A Treatise on Argumentation,* as the process by which speakers enhance the significance of certain elements of their message in the minds of their audiences: "[O]ne of the preoccupations of a speaker is to make present, by verbal magic alone, what is actually absent but what he considers important to his argument or, by making them more present, to enhance the value of some of the elements of which one has actually been made conscious" (1971, 117).[9] Relying on the concept of presence, chapters 2 and 3 illustrate how the historical context of welfare in America lends presence to such values as work, family, and individual responsibility, enhancing the primacy of those values in the minds of witnesses and legislators.

Second, legislative discourse privileges some testimony as authoritative and discounts other forms of evidence as irrelevant. McKerrow explained that "discourse insinuates itself in the fabric of social power and thereby 'effects' the status of knowledge among the members of the social group" (1989, 92). In the case of welfare, the largely unfavorable depictions of welfare recipients and their families justify the exclusion of welfare recipient testimony from the hearings and debates with few exceptions. In contrast, welfare scholars, legislators, religious leaders, and welfare program managers receive considerable time on hearings panels, guaranteeing an audience for their views.

Third, discourse rules of the legislative process also favor dominant ideologies. Explaining this phenomenon in *The Archaeology of Knowledge and Discourse on Language,* Michel Foucault noted that "in every society the production of discourse is at once controlled, selected, organised and redistributed according to a certain number of procedures whose role is to avert its powers and its dangers, to cope with chance events, to evade its ponderous, awesome materiality" (1972, 216). As explained in chapter 3, the Republican party dominated the 104th Congress. As a result of this plurality, Republican leaders were afforded the privilege of selecting the majority of the witnesses and determining the order and structure of the hearings panels. In a Foucaultian manner, the Republicans largely controlled who could speak and on what topic, and they invited groups of witnesses whom they knew would support the Republican welfare reform plan.

Ultimately, this book makes several important contributions relevant to theorists and practitioners interested in rhetoric and public policy. First, the book provides an extensive account of how depictions (representations of welfare recipients and their families) function in public moral argument, thereby expanding our knowledge of depictive rhetoric. Second, this book makes a significant contribution to narrative theory, demonstrating that some narratives powerfully constrain an audience's ability to judge stories critically and may encourage elitist arguments. Third, this study builds on Perelman and Olbrechts-Tyteca's concept of presence, demonstrating how presence can be achieved with multiple rhetors and multiple texts. This book also suggests that historical context can accomplish presence. In the case of welfare, the historical context surrounding reform deliberations frames the legislative process, providing a conceptual backdrop upon which legislators test and refine their ideas. This historical conceptual field acts as a filter that privileges certain forms of argument as authoritative and dismisses others as inconsequential. In the end, this book contributes to a theory of congressional rhetoric, contending that historical context and rhetorical depictions, not the quality of the arguments, may exert more persuasive appeal in the construction of social policy.

ORGANIZATION OF THE BOOK

This book is divided into three sections. Part I, "The Changing Faces of American Welfare Policy: Historical Roots of Contemporary Welfare Legislation," provides the sociohistorical context for the study. The argument developed in this first part is that the historical depictions of welfare recipients, providers, and the system continue to shape the contemporary welfare debate and legislative activity, lending presence to values of work, family, faith, and individual responsibility.

Chapter 2, "American Social Welfare Policy in Context, 1600–1935," chronicles the story of welfare reform from colonial America to the 1935 Social Security Act reforms. It also provides an account of significant steps in welfare reform debates, including societal views about welfare and the legislative acts that punctuate public opinion and perceptions. During this period, responsibility for public assistance evolved from familial and local obligations to state efforts and, eventually, to national federal initiatives.

Building on chapter 2, the third chapter, "American Social Welfare Policy in Context, 1936–2003," recounts the story of welfare reform in America following the 1935 Social Security Act to the 1996 Personal Responsibility and Work Opportunity Reconciliation Act and reauthorization discussions. Throughout this period, responsibility for welfare reform devolved from largely federal initiatives to state and local efforts. Chapter 3 presents a view of contemporary welfare policies as a realization or encapsulation of sociohistorical views on welfare.

Part II, "Rhetorical Constructions of Welfare Recipients and Welfare Families in U.S. Congressional Hearings, Debates, and Legislation," focuses on the central representations of welfare recipients that are emergent in contemporary legislative deliberations. Chapter 4, "'Are We Going to Now Govern by Anecdote?': A Portrait of the Misfortunate, the Feckless, the Young, and the Fathers," examines four prominent depictions of welfare recipients constructed in the hearings and debates. Relying on a narrative approach, this study challenges the democratic and participatory functions of the narrative paradigm as conceived by Walter Fisher. The central argument developed in this chapter is that some narrative forms facilitate elite discourse, discourage the inclusion of alternative public views, and delegitimate particular public voices.

Chapter 5, "Legislating a 'Normal Classic Family': The Rhetorical Construction of Families in American Welfare Policy," discusses the policy construction of mothers, fathers, and families on welfare. The chapter reviews how, throughout the legislative process, witnesses and legislators have related stories about families on welfare and compared welfare families with an ideal nuclear family. The main argument of the chapter is that centuries-old depictions of welfare families influence legislation that affirms a historically privileged family structure based on the family-wage model. Chapter 5 demonstrates that the ideologically driven legislation that promotes marriage has profound implications in terms of race, gender, and class. The chapter further contends that contemporary welfare legislation is ill equipped to address the material situations of many impoverished families.

Part III, "The Rhetorical Force of Depiction in American Welfare Policy," examines the persuasive force of anecdotal evidence in the construction of the 1996 PRWORA and its subsequent reauthorization proposals. Chapter 6, "In Search of an Exigence to Warrant Welfare Reform: Public Opinion, Policy Research, and Anecdotal Evidence," explores the role of different forms of evidence in welfare policy deliberations. Throughout the congressional hearings and debates, legislators had access to a considerable body of policy research and public opinion. A discursive examination of the congressional hearings and debates on welfare, however, suggests that policy research and public opinion played a surprisingly limited role in warranting policy changes in the 1996 act and subsequent reauthorization proposals. Instead, legislators privileged depictions as sources of evidence, even when the depictions were not supported, and in some cases were contradicted, by other kinds of evidence. Consequently, this chapter underscores the significant evidentiary value of depictions as warrants for public policy.

The final chapter, chapter 7, "American Welfare Policy and the Ineluctable Appeal of Language: Conclusion and Implications," explores the implications of this study for rhetorical theorists and for public policy practitioners. In particular, this chapter summarizes the dynamics of power inherent in public policy formation by reviewing how the historical welfare context, legislative rules and procedures, and rhetorical depictions function together to legitimate or discredit specific kinds of testimony, evidence, and arguments. The link among historical values, depictions of welfare recipients and families, and the corresponding legislation evinces the significance of language and ideology in shaping policy change. Indeed, as chapter 7 concludes, historical context and rhetorical depictions may exert even greater rhetorical force than traditional arguments associated with deliberative hearings in determining the forms of evidence legislators perceive as salient and the policy solutions legislators perceive as effective.

NOTES

1. For example, on several occasions in both the hearings and debates, Representative Lynn C. Woolsey (D-Calif.) testified about her own experience getting off of welfare: "During the three-year period that I relied on these [welfare] programs, I always knew that I had an advantage over other welfare recipients, an advantage that enabled me to make it through the welfare system. First, my children and I were very healthy,... I was also educated and you have to know I was assertive" (House Committee on Government Operations 1994, 3, 6; *Cong. Rec.* 1995, H3377). Representative Maxine Waters (D-Calif.) also related her welfare experience: "There is nothing wrong with welfare children. There is nothing wrong with welfare parents. Some of us do make it to Congress, where we can speak up for welfare families and talk about what is really needed" (House Committee on Ways and Means 1994a, 587; *Cong. Rec.* 1995, H3772). See also the related comments of Wisconsin State Representative Antonio Riley (D): "As a former welfare recipient myself, and now as a representative of some of the poorest central city neighborhoods in Wisconsin, I am intimately familiar with the affects of welfare on real people in real life" (Senate Committee on Finance 1994b, 34).

2. This case is also referenced in the following hearings and debates: House Committee on Ways and Means 1995b, 534; 1995g, 119; *Cong. Rec.* 1995, H3382, H3506.

3. Despite several studies on public policy debates and legislation, communication scholars have not yet examined the negotiation and construction of public policy as a *rhetorical process*, beginning with bill proposals, congressional hearings, and congressional debates. Making a similar point, Janice Schuetz noted in her study of legislative argumentation that research in the communication discipline "seldom examines a large segment of the political process or the development of one argument through the hierarchy of the decisional process" (1986, 223). Going further, Craig Allen Smith and Kathy B. Smith contended, "Scholars have rarely studied the rhetoric of political institutions.... It should, therefore, come as no surprise that there is, as yet, no theory of...congressional rhetoric" (1990, 251). More recently, rhetorical scholar Linda Miller concluded that despite a few empirical studies of public controversies in legislative contexts, "the relationship between public argument and policy change remains unclear." Consequently, she called for "further analysis of the formation of a variety of public policies at the municipal, state or federal legislative levels" (1999, 375).

4. As a series of discursive practices that eventually became codified into law, the congressional hearings and debates over welfare reform merit careful consideration by communication scholars because they provide insight into the policy formation process. As Cynthia Cooper noted in her study of congressional hearings over television violence, "Congressional hearings may be a window into legislative policy making. Ever since the first hearing was held in 1792,... subcommittee hearings have been an important tool for information-gathering essential to informed decision making" (1996, 11). Indeed, over several centuries, communication scholars have developed a sustained and lively interest in the relationship between rhetoric and public policy. Early accounts of oratory reflect an emphasis on public speaking in the deliberative arena (Kennedy 1980, 3–40). In his *Art of Rhetoric,* Aristotle claimed that legislation is one of "the most important questions upon which the would-be deliberative orator must be well informed" (1.4:13). In more recent years, communication scholars have refined and expanded policy-making studies, investigating the specific role of rhetoric in public policy formation. A clear example of this sustained commitment is the 1998 inauguration of *Rhetoric & Public Affairs*, which has a mission statement welcoming manuscripts that explore "traditional arenas of rhetorical investigation" including "executive leadership, diplomacy, political campaigns, judicial and legislative deliberations, and public policy debate."

5. Other studies that highlight the role of language in policy formation include Edelman 1977, 1988; Fineman 1995, 20–24; Halloran 1978; and Schram 1995, 2000.

6. I take my definition of narrative from Walter Fisher (1995), who stated that when narratives are not the master term of rhetoric, they are a rhetorical "figure: simply storytelling, an art, a mode of expression, or a genre" (170). Chaim Perelman's and L. Olbrechts-Tyteca's definition of argument is appropriate for the purposes of this study. According to Perelman and Olbrechts-Tyteca, "efficacious" arguments are structures (methods and proof) that succeed in increasing an audience's adherence to claims "in such a way as to set in motion the intended action...or at least in creating in the hearers a willingness to act which will appear at the right moment" (1971, 45, 47). Rhetors achieve this goal by making one choice seem rational through an appeal to shared objects of agreement and inference rules (62).

7. Drawing on Osborn's work on depictive rhetoric, I define "depictions" as strategic pictures that vividly and powerfully portray common values and goals (1986, 79). Depictions may exist as single words or they may encompass anecdotes and short stories. For instance, the term "welfare queen" implies a story of a dysfunctional welfare recipient who is unskilled and uneducated, bears multiple children, and takes advantage of the welfare system. Similarly, short stories about specific welfare recipients may also serve as depictive rhetoric.

8. This implied audience is discussed in greater detail in Edwin Black's (1970) "Second Persona."

9. Michael Osborn also addressed the concept of presence (1986, 80).

Chapter 2

American Social Welfare Policy in Context, 1600–1935

> Public welfare has been a political concern virtually from the moment public responsibility for the poor was codified in the Elizabethan poor laws of 1600.... In important respects, the character of the welfare debate has not changed much over time. The tenor of the debate endures because it touches upon the most sensitive of societal issues: work, family, sex, abortion, personal responsibility, and community integrity. It is a proxy for fundamental questions about the quality of life in society and about how to allocate personal and public responsibilities.
>
> Corbett 1995, 43

Throughout American history, public officials, scholars, and concerned citizens have debated key components of the welfare system, including the root causes of welfare dependency (e.g., individual behaviors, structural barriers); the goals of welfare reform (e.g., poverty reduction, self-sufficiency, aid to children); the best methods for achieving welfare reform (e.g., penalties or rewards, job training programs, behavioral modification); and the most cost-effective and results-oriented forms of intervention (e.g., national government legislation, charitable responses, state and local programs). Embedded in these discussions are competing depictions about welfare recipients, including their behaviors, attitudes, values, and beliefs. These diverse views of welfare recipients, in turn, shape public perceptions of who deserves welfare and who does not, what are appropriate forms of welfare, and who has social responsibility for providing public aid. These perceptions of welfare are gradually institutionalized in the form of local, state, and national policies, such as the Elizabethan Poor Laws, the Social Security Act of 1935, the Family Support Act of 1988, and,

more recently, the Personal Responsibility and Work Opportunity Reconciliation Act of 1996 (PRWORA). Even as these policies and laws specify
causes of poverty, typical welfare recipients, and the goals of welfare
reforms, they also legitimate, indeed codify, American values and ethics.

This chapter traces various narratives of welfare reform in American
history that are embedded in welfare legislation. Specifically, the chapter
surveys three centuries of welfare reform legislation, from 1600 to 1935.
The aim of this historical review is not to identify new historical material
on welfare but rather to describe a general framework for the representations of welfare recipients that powerfully shape welfare legislation. This
general framework provides the historical background and context to analyze the congressional hearings over the PRWORA.

Notably, one of the arguments of chapters 2 and 3 is that the historical
context of welfare reform in America lends presence to certain values (e.g.,
values about family and work). These values exert a powerful influence
on the contemporary hearings, debates, and resulting legislation. The contextual frame predisposes legislators and witnesses to interpret information in particular ways. Chaim Perelman defined the concept of presence
in *The Realm of Rhetoric:* "Every argument implies a preliminary selection
of facts and values, their specific description in a given language, and an
emphasis which varies with the importance given them.... Choosing to
single out certain things for presentation in a speech draws the attention
of the audience to them and thereby gives them a *presence* that prevents
them from being neglected" (1982, 34–35, emphasis in original). According to Perelman, individual rhetors can accomplish presence in three
ways: (1) through data selection, (2) through data interpretation, and (3)
through stylistic figures. For example, every argument involves a "preliminary selection of elements that are to serve as the starting point of the
argument...By the very fact of selecting certain elements and presenting
them to the audience, their importance and pertinency to the discussion
are implied. Indeed, such a choice endows these elements with *presence*,
which is an essential factor in argumentation and one that is far too
much neglected in rationalistic conceptions of reasoning" (1971, 115–116,
emphasis in original). In addition to selecting data, rhetors can also
emphasize one interpretation of events over another, thereby encouraging
audiences to see some interpretations as favorable, or more present, than
others (121–22). Furthermore, through stylistic techniques, or "forms of
expression" such as rhythm, for example, rhetors can distinguish certain
accounts in the minds of their hearers (143).

This discussion of welfare reform history suggests a fourth way presence is accomplished—through historical context. Certainly, Perelman
recognized the importance of context: "[E]very conceptual thought is
inserted into frameworks that are already completely formed, which one

must use and manipulate so as best to serve the necessities of action upon others" (1971, 127). Building on Perelman's work, this book demonstrates how such a preexisting framework can lend presence to particular values and beliefs, influence data selection, and bias data interpretation. Indeed, the very context constrains possibilities for what legislators in contemporary debates can make present.

This chapter continues with a discussion of the meaning of welfare and some of the major themes in welfare policy that span American history, from colonial times to the present. The chapter then explores how prevailing social depictions of welfare recipients, welfare providers, and the welfare system in general, as well as the motives and values ascribed to those depictions, shaped public policies and legislation from 1600 to 1935. After addressing the Elizabethan Poor Laws in England and colonial America, this chapter examines other major welfare public policies, including the nineteenth-century Poor Law reforms, mothers' pensions, and the Social Security Act of 1935.

THE CHANGING FACES OF AMERICAN WELFARE POLICY: CENTRAL ISSUES

> Americans have a long history of helping the poor and just as long a history of trying to ensure that those who receive our help are deserving of it. (Cammisa 1998, 59)

Before addressing central themes in American social welfare policy, I want to clarify what I mean by the term "welfare." I use this term broadly to refer to private charity, volunteer organization, and local, state, and federal government programs designed to provide public assistance to poor families. I include in my definition such assistance programs as almshouses (long-term facilities of employment, housing for those unable to work, and free hospitals), mothers' pensions, and AFDC. Although they might be just as accurately labeled welfare (and theoretically are forms of welfare), many government programs designed to improve the well-being of citizens remain outside the scope of this study and are therefore not included in my definition of welfare. Because program benefits such as Medicare, social security, home mortgage tax deductions, medical expense deductions, corporate subsidies, and capital gains tax limits are associated with employment, the American public typically characterizes these program benefits not as welfare but rather as acceptable social insurance and earned entitlements.

A brief journey through American welfare policy history from colonial times to the present reveals four central and recurrent themes. Stated as questions, the major themes are, Who or what is responsible for poverty?

Who should provide assistance? What are the goals of aid? Who deserves assistance and for what reasons? Throughout history, concerned citizens, government officials, and welfare recipients have engaged in vigorous debates to answer these questions (Cammisa 1998, 25). The answers to the questions shape public perceptions of social welfare as well as welfare legislation.

In an attempt to answer the first question of who is responsible for poverty, the American public has typically focused either on the individuals themselves or institutional structures. The notions of individualism, self-determination, free will, and personal responsibility have their roots in the Protestant tradition. Popular myths and stories of the American dream, Horatio Alger, and manifest destiny support a profound belief in the power of individuals to overcome adverse situations and succeed through hard work and self-determination. In times of public faith in individualism, welfare policies fault individual character flaws, such as indolence and immorality, for poverty. As a result, the policies stress the need for rehabilitating individuals and deterring deviant poor from a life of dependency.

For a variety of reasons, individualistic explanations for poverty are not always privileged. Particularly in times of economic distress, such as the Great Depression, the public blames poverty on flaws inherent in institutional structures. From this perspective, the government must intervene with legislation to serve as a safety net for individuals who experience periodic bouts of economic misfortune despite their best efforts. As public perceptions increasingly favor structural causes of poverty, welfare policies emerge to provide all individuals with the opportunities to succeed. Instead of punitive measures associated with individualistic explanations, structural interpretations favor direct relief (e.g., cash and in-kind assistance) as well as policies (e.g., social insurance) designed to prevent depraved conditions. Significantly, however, both individualistic and structural explanations for poverty are predicated on the same underlying philosophy. Both strategies assume that individuals will be able to overcome adversity through their own efforts after either they or the system reforms.

A second and related theme in welfare history concerns questions of who is responsible for providing aid. Since colonial times, welfare policies have specified a number of different aid providers: private charities, volunteer organizations, and local, state, or federal governments. As welfare policy scholar Anne Marie Cammisa insightfully observed, the question of who should provide aid closely correlates with who or what is responsible for poverty.

The first [philosophy] focuses on the ability of an individual to succeed in a free market economy. In a capitalist society, individualism and free choice are valued, and the government is expected to intervene as little as possible in the economic decisions of individuals. Too much government interference stifles creativity and innovation and encourages laziness.... The second philosophy, community, posits that individuals must take responsibility for one another. The idea of community is based on the Judeo-Christian tradition that runs through much of American social thought. Those who are well-off have a responsibility to take care of those who are less fortunate. As a community, if one of our number is in difficulty, we are under an obligation to help him or her. Community begets charity. (1998, 17)

Further complicating the issue of relief provision is America's faith in federalism and suspicion of big government. Of particular relevance to postcolonial welfare policies is that the U.S. Constitution does not grant the federal government jurisdiction over relief. Because all powers not directly accorded to the federal government devolve to the states, relief is implicitly a state government responsibility (Axinn and Stern 2001, 37; Katz 1996, 225). At various points in history, however, when state and local relief efforts have been insufficient to combat systemic poverty, negotiating a relief partnership between federal and state governments has been important. Increased state and federal government roles in relief provision invariably affect the extent and nature of local and volunteer activities. As will be evident in the following survey of welfare legislation, American welfare policies rely, to varying degrees, on many different relief providers and relief strategies.

A third recurring theme in social welfare policy is a struggle over the goals of assistance. At different times in American history, welfare policy has attempted to perform one or more of the following functions to prevent poverty: assist needy individuals, reform recalcitrant individuals, or deter unworthy individuals from applying for aid.[1] Welfare polices that reflect goals of assistance frequently offer aid to poor individuals in the form of cash benefits or in-kind relief, such as food or shelter. In theory at least, such policies correct for personal tragedies (loss of breadwinner) or structural problems (economic recession) by providing a living wage to qualified individuals. Other policies attempt to reform individuals by making benefits contingent on behavioral modification. For instance, welfare policies may mandate participation in counseling or work training programs as a condition of receiving assistance. A final major function of relief reflected in welfare policies is deterrence. As the quotation at the start of this section suggests, a major dilemma of welfare policy is providing adequate care for people who genuinely require assistance while simultaneously deterring those who are perceived as not requiring assistance from aid applications. Punitive in nature, deterrence policies endeavor to make welfare undesirable to potential applicants through such measures as tedious application procedures, intense supervision, and strict work requirements. As is evident by a long history of welfare policy reforms, welfare legislation has not yet satisfactorily achieved assistance, deterrence, and reformation objectives.

A fourth and final major theme that runs throughout American welfare history is assessing who deserves aid. Phrasing the issue in a slightly different manner, law professor Joel Handler and social welfare professor Yeheskel Hasenfeld commented: "[T]he heart of welfare policy centers on the question of who is excused from work—who can claim material support that is not the product of his or her own effort. In short, when is the failure to support oneself and one's family justified?" (1991, 16). The question of who deserves aid is a significant one, especially when a more obvious question may be, Who needs aid? Unfortunately, in American welfare policy history, the truly needy do not always correlate to the truly deserving. In other words, social constructions of deserving poor do not include all people who live at or below subsistence levels. Thus, to speak of social welfare policy at any point in time is to speak of the deserving poor (worthy of public aid) and the undeserving poor (unworthy of public aid).

Worthy poor are defined as the people who are poor through no fault of their own. Generally, those people we consider worthy poor have fallen into poverty because of age, temporary unemployment, or disability.... The *unworthy poor,* on the other hand, are those whom society sees as responsible for their own poverty, or at least as capable of getting themselves out of poverty. (Cammisa 1998, 5, emphasis in original)

Although the two categories have remained constant from colonial times to the present, the types of people considered worthy or unworthy have changed. Debates over worthy and unworthy poor also invariably include discussions about who is considered able-bodied and, thus, a part of the labor force. Because they are able-bodied and at least theoretically capable of earning a living wage, some individuals are labeled unworthy of public assistance. In contrast, individuals defined as incapable of earning an income to support themselves and their families are usually viewed as worthy of public assistance.

The criteria that various publics have used to determine worthy and unworthy status are fraught with racial, gender, and class overtones. For instance, in colonial times, black men, women, and children were automatically excluded from welfare policy, implicitly making them unworthy of assistance. Later welfare policies maintained racial prejudice through settlement laws and by excluding black-dominated professions, such as domestic servants and agricultural workers, from social insurance coverage. Today, with few exceptions, legal and illegal immigrants are largely excluded from public assistance.[2] Welfare policies also exhibit a gender bias by creating categories of deserving and undeserving women. Unwed, divorced, and separated mothers, particularly those of marginalized groups, have engaged in a centuries-old struggle to achieve legitimacy as deserving poor in welfare policies. Moreover, at various points in history, prevailing social views have defined certain categories of women as worthy or unworthy of public assistance, based on racial, gender, and class biases. In general, widowed, middle- and upper-class, white mothers have been considered outside of the labor force and, therefore, worthy of public assistance. In contrast, lower-class, minority, unwed, divorced, and separated mothers have been defined implicitly as able-bodied laborers and, by association, unworthy of public assistance. In an attempt to identify and eliminate the unworthy from welfare rolls, racial, gender, and class biases have infiltrated nearly every major piece of American social welfare legislation. As Michael B. Katz summarized in his historical account of welfare reform, "Indeed, it is only a slight exaggeration to say that the core of most welfare reform in America since the early nineteenth century has been a war on the able-bodied poor: an attempt to define, locate, and purge them from the rolls of relief" (1996, 19). In many ways, the same statement holds true today.

All of these major themes have become woven into the fabric of public welfare legislation. Tracing each major thread through significant pieces of legislation provides a glimpse into prevailing social views of the welfare system that inform both historic and contemporary public policies. Each of the following sections begins by juxtaposing two quotations. The first is from the period being discussed, and the second is from deliberations surrounding the 1996 act. The comparisons exhibit a striking resemblance, illustrating how historical ideologies pervade contemporary policy deliberations.

TRACING CENTRAL WELFARE ISSUES IN HISTORIC WELFARE LEGISLATION

The Elizabethan Poor Laws in England and America

> And be it further enacted, That the father and grandfather, and the mother and grandmother, and the children of very poor, old, blind, lame and impotent person, or other poor person not able to work, being of a sufficient ability, shall, at their own charges, relieve and maintain every such poor person in that manner. (An Act for the Relief of the Poor, 43 Elizabeth, 1601, quoted in Axinn and Stern 2001, 11)

> *Welfare Reform Through Kinship Care:*...Currently, most welfare programs look only at the cash income of the custodial single parent without regard to the availability of voluntary kinship or extended family assistance. The attached proposal provides that welfare eligibility should be determined by examining all resources that are available voluntarily through the child's kinship network. (House Committee on Ways and Means, 1995c, 1150)

Several social policy and welfare reform scholars identify the Elizabethan Poor Laws of 1601 as the originators of the modern welfare state.
The English Parliament passed the Poor Laws of 1601 in response to a
series of difficulties that had plagued the continent for centuries. Examples
of such social, political, and economic unrest included famine, unemployment and labor supply problems, urbanization, small rebellions, wars, epi-
demics, and an increase in the number of vagabonds and others seeking
relief. The Poor Laws contained a number of provisions, including the dif-
ferentiation of poor people into categories (children, able-bodied, and
those unable to work), local tax collection to support local relief efforts,
family responsibility to care for dependent relatives, local government
financing and administration of relief in the absence of family care, and settlement or residency laws. Implicitly, the laws also incorporated a number
of provisions designed to deter individuals from applying for aid (using
severe punishment, such as whipping or death, to force individuals to
work for aid); to reform individuals (using overseers to closely monitor the
poor to ensure proper behavior); and to assist needy individuals (providing cash payments or food and shelter). Such legislation reflected economic
needs for ensuring a productive labor force and reducing the number of
dependents on local governments. Furthermore, the laws specified who
was responsible for relief, thus transforming welfare accountability from
religious institutions (as was the case prior to and during the initial stages
of the Middle Ages) to secular local governments.[3]

Implicit in the Poor Laws were social perceptions of welfare and welfare
recipients. Most important, the English Poor Laws imposed a moral order
on welfare receipt by distinguishing between worthy and unworthy poor,
often equating immorality with poverty. Poor Laws also established two
forms of relief that mirrored the distinction between worthy and unworthy
poor. Outdoor relief (e.g., firewood, food, medical supplies) supported
people in their own homes and outside of public institutions. Those individuals considered worthy typically received outdoor relief. In contrast,
indoor relief (such as almshouses and apprenticeships) provided individuals with food, shelter, and work opportunities inside public institutions.
Typically, unworthy poor, or at least those considered less worthy, received
indoor relief (Coll 1971, 1–16; Dolgoff, Feldstein, and Skolnik 1997, 41–64).

Another important theme embedded in the English Poor Laws was an
emphasis on the work ethic. Religious influences, such as Martin Luther's
teachings and Calvinism, also made their mark on Poor Laws, highlighting individual responsibility and the importance of work as a prerequisite
for righteousness.

The values of Calvinism very much affected our ideas on social welfare through
the centuries. The Calvinism of England in particular stressed personal responsi-

bility and discipline and an intense individualism in social affairs. Pauperism was viewed as a question of character. Calvin himself condemned indiscriminant alms-giving and urged ecclesiastical authorities to visit families regularly to see if they were idle, drunken, or otherwise undesirable. (Dolgoff, Feldstein, and Skolnik 1997, 49–50)

The Poor Laws reflected prevailing conceptions of individuals as being responsible for their own success or failure, which resulted in public sus-picion of direct cash relief and public preference for work relief as the main form of welfare.

The English Poor Laws Influence American Colonial Laws

English values emphasizing personal responsibility, the work ethic, and categories of worthy and unworthy poor heavily influenced the welfare policies of colonial America and continue to have a lasting impact on the American welfare system. Social policy scholar Mimi Abramovitz argued that the first public aid laws adopted by colonial legislatures, including those of Plymouth Colony (1642), Virginia (1646), Connecticut (1673), and Massachusetts (1692), were heavily informed by religious doctrine and the Elizabethan Poor Laws (1996, 75–79). The English Poor Laws, which con-tinue to have a profound impact, have had a "tremendous and lasting influence . . . upon social welfare policy and programs, first in the Ameri-can colonies and subsequently in the United States" (Axinn and Levin 1997, 81; see also, Coll 1971, 19).

Early American Poor Laws served a vital function in the settlements by providing public assistance to the colonists, many of whom had been pau-pers, vagrants, or indentured servants in England and who, therefore, lacked financial resources (Coll 1971, 1; Jernegan 1980, 178, 198). Because the survival of the colonial communities rested on hardworking, responsi-ble, thrifty, and frugal family units, and because costs of caring for the poor were quite high, early welfare laws encouraged the formation of sta-ble, well-ordered, and disciplined nuclear families (Abramovitz 1996, 77–78). The driving force of colonial Poor Laws was not so much to help the poor, as it was to protect society. In an effort to reduce public relief costs and reflect the importance of community, families bore initial responsibility for caring for their poorer relatives. Only when families could not assume financial responsibility did local governments offer aid. Private charity was also prevalent, and wealthier community members frequently housed less fortunate neighbors, sometimes at public expense (Axinn and Levin 1997, 22; Brown 1940, 11; Cammisa 1998, 29; Coll 1971, 20–21; Katz 1996, 14). Further, communities restricted aid to white families within the locality who were considered unemployable, including the elderly, sick, disabled, temporarily wounded, and widows with young children (Axinn and Levin 1997, 15; Jernegan 1980, 195). Despite these rather stringent criteria, many parishes expended almost a third of their annual budget on the care of poor people (Jernegan 1980, 183–84, 199, 204–5).

A brief review of colonial Poor Laws of settlement, outdoor relief, and child-care provisions illuminates key colonial values and perceptions of poverty that shaped colonial responses to poverty. Settlement laws emphasized local and familial responsibility to care for the deserving poor within the community. In response to society's intolerance of immigrants, paupers, and unskilled newcomers, early settlement laws enabled communities to remove undesirables from their localities. Only "those few who could ensure their financial independence and future contribution to the community were permitted to remain and to acquire settlement" (Axinn and Levin 1997, 22). Careful screening of the financial situation and skills of newcomers resulted in officials warning many to leave (Coll 1971, 19–21; Jernegan 1980, 192–95). Reflecting an implicit gender bias, such laws were particularly harsh on some women who, without resources or male breadwinners, often had great difficulties satisfying settlement requirements (Abramovitz 1996, 80–82; Coll 1971, 20).

An early form of entitlement, outdoor relief was the most common form of aid to poor deserving whites in colonial times. Perhaps reflecting colonists' mistrust of the very category of deserving poor, outdoor relief typically provided eligible poor persons with basic necessities rather than cash aid. In fact, the colonial parishes and local governing bodies collected taxes and donations specifically for outdoor relief. Only in rare instances did local governments distribute cash payments to poor persons (Axinn and Levin 1997, 19; Coll 1971, 35; Jernegan 1980, 181–88; Koon 1997, 22). In addition, local communities imposed a variety of fines on community members for infractions of the work ethic and church attendance, using such monies to support relief funds (Jernegan 1980, 197).Outdoor relief also allowed some poor women to conform to the colonial family ethic of women as homemaker (Abramovitz 1996, 85).

Whereas most deserving poor earned assistance in the form of outdoor relief, able-bodied poor (typically single women, unmarried mothers, men, and minorities) sought alternative forms of relief. Usually, the able-bodied exchanged their labor for a place to board (e.g., a poorhouse or a neighbor's home) or for cash assistance. An early form of workfare, this indoor relief provided individuals with work and shelter outside of their own homes in institutions or the homes of others. Indoor relief consisted of farming out (auctioning off skills to the lowest bidder), putting out (a form of home manufacturing), or placing people in almshouses and workhouses (Abramovitz 1996, 86–90; Coll 1971, 21–22; Jernegan 1980, 203; Kennedy 1979, 21; Matthaei 1982, 53–54, 62–65, 126; Tanner 1996, 35).[4] The emphasis on hard work and individual responsibility evident in indoor relief was consistent with the Protestant tradition that many colonists inherited from England. By equating hard work with righteousness and idleness with sin, religious sentiments endorsed welfare legislation with work requirements. In addition, although recipients preferred outdoor relief, indoor relief and workfare drew on women's homemaking abilities (e.g., sewing), allowing them to conform to social views of femininity.[5]

Although colonial laws provided several forms of aid, they also included deterrents to discourage potential aid recipients from seeking relief and to encourage an industrious community. For example, in cases of destitution, ungovernable conduct, and unfit parenting, colonial laws permitted government officers to remove children from their families and to apprentice or indenture the children to proper families. Authorities could also force both children and adults to work in houses of correction or workhouses (Abramovitz 1996, 78, 91; Axinn and Levin 1997, 17–20). Colonial Poor Law officers hoped that these policies would enable proper families to inculcate pauper children with morality, a strong work ethic, and other important values (Abramovitz 1996, 93).

Colonial laws also provided for overseers who acted as a deterrent to indolence. Essentially, the laws compelled overseers to inspect families and report the presence of idle members to the local court or justice of the peace. The laws further empowered community overseers to find work for all able-bodied and idle "rogues, vagabonds, and common beggars," often by placing such individuals in local workhouses (Jernegan 1980, 199–209). The Poor Laws of the Massachusetts Bay Colony, expressed in *An Act of Supplement to the Acts Referring to the Poor of 1692,* provide an excellent example of the colonial preoccupation with the work ethic.

And, for the better preventing of idleness, and loose or disorderly living, . . . the selectmen or overseers of the poor, . . . are further impowred . . . to set to work all such persons, married or unmarried, able of body, having no means to maintain them, that live idlely and use or exercise no ordinary and daily lawful trade or business to get their living by. . . . And the selectmen or overseers of the poor . . . are hereby ordered . . . to complain and inform against any transgressions thereof to one or more justices of the peace, . . . who are hereby respectively required and impowred, upon due conviction of the offender or offenders for living idely or disorderly, . . . to commit or send such offenders to the house of correction or workhouse. (quoted in Axinn and Stern 2001, 33)

This act, typical of Poor Laws of the time, further intended that all persons under the age of 21 "live under some orderly family government." The law applied to those who received alms as well as those who did not, thus providing disincentives to able-bodied persons who might consider unemployment, encouraging adherence to a work ethic, and institutionalizing family responsibility for the paupers who were unable or not expected to work.

Another form of stigmatizing both worthy and unworthy poor included requiring all people who received public relief to wear symbols on their clothing (Axinn and Stern 2001, 21). In her historical study of welfare, Josephine Brown, social worker and federal relief administrator assistant during the Franklin Roosevelt administration, stated that many localities required paupers to take an oath that they were completely destitute before local governments would administer relief (1940, 15). Abramovitz further asserted, "In some colonies, paupers forfeited all civil and social rights; they could be jailed, sold at auction, or indentured at the discretion of local officials; and, like most of the landless, they had no right to vote" (1996, 86; see also, Brown 1940, 10).[6] Thus, to be a pauper in colonial America was the lowest state to which a white person could descend, with the exception of being a prisoner (Brown 1940, 15).

In sum, many of the four major welfare themes discussed earlier pervaded the colonial Poor Laws. In general, the public assigned responsibility for poverty to structural causes and calamities outside of an individual's control (e.g., physical disabilities, harsh weather). In part and as a result, the local community assumed responsibility for providing relief to needy families. Religious overtones pervaded colonial views of and responses to poverty. By explaining the existence of poor people as one natural, albeit unfortunate, aspect of God's plan, Puritan theology condoned hostility toward laziness and supported putting people to work as a means for community members to live godly lifestyles in accordance with religious beliefs (Abramovitz 1996, 144; Jernegan 1980, 199, 208).

The emphasis on familial responsibility to care for the less fortunate members, as well as the prevalence of private charity, reflected the major goals of welfare policies to assist needy individuals. Through measures that stigmatized public assistance, the colonial Poor Laws also stressed deterrence. Apparently local communities feared that individuals might take advantage of local relief efforts at a time when communities could not afford to support many individuals and community survival depended on individual hard work. As a result, deterring potential aid-seekers was viewed as critical to long-term community survival. Evidence of individual reform is also present in colonial welfare policy. Colonial overseers hoped that measures such as child apprenticeships and workhouses would reinforce the value of work and enable individuals to become productive, self-supporting members of the community.

Finally, the colonial Poor Laws supported conceptions of deserving and undeserving poor. In general, persons with physical disabilities, widows, or individuals perceived as incapable of working and supporting their families were considered most deserving of aid. Such families received cash assistance or in-kind relief from other family members or through charity. Less-deserving persons (able-bodied men, women, and children) sought aid in the form of indoor relief. Racial biases permeated the distinctions between worthy and unworthy poor, defining black women, men, and children outside the public relief system. As such, the black community constituted part of the undeserving poor.[7] Settlement laws also defined immigrants and members outside of the locality as undeserving of public funds. Cammisa concisely characterized colonial Poor Law relief: "Localities were the focal point of assistance, families and private individuals were expected to contribute to the care of impoverished community members, assistance only went to members of the community, and a distinction was drawn between the truly needy and those capable of working" (1998, 29).

Nineteenth-Century Poor Law Reforms

> The degraded, vicious and idle…are continually rearing a progeny who, both by hereditary tendencies and the associations of early life, are likely to follow in the footsteps of their parents.… It is in the highest degree contrary to sound policy to keep such families together; in fact, the sooner they can be separated and broken up, the better it will be for the children and for society at large. (Hoyt 1877, 195–96)

> A primary cause of intergenerational welfare dependency is the adverse impact of the welfare environment upon children. To break intergenerational welfare dependency requires, where possible, the separation of children from the welfare environment and their placement into family situations that will be conducive to rejection of the welfare career. (Ronald K. Henry, cofounder of the Men's Health Network, House Committee on Ways and Means, 1995c, 1292)

For a variety of reasons, including increased costs of providing relief to poor people, massive increase in population (which multiplied six times between 1800 and 1860), a discontented labor force, racial tensions, labor shortages, and a series of economic depressions, Poor Laws came under scrutiny in the early 1800s (Abramovitz 1996, 137–41; Axinn and Levin 1997, 36, 42). Social historian Paul Boyer underscored the consequences of this social upheaval on the welfare population in America: "Somewhat illogically, the urban poor were singled out as both cause and victim of a frightening array of moral and social evils" (1978, 86). Whereas families had been the first form of welfare in colonial days with family members obligated to care for poorer relatives prior to seeking public aid, the state in the postcolonial period assumed a more active role. With growing urbanization and the geographical break up of families, extended kinship ties dissolved and many individuals could no longer rely on relatives for welfare assistance. Instead, families requested aid from state and federal sources (Axinn and Levin 1997, 41–42; Katz 1996, 4–10).[8]

With such changes came new explanations for poverty, distinct from those endorsed in colonial times. In contrast to the colonial era, reformers of the post-colonial period faulted individual behavior, rather than structural inequities, for poverty.

The poor law reforms—the contraction of outdoor relief, the rise of institutional care, and the growth of private charities—conceived and implemented in the first half of the nineteenth century, represented a major shift in the provision and philosophy of public aid. A new explanation of poverty emerged at this time and helped to rationalize the changes.... The rise of the market economy brought forward a new individualistic and moralistic explanation which focused instead on the characteristics of the poor. (Abramovitz 1996, 144; see also, Axinn and Stern 2001, 49)

Believing that those who worked hard and lived frugally would not suffer pauperism, many people faulted the poor, locating the root causes of poverty in a pauper's preference for indolence, lack of initiative, and moral degeneracy. The 1818 annual report of New York's Society for the Prevention of Pauperism, for example, cited "ignorance...idleness... intemperance in drinking...lotteries...[and] imprudent and hasty marriages" as among "the more prominent of those causes of poverty" (Axinn and Stern 2001, 68).

Several factors account for these new perceptions of welfare recipients. The convergence of complementary discourses that emerged prior to and during the nineteenth century, such as Enlightenment principles, religious doctrines of the Second Great Awakening, liberal economics, Social Darwinism, and eugenics philosophies, contributed to the focus on individual responsibility. For instance, eighteenth-century Enlightenment principles had an increasing influence on public views of social welfare. With its focus on humanism and the equality of all people, Enlightenment intellectual thought reinforced individualism.

At first, this theory encouraged a sense of community with those in poverty: As equal human beings, the impoverished should be treated with compassion. However, Enlightenment thought also encouraged individualism and personal responsibility and eventually contributed to a belief that the poor were responsible for their poverty, since they had equal opportunities to rise above it. (Cammisa 1998, 30)

In the late 1780s and the 1790s, the Second Great Awakening swept across frontier America, eastward toward New England and New York State.

According to welfare historian Michael B. Katz, "[I]n the wake of the revival, church membership increased from about one person in fifteen in 1800 to one in eight by 1835" (1996, 62). The primary mission of these revivals was to bring about spiritual, not material, relief through the distribution of Bibles and later tracts. By the mid-1830s, religious society members "began to lose [their] early optimism…and began to blame the poor themselves for their misery" (63). This shift in thinking complemented classical liberal economic theories. Liberal economics supporters believed that relief programs caused poverty by destroying an individual's desire to become independent and self-sufficient and encouraging dependence on handouts (Abramovitz 1996, 146).

Concurrent with the rise of religious societies and missions on the east coast, many scholars, such as Herbert Spencer, began to apply principles of science to social thought. By 1852, Spencer had already published two articles in which he developed a theory of social selection. He coined the term "survival of the fittest," which was later made famous by Charles Darwin. In his extensive account of sociopolitical thought, William Ebenstein wrote, "As early as 1842 Spencer contributed to the *Nonconformist* a series of letters called *The Proper Sphere of Government*," which contained his "political philosophy of extreme individualism and *laissez faire*, which was little, if at all modified in his writings of the subsequent sixty years" (1969, 637). In his work, Spencer enumerated responsibilities outside the sphere of the state, including aid to the poor.

Later in the nineteenth century, the philosophies of Social Darwinism and eugenics solidified societal perceptions of paupers as being responsible for their poverty. Applying biological theories of evolution to social phenomena, Social Darwinists believed that individuals bore personal responsibility for their position in society; that status was achieved through hard work, initiative and ability; and that poverty signaled inherent individual weaknesses (Abramovitz 1996, 148; Kennedy 1979, 132). Moreover, eugenics advocates argued that pauper traits were genetic and, therefore, passed on biologically from one generation to the next. As Richard Hofstadter wrote in *Social Darwinism in American Thought*, eugenics "proved to be the most enduring aspect of Social Darwinism… offer[ing] support to the common view that disease, pauperism, and immorality are largely controlled by inheritance" (1965, 161). Katz elaborated: "[E]ugenics offered a simple, scientific explanation [for poverty]: whatever the defect—and it might pop out as criminality, insanity, feeble-mindedness, or moral imbecility—its origins lay deep and ineradicably within dependent people themselves. Eugenics, then, tossed the mantle of science over the ancient distinction between the worthy and the unworthy poor" (1996, 189). These scientific perspectives justified a negative, even contemptuous, view of paupers. The scientific arguments further discouraged examining structural causes of poverty and encouraged blaming the poor for their condition.

The union of such disparate discourses as Social Darwinism, eugenics, laissez-faire economics, and Enlightenment principles provided the warrants for eliminating poverty (paupers and indigents) through a survival-of-the-fittest strategy that consisted of abolishing outdoor relief, sterilizing paupers, breaking up families by placing members in separate institutions, and closely supervising indigents (Coll 1971, 41–43; Katz 1996, 188–92). In sum, "At an early date in America's urban history, then, a significant group of reformers had dismissed the slum family as a social failure and moral disaster—a flawed institution that could, in all good conscience, be thrust aside in favor of new instrumentalities of moral nurture" (Boyer 1978, 40).

The Poor Law Reforms and societal responses to welfare needs in the first half of the nineteenth century reflected this shift in perceptions of welfare recipients, the goals of welfare reform, and responsibility for enacting reform. American child welfare scholars Andrew Billingsley and Jeanne M. Giovannoni incisively observed, "Our social reforms of the nineteenth century were movements not so much of reform for the poor as reform of the poor" (1972, 22).

Policies encouraging a decrease in outdoor relief, an increase in private charities, and a rise in institutional care (e.g., orphanages and asylums) all sanctioned, either implicitly or explicitly, the practice of breaking up families in order to help them. First, arguments against outdoor relief included public beliefs that such aid deprived poor people of independence and self-respect as well as fostered indolence and immorality. As a result, many state commissions, particularly late in the nineteenth century and during severe depressions, recommended abolishing relief, especially outdoor relief (Coll 1971, 43–60; Katz 1996, 17–19, 37–43). Most large cities cut back spending on outdoor relief while several other states, including Delaware, and cities, such as Philadelphia and Chicago, closed down outdoor relief programs altogether (Abramovitz 1996, 147–49; Axinn and Levin 1997, 52; Coll 1971, 58–59). Many public officials, however, recognized the necessity of outdoor relief and continued to provide it, frequently in amounts equal to or less than required for subsistence. Welfare officials believed that meager funds discouraged dependence and encouraged industriousness on the part of recipients (Brown 1940, 16–17; Coll 1971, 32–33, 39; Katz 1996, 54–59).

Second, and spurred by the Second Great Awakening, private charities increased in number, although still making a distinction between deserving and undeserving recipients. The private charities "favored married women or previously married women who lacked a male breadwinner through no fault of their own—widows, the wives of sick, disabled, and temporarily unemployed men, and/or others defined as deserving of help. In contrast, they frequently denied aid to, separated, or otherwise penalized unwed mothers, abandoned wives, and wives of permanently unemployed men" (Abramovitz 1996, 151). Some private charities, again reflecting prevailing social scientific theories and beliefs, supplied poor women with moral advice rather than financial aid in the hopes of sustaining and cultivating behavior commensurate with independence and self-sufficiency (Abramovitz 1996, 151–52; Katz 1996, 60–87).[9] These strategies mirrored society's concerns about poor people—that paupers were poor because of their character flaws and that poor individuals were a growing threat to social stability (Boyer 1978, 89–90).

Third, and concurrent with cutbacks of outdoor relief and the rise of private charities, institutional care became increasingly important as a means of caring for the poor and instilling work and moral ethics in inhabitants through labor and discipline. Almshouses were the primary form of care for the poor until the late nineteenth century (Axinn and Levin 1997, 46–59).[10] Humanitarian, Social Darwinist, and economic goals drove the popularity of the poorhouse. The main purposes of poorhouses were to end the harsh practice of auctioning off poor persons to the lowest bidder, to inculcate paupers with the work ethic, to reduce the costs of pauper care, and to deter people from seeking relief. The poorhouses also promised to transform the character of inmates, improve the lives of children, and provide work and educational opportunities for the poor (Katz 1996, 25–36).

Orphanages, another form of institutional care, also gained ascendancy during this time as a means of addressing child welfare. The Poor Reform Laws continued the colonial practice of removing children from their homes, indenturing them to families who could instill in them the work ethic and proper values, or placing them in orphanages, with one important exception—"No longer did parents need to commit a crime, act immorally, or abuse their offspring before reformers urged authorities to step in and remove their children. Extreme poverty itself had become evidence of their incompetence and adequate grounds on which to break up their families" (Katz 1996, 112). After removing children from their homes, institution officials discouraged all further contact between children and their parents or other relatives to ensure a rapid and comprehensive reform of the children (Axinn and Levin 1997, 55). Research of the time supported such actions. Charles Hoyt's *Report,* one of the most influential studies on pauperism in the late nineteenth century, concluded in a passage that bears repeating.

[B]y far the greater number of paupers have reached that condition by . . . vices and weaknesses [which] are very frequently, if not universally, the result of tendencies which are to a greater or less degree hereditary.... The degraded, vicious and idle ... are continually rearing a progeny who, both by hereditary tendencies and the associations of early life, are likely to follow in the footsteps of their parents.... It is in the highest degree contrary to sound policy to keep such families together; in fact, the sooner they can be separated and broken up, the better it will be for the children and for society at large. (195–96)[11]

Breaking up "the line of pauper descent" by forcing parents and children into institutions was an effective strategy consistent with prevailing social conceptions of poverty and philosophies, such as Social Darwinism and eugenics. After all, if parents required aid because of defects in their moral character and social values, and if such flaws could be passed genetically to their children, then an obvious solution was to remove children from parental custody and reform them immediately (Billingsley and Giovannoni 1972, 22).

Examining the nineteenth century Poor Law Reforms through the lens of the four major welfare themes reveals that, almost without exception, postcolonial welfare reforms addressed poverty as inherent in individuals and external to such factors as the economy. During this era, societies held individuals accountable for their own success or failure and allocated responsibility for alleviating poverty to local, public, and voluntary associations. The goals of welfare reform were largely aimed at rehabilitating deviant individuals. In fact, the primary objectives of almshouses, workhouses, orphanages, local charities, and other institutions were to remove the social undesirables from society and confine them in institutions geared toward character reformation until such time when individuals could demonstrate their conformity to social norms, values, behaviors, and attitudes. A focus on the individual as responsible for poverty even pervaded the philosophies of charity organizations. Underlying the strategies of major reform movements and societies, such as the Charity Organization Society, was "the assumption that the urban poor had degenerated morally because the circumstances of city life had cut them off from the elevating influence of their moral betters" (Boyer 1978, 149; see also, Cammisa 1998, 31). Paul Boyer provided an extended example of this phenomenon in his discussion of the American Sunday School Union and Sunday school reform. Boyer reported that Sunday school leaders believed that Sunday school was a "superior socializing agent" to home life, particularly in the case of the urban poor. In addition, Sunday school literature reflected hostility toward the poor with "references to the 'ruinous' influences of 'intemperate,' 'profane,' dishonest,' 'brawling,' 'licentious,' 'profligate,' and 'vicious' parents" (1978, 39–53). Sunday school reformers believed they had to educate children in morality to prevent those children from adopting the habits and lifestyles of their parents.

Deterrence was also an important component of nineteenth-century welfare reforms. Threats of child removal, indentureships, and poor workhouse conditions ensured an unappealing image of relief. The attempt of poorhouses to accomplish the twin goals of deterrence and reform did not succeed: "Irreconcilable contradictions had been stamped into the foundations of the almshouses. The almshouse was to be at once a refuge for the helpless and a deterrent to the able-bodied; it was supposed to care for the poor humanely and to discourage them from applying for relief. In the end, one of those poles would have to prevail" (Katz 1996, 25).

As in colonial times, many people continued to recognize two classes of poor people (worthy and unworthy). But whereas colonial policies emphasized assisting the worthy poor, nineteenth-century policies focused on deterring and rehabilitating the unworthy poor. Notably these deserving and undeserving categories corresponded with another important nineteenth-century distinction between poverty (deserving poor), and pauperism (idle vagrants and beggars who seemingly lacked industry and good moral character) (Jernegan 1980, 200–201, 203; Katz 1996, 19). Charles Hoyt's *Report* provides an apt illustration of this distinction.

The number of persons in our poor-houses who have been reduced to poverty by causes outside of their own acts is, contrary to the general impression, surprisingly small. These two classes of persons ought not to be confounded; neither ought they to be compelled to associate with each other. The whole policy of the State should move in the direction of caring for the really unfortunate and worthy sick poor in hospitals, while a vigorous system of labor should be organized and administered for the vicious and unworthy. (1877, 196)

This distinction between poverty and pauperism "helped in deciding who should go to the poorhouse: 'Paupers' went to institutions as punishment for their moral failings, and the worthy received outdoor relief to help them through difficult times" (Cammisa 1998, 32). Preoccupied with deterring unworthy recipients, public perceptions reinforced the notion that the majority of welfare dependents were able-bodied and, therefore, unworthy of public aid. Contrary to public perceptions, however, considerable statistical evidence existed to suggest that most people who required public assistance were unable to work due to circumstances beyond their control. Matthew Carey's 1833 study of canal workers, for example, provided empirical evidence that blurred the public's sharp distinction between worthy and unworthy poor. Carey demonstrated that most public dependents were in need of assistance (unable to work or earn a living wage) and were therefore deserving poor (Axinn and Stern 2001, 51–57; Coll 1971, 35).[12] This strong conflicting evidence was virtually ignored, and prevailing public views that individual behavioral defects caused public dependence continued to shape welfare legislation.

Racial and gender biases helped shape distinctions between unworthy and worthy poor, resulting in policies that were especially harmful to minority groups as well as to men. As in colonial times, black women, men, and children remained part of the undeserving poor and were therefore largely outside the public welfare system. With the exception of the federally funded Freedman's Bureau, black people relied on their own community structures to provide aid. "To speak of workers in the South is to speak largely of slaves and, therefore, to speak of no public social welfare programs. Free blacks were left to help themselves" (Axinn and Stern 2001, 42; see also, Tanner 1996, 41–44). In addition, the public was suspicious of nonworking men, referring to them as able-bodied tramps who did not deserve public welfare. A powerful, although false, societal belief in the availability of work for all able-bodied workers who desired employment combined with persistent reform efforts to remove men from poorhouses, forced many poor men to seek aid elsewhere (Katz 1996, 90–92, 95–102).

In sum, nineteenth-century welfare reforms elevated individual explanations of poverty over structural ones, advocated local responsibility for relief, and concentrated efforts on reforming and deterring the poor. Indoor relief surpassed outdoor relief in popularity as welfare policies increasingly made relief contingent on behavioral change. In a somewhat paradoxical fashion, welfare policies encouraged the formation of strong, stable families and communities by separating some individuals from their families and their communities.

Mothers' Pensions in the Early Twentieth Century

The mother is the best guardian of her children.... [W]ork...outside of the home inevitably breaks down the physical, mental and moral strength of the family and disrupts the home life through an inadequate standard of living and parental neglect.... [A] system of direct governmental aid to the widowed mother with children should be considered not as an alternative to, but as a necessary and integral part of social insurance. (New York State, *Report of the Commission on Relief for Widowed Mothers* 1914, 7, 9–10)

While work requirements are appropriate for many people, mothers are the most important influence in a young child's life. Work requirements should be compatible with raising a family and guiding young children. I believe a 20-hour work week requirement for mothers with young children...is reasonable. (Senator Dianne Feinstein [D-Calif.], *Cong. Rec.* 1995, S19166)

The early twentieth century was marked by the introduction and passage of numerous reforms on both the state and federal levels concerning such issues as women's suffrage, labor conditions, and family welfare (Axinn and Levin 1997, 123–63; Coll 1971, 73–82). These reforms reflected another ideological shift in societal conceptions of poverty, even as they critiqued nineteenth-century strategies of family breakup, institutional care, and charity organization relief. Whereas the nineteenth century was largely characterized by an emphasis on reforming individual character flaws, the late nineteenth and early twentieth centuries witnessed a reconsideration of social and economic causes of poverty (Coll 1971, 60). Simply stated, reformers acknowledged that circumstances outside of an individual's control exerted a more profound influence on one's economic stability than did individual character flaws (Axinn and Levin 1997, 132; Boyer 1978, 224–25). Long working hours, depressed wages, and hazardous working conditions led reformers to conclude that for families to maintain their economic security they must be protected from institutions such as large corporations and industries. Concrete evidence of this shift in thinking is a resurgence in outdoor relief provisions, from $1.6 million in 1911 to $14.7 million in 1925 in the nation's 16 largest cities (Tanner 1996, 37). In addition, many reformers believed that such protection could only come from state and federal legislation. Reflecting prevailing social sentiments, the federal government established a Children's Bureau in the Department of Labor in 1912 to investigate and report on the welfare of children (Coll 1971, 73).

Several factors account for this shift to a more holistic view of poverty, including the influence of Progressivism, the growth of social work and public welfare as recognized professions, and several economic crises. First, throughout the Progressive Era, reformers approached poverty comprehensively and addressed a variety of issues, including rising poverty levels in urban areas, deteriorating working-class conditions, and worsening levels of institutional care (Ehrenreich 1985, 24–25). Despite unparalleled growth in manufacturing, communications, and industry in the United States during the first part of the twentieth century, a 1915 Commission on Industrial Relations report noted that "50 to 66 percent of working-class families were poor" with at least one-third living in "abject poverty" (Axinn and Stern 2001, 127). In addition to this rise in poverty, citizens were gravely concerned about overcrowded and unsanitary living conditions in urban areas, as well as long work hours and working conditions, particularly for women and children (Coll 1971, 63–66). Moreover, state reports supported growing public sentiment that when women worked, family life, living standards, and child well-being suffered (Abramovitz 1996, 190–95; Handler and Hasenfeld 1991, 65–66).

Critics also began to question the individually targeted institutional approach as well as the effects of breaking up families and forcing children, mentally ill persons, criminals, and paupers into labor programs. These programs actually cost more than outdoor relief and reformers faulted many institutions for being poorly financed, overcrowded, unclean, ill ventilated, mismanaged, corrupt, and generally unable to provide adequate care or an environment conducive to rehabilitation efforts (Abramovitz 1996, 159; Axinn and Stern 2001, 59–62; Coll 1971, 25–28, 31, 39; Katz 1996, 3–36). Finally, critics cited abusive care, high infant mortality rates, and punitive disciplinary approaches as evidence of ineffective and low-quality care.

In addition, social work methods became more sophisticated and engendered a sense of public confidence in the social worker's ability to establish adequate casework files on families and to train mothers in proper child and home care. With the promotion of field research and schools for social work professionals, such as administrators, settlement house workers, analysts, and lobbyists, came statistical information on the extent of poverty (Abramovitz 1996, 198–200; Gordon 1994, 167–81; Kennedy 1979, 130–56). Settlement house workers as well as members of organizations, such as the Charity Organization Movement (1877), Women's International Union Labor League (1899), and Women's Trade Union League (1903), collected data and relied on these statistics and social work methods to justify and advocate reform (Kennedy 1979, 132–56).[13] Further, a rise in juvenile courts, child guidance programs, and public welfare boards reflected the growing mass of public welfare issues that some critics argued had surpassed the power of private charities to address (Abramovitz 1996, 199–200).

Economic conditions also precipitated a more holistic view of poverty. More specifically, a severe depression from 1893 to 1897 challenged two major prevailing nineteenth-century conceptions of poverty: (1) poverty resulted from individual character flaws and moral deficiencies, and (2) moral uplift strategies could correct such individual character defects. Instead, the economic crisis seemed to suggest larger structural causes for poverty beyond any individual's control, thereby fueling criticism of the efforts of private charities and state and local institutions to reform the individual pauper (Boyer 1978, 154).

The old Social Darwinist explanations characteristic of the late nineteenth century, which saw individual physical, mental, or moral weaknesses as the source of economic disadvantage, went into eclipse, and the dominant modes of social thought shifted to environmentalist explanations. The poor came to be seen as victims of external forces—unemployment, bad housing, disease, and accidents—which they could not be expected to control through strength of character alone. (Ehrenreich 1985, 43)

These criticisms of institutional care, innovations in social sciences and child psychology, professionalization of welfare, negative perceptions of women working, and economic crises ushered in some important changes in welfare legislation (Katz 1996, 128–34).

Most significant for the purposes of this project was the advent of mothers' pensions in 1911. Mothers' pensions responded to a growing public concern with preserving the family, protecting children, and supporting women's primary roles as wife and mother. Recognizing the magnitude of this radical shift in welfare policies, Katz asserted:

This emphasis on family preservation reflected a major shift in reform thought. Recall that only a couple of decades earlier, the same sorts of people advocated family breakup not just when parents drank, stole, or seemed otherwise immoral and neglectful but, even more, when they were so poor that they had to ask for relief.... Within less than twenty years, family breakup had virtually disappeared as the strategy of first resort.... Once family breakup was rejected, the campaign against outdoor relief, which already had run out of steam, was doomed, and, even more, some sort of mothers' pensions had to follow. (1996, 129)

Reproducing the entitlement language of outdoor relief programs, progressive reformers introduced mothers' pensions as a means of providing cash assistance to deserving mothers, thereby enabling mothers to remain home to care for their children (Gordon, 1994, 56–58).

Even the federal government sanctioned such social views of women's proper roles as wife and mother and prioritized the preservation of families. In a letter to President Theodore Roosevelt, members of the Committee on Resolutions expressed the findings of the 1909 Conference on the Care of Dependent Children. Notably, the committee's report retained distinctions between worthy and unworthy poor, even as it affirmed the traditional nuclear family as normative.

Home life is the highest and finest product of civilization. It is the great molding force of mind and of character. Children should not be deprived of it except for urgent and compelling reasons. Children of parents of worthy character, suffering from temporary misfortune, and children of reasonably efficient and deserving mothers who are without the support of the normal breadwinner should as a rule, be kept with their parents, such aid being given as may be necessary to maintain suitable homes for the rearing of the children.... Except in unusual circumstances, the home should not be broken up for reasons of poverty, but only for considerations of inefficiency or immorality. (*Cong. Rec.*, 60th Cong., 2d sess. 1909, 43, pt. 3:2364)

Despite federal support, the mothers' aid program was highly controversial and sustained powerful critiques against program implementation. The majority of opponents raised objections to the use of public funds to finance the pensions in a form akin to the discredited outdoor relief. Critics also questioned why professionals (i.e., social workers) were not administering the money or monitoring recipient progress. Others cited problems with the pension program's limited implementation (Axinn and Levin 1997, 152; Bremner 1971, 348–97; Bremner 1974, 519; Coll 1971, 76–77; Handler and Hasenfeld 1991, 70–73).

Although 48 states had adopted a form of mothers' pensions by 1921, the programs were narrow in scope for several reasons. First, as state-controlled, permissive (not mandatory) programs, mothers' pensions were not universally applied across the country; neither did implementation of the programs occur quickly. "At no point prior to the 1935 Social Security Act did more than half the counties in the United States actually provide Mothers' Pensions" (Abramovitz 1996, 194; see also, Brown 1940, 26–32). In addition, the program discriminated among women, particularly in terms of race and class. For the most part, the pensions helped white women whose husbands were absent due to death, imprisonment, or physical or mental incapacitation, whereas divorcees, unmarried women and mothers, and women of minority groups remained largely ineligible (Abramovitz 1996, 201; Axinn and Levin 1997, 133–35, 144–45; Goodwin 1997, 160–69, 185–88; Gordon 1994, 111–43). Those who qualified for aid received pensions only after enduring an intense and reportedly humiliating investigation process that verified the women's status as deserving and their provision of a suitable home. Moreover, aid recipients experienced frequent follow-up visits under the close scrutiny and supervision of administrators (Coll 1971, 79). This process reflected the views of many charity organizations, which believed that public aid "demoralized the poor, provided a disincentive to work, and contributed to a decline in familial responsibility, particularly on the part of fathers toward their families" (Goodwin 1997, 38).

Finally, critics faulted the pensions for awarding funds in amounts below or at subsistence level (Coll 1971, 79; Katz 1996, 133). As a result, many women had to work in addition to their pensions to make a living wage. Consequently, mothers' pensions did not fulfill their intention to pay women to remain at home and care for their children. Instead, the pensions reinforced societal values of independence, hard work, and self-sufficiency and continued a long-standing American tradition of requiring able-bodied men and women to work even when they received a pension (Goodwin 1997, 7, 169–81). Handler and Hasenfeld explained the double bind such welfare policies placed on poor women in particular: "Labor discipline forced poor mothers to work by restricting relief. Patriarchy and the domestic code condemned them for working. Child protection declared them socially deviant and threatened to take away their children" (1991, 22). Such criticisms, combined with political conservatism, lack of uniformity in arguments for mothers' pensions, and financial constraints, eventually caused proponents of mothers' pensions to shift their arguments for aid from ensuring justice for deserving mothers to protecting child welfare (Goodwin 1997, 18, 189).

Despite its policy of aiding only deserving women, mothers' pensions did provide relief for a significant number of women and their families while simultaneously increasing public favor of outdoor relief programs. By 1934, for example, at least 110,000 families of the nation's 1.4 million female-headed households received mothers' aid (Abramovitz 1996, 315; Brown 1940, 330). Coll made a similar point, contending, "Although mothers' aid was far from comprehensive either in coverage or in adequacy of grants, these programs did serve to reaffirm the long American tradition of public aid to the needy in their homes" (1971, 80).

As in previous eras, several major themes permeate mothers' pension legislation. First, in answering the question of who was responsible for poverty, public opinion and mothers' pension legislation focused more on structural causes. Premised on the importance of home life for children, mothers' pensions reflected prevailing social conceptions that women should not work outside of the home because their primary duties were to raise children and keep the home. More important, the pensions also posed work and family as mutually exclusive options. The pensions further codified the notion that some people, namely women and children, required economic and legal protection from institutions (Axinn and Stern 2001, 152).

Second, mothers' pensions continued a centuries-old tradition of separating worthy and unworthy recipients along racial, class, and ethnic lines, frequently discriminating against many minority women and reserving aid largely to widowed, white mothers (Tanner 1996, 41–44). Mothers' pensions also fortified some gender-specific attitudes about women's place at home and the responsibility of men to earn living wages.

The mothers' pension…proved a poor vehicle in which to advance women's rights.… The family wage ideal ascended as the framework that shaped social policy. It institutionalized a gender system that recognized the location of women's labor in the home and a system of social insurance that based its benefits upon contributions made predominantly from primary-sector jobs.…In a system increasingly defined by wage labor participation, the official standard of the family wage eclipsed women's labor at home and effectively made women's wage-earning invisible. (Goodwin 1997, 187)

In so doing, mothers' pensions "linked aid to the dependency of women" and "did not provide assistance for women to become independent" (Cammisa 1998, 37). The institutionalization of women's dependence spurred critiques of the welfare system beginning in the 1940s.

Third, and contrary to the stated goal of mothers' pensions to provide assistance to needy families, the pensions principally served a rehabilitative function. By attaching conditions (e.g., morally fit) to cash relief, mothers' pension caseworkers supervised recipient behavior to ensure compliance with traditional family behaviors, morals, and values. The mothers' pensions also reinforced the work ethic outside of the home. As already noted, the below or at subsistence level pensions, in practice, became supplements and safety nets for wage-earners rather than replacements for earnings. As a result, many mothers were forced to assume a dual role of wage-earner and caretaker. Handler and Hasenfeld concluded: "Despite the rhetoric of many reformers, these children and their parents [poor families] were still part of the general mass of poverty, the category that was undeserving.... In other words...both adults and children, as a category, were in no sense excused from work" (1991, 64).

Finally, the era of mothers' pensions marked a shift in prevailing views of who was responsible for poverty relief. Although the majority of public welfare efforts prior to this time emanated from local welfare departments or private organizations, the mothers' and children's pension programs instigated the expansion of public assistance to the state and federal levels. As Goodwin succinctly stated, "the infrastructure they [mothers' pensions] helped to develop signaled a reorganization of public welfare within the local state from political parties to state agencies" (1997, 183). Going further, Abramovitz argued that the mothers' pensions "foreshadowed the inclusion of a program to aid dependent children in the historic Social Security Act of 1935" (1996, 205). With their strident appeals to the public sector for financial support, mothers' pensions impelled the formation of public bureaucracies to facilitate welfare relief and heralded a new direction in government responsibility for welfare.

Social Security Act of 1935: Aid to Dependent Children (ADC)

The Social Security Act of 1935. An Act to provide for the general welfare by establishing a system of Federal old-age benefits, and by enabling several States to make more adequate provision for aged persons, blind persons, dependent and crippled children, maternal and child welfare, public health, and the administration of their unemployment compensation laws. (Public Act No. 271, 74th Congress, H.R. 7260)

If you read the preamble of the Constitution, it's quite explicit that the role of the general welfare is one of the mandates of the Constitution. Government has a role, can play a role, and I think they should in this process, especially at this time in our history. (Matthew G. Martinez [D-Calif.], House Committee on Education and Labor, 1994c, 4)

During the early part of the twentieth century, the Great Depression and its attendant catastrophes marked another major shift in public perceptions of welfare, reinforcing the public's growing acceptance of welfare problems as the product of inherent flaws in economic, social, and political structures. On October 24, 1929, the stock market crashed, signaling the beginning of a severe depression and economic hardship that lasted for nearly 12 years. During the early 1930s, banks closed, industries failed, farmers declared bankruptcy, wages fell, and unemployment rates rose at an alarming rate to nearly 25 percent in 1933 (Axinn and Stern 2001, 168–75; Brown 1940, 145–46; Piven and Cloward 1971, 45–79; Tanner 1996, 45). According to Cammisa, "[T]he depression was not only characterized by bank runs, but also by soup and bread lines as people on limited incomes queued up for limited resources" (1998, 39). Equally disastrous was that approximately 60 percent of the nation's population earned incomes that were below the amount necessary to meet basic necessities, while 40 percent of American citizens had no financial reserves to rely on when the depression began (Axinn and Stern 2001, 168).

With about 10 percent of the population dependent on unemployment aid in the face of an economic catastrophe, the public was forced to adopt another view of poverty. Individually based explanations could no longer account for such high poverty rates, nor could local and state temporary relief systems provide sufficient funds or comprehensive care to meet relief demands. As a result, society sought alternative and material causes for poverty in addition to alternative sources of aid (Katz 1996, 218).

Despite an inherited colonial suspicion of excessive federal government involvement in state and local affairs, many citizens throughout the latter nineteenth and early twentieth centuries advocated national government involvement in public relief. Organized and spontaneous expressions of worker dissatisfaction,[14] combined with the inability of local and state financial reserves to provide relief for rapidly growing welfare caseloads, virtually compelled the federal government to intervene in public welfare.[15] President Herbert Hoover, however, was reluctant to approve federal aid proposals, believing that aid demoralized recipients, self-help and industry alleviated poverty, and the free enterprise system would restore prosperity (Trattner 1994, 274–79). Not until nearly two years after the onset of the Great Depression did the federal government initiate emergency legislation to deal with the economic crisis. The programs established as part of the New Deal, during President Franklin Delano Roosevelt's legendary first 100 days and later, marked a major shift in public welfare program financing and administration from private organizations and state and local governments to the federal government.

Although early programs, such as the Federal Emergency Relief Administration (FERA) of 1933,[16] did provide temporary assistance to needy families, they were intended to be short-lived, a fact expressed by President Roosevelt in a January 4, 1934, address to Congress:

The lessons of history, confirmed by the evidence immediately before me, show conclusively that continued dependence upon relief induces a spiritual and moral disintegration fundamentally destructive to the national fibre. To dole out relief in this way is to administer a narcotic, a subtle destroyer of the human spirit. It is inimical to the dictates of sound policy.... Work must be found for able-bodied but destitute workers.... The Federal Government must and shall quit this business of relief. I am not willing that the vitality of our people be further sapped by the giving of cash, of market baskets, of a few hours of weekly work cutting grass, raking leaves or picking up papers in the public parks. We must preserve not only the bodies of the unemployed from destitution but also their self-respect, their self-reliance and courage and determination. (19–20)

Apparently, prevailing social views on welfare still supported the idea that relief was destructive to the values, attitudes, and actions of recipients. Further, FERA staff feared that direct relief promoted dependency and instigated a "gimme" syndrome, wherein people felt they deserved relief (Piven and Cloward 1971, 81). As a result, administrators did not wish to make FERA more attractive than work and imposed a means test on the meager benefits. Thus, to qualify for aid, potential recipients had to present themselves at a relief station and demonstrate to the satisfaction of a social worker that they were needy (Trattner 1994, 286). Axinn and Levin commented on the lasting effects of FERA administration, stating that FERA "established certain operating principles that were to have negative consequences in later years: administrative discretion, rather than legal definitions, for establishing eligibility aid; a professional casework service orientation toward relief giving; and a subtly pervading, if unnoted, reservation that relief was somehow a necessary evil" (1997, 186). Because FERA benefits varied from state to state and applications involved a lengthy interview process, this form of public aid carried the historical stigma of public assistance that was often discriminatory toward minority groups (Katz 1996, 226–28; Trattner 1994, 283).

Eager to encourage the work ethic and elevate the dignity of the poor, the federal government also instituted more publicly popular work-relief programs, such as the 1933 Civil Works Administration and the 1935 Works Progress Administration (WPA—later, after 1939, termed the Work Projects Administration). As these names suggest, work-relief programs provided employment opportunities for more than eight million Americans, even as those programs replaced the temporary cash relief provided by FERA, which was phased out in June 1936. These work-relief programs attached no stigma of a means test on relief and paid benefits more consistent with current wages (Trattner 1994, 286). Even so, the security wage of work-relief programs, although higher than relief payments, frequently fell below prevailing wages. The goal of this strategy was to encourage recipients to view aid as temporary and seek permanent employment (Piven and Cloward 1971, 82–84, 95).

Of course, the federal government did recognize the existence of deserving poor who simply could not work. In his January 4, 1935, congressional address, President Roosevelt expressed the government's position of upholding state and local responsibility for such unemployables, thereby distinguishing between worthy (supported by the federal government) and unworthy (supported by states and localities) poor: Those persons "dependent upon local efforts" in the past shall be maintained by "[s]tates, by counties, by towns, by cities, by churches, and by private welfare agencies" (1938, 20). The termination of FERA, combined with the inability of WPA to provide work for all of the able-bodied and with the federal government's insistence on state and local responsibility for unemployables, resulted in criticism from social workers, welfare agencies, and state and local officials. Such critics were angered that Roosevelt had not transformed FERA into a federal social work–public welfare department designed to alleviate the effects of destitution throughout the nation (Brown 1940, 169–70).

On August 15, 1935, President Roosevelt approved longer-term relief in the form of the Social Security Act of 1935, the major thrust of the New Deal. Essentially, the New Deal created a welfare system with four major types of relief, which are still in existence today: general relief, work relief, categorical assistance, and social insurance. Together, these four categories covered individual loss of income in three main cases: temporary loss of job (Unemployment Compensation), inability to participate in the labor force (Federal Old Age Insurance, Old Age Assistance, Aid to the Blind, Aid to Dependent Children) and health and welfare issues (Maternal and Child Health Services, Services for Crippled Children, and Child Welfare Services) (Axinn and Levin 1997, 188–89; Brown 1940, 327–28).[17] Of the different types of relief, categorical assistance was, and continues to be, the most controversial (Cammisa 1998, 43–45). As its name implies, categorical assistance provides aid to individuals who qualify for assistance based on membership in certain categories, such as the blind, aged, and families with dependent children (the largest component of categorical assistance). The most important form of assistance for the purposes of this book is Title IV of the Social Security Act, Aid to Dependent Children (ADC). This program is the predecessor of Aid to Families with Dependent Children, a program replaced by the Temporary Assistance for Needy Families (TANF) block grant as part of the 1996 Personal Responsibility and Work Opportunity Reconciliation Act.

Aid to Dependent Children (ADC)

Essentially, ADC was a more comprehensive version of the mothers' pensions (Abramovitz 1996, 315–16). Unlike social insurance programs, which were entirely administered by the federal government, ADC was a federally aided, state-administered program. The federal government matched state expenditures only if the states chose to participate in the categorical assistance programs (Cammisa 1998, 44). Despite a favorable review by the Committee on Economic Security, however, ADC received little attention during congressional hearings begun in January 1935 (Gordon 1994, 253–85). This fact had profound implications for the ADC administration.

The inattention to provisions for dependent children resulted, first, in the administration of ADC along with the adult categories of assistance. The original intent that the program be under the jurisdiction of the Children's Bureau was thus ignored. Second, the phrase "aid to dependent children" was defined to mean money payments with respect to a dependent child or children and not to include caretakers. Third, the grant-in-aid formula limited federal payments to one-third of a total of $18 per month per family provided for one dependent and to one-third of $12 per month provided for additional dependent children. (Axinn and Levin 1997, 191; see also, Goodwin 1997, 192)

Reforms to ADC in 1950 provided federal matching funds for the child's caretaker. Once children reached adulthood, the program reclassified the mothers as able-bodied and ceased to provide them with aid. Notably, matching and reimbursement amounts for the ADC program were lower than for any other public assistance program at that time, again reflecting the program's relatively low priority (Abramovitz 1996, 316).

In addition to lower federal funding levels, modest ADC benefits, slow ADC implementation, and eligibility rules limited the scope and effectiveness of the program. First, as with mothers' pensions, ADC grants were insufficient for raising a family above the poverty level, reflecting the historical dilemma of aiding the poor and promoting the work ethic. Second, many states delayed ADC program implementation in spite of federal mandates. For instance, although most states (42) had established the Old Age Assistance program for the elderly poor in 1936, only 26 had instituted an ADC program. By 1939, 10 states still lacked an ADC program (Abramovitz 1996, 316).

Third, and in contrast to other entitlement social security programs such as social insurance, the ADC program constituted a nonwork and means-tested form of relief, whereby individuals had to pass eligibility requirements and demonstrate their need for assistance prior to receiving aid. By restricting relief to single-parent families, legislation upheld the work ethic and prevented two-parent families from taking advantage of public assistance. In addition, the congressional committee reports and early versions of the Social Security Act bill implicitly allowed states to continue the mothers' pension philosophy of suitable home and fit parent provisions (Abramovitz 1996, 317). If public agencies deemed mothers to be unfit or incapable of providing adequate care, they could deny aid, leaving the families to fend for themselves (Abramovitz 1996, 318; Handler and Hasenfeld 1991, 105). Furthermore, some states instituted employable mother rules, which prohibited able-bodied mothers of school-aged children from receiving relief. Critics argued that these rules were used to discriminate against black women in particular (Gordon 1994, 275–77). Embedded in such regulations was the public perception that without enforcement, undeserving mothers, especially those of minority groups and lower classes, would continue bearing children to maintain relief benefits. Finally, although most New Deal programs attempted to prevent racial and class discrimination, they did not ultimately aid many black Americans. "By excluding agricultural and domestic workers, the Social Security Act left two-thirds of employed blacks with no protections for old age or unemployment.... At the same time, New Deal housing policies also discriminated against blacks and promoted residential segregation, because the Federal Housing Authority redlined black neighborhoods and refused to insure mortgages within them" (Katz 1996, 252–53).[18] As a result of the discrimination implicit in many of the social security programs, the small, poorly financed ADC program designed for widows became an increasingly important and controversial means of relief for black Americans and other minority groups.

The social welfare changes of the 1930s marked a significant departure in societal views of who was responsible for relief provisions and who was responsible for poverty. First the Social Security Act legitimized federal responsibility for welfare relief. Second, the Great Depression and related economic crises heralded new perceptions of the causes of poverty. Abandoning biological, genetic, and individually focused explanations of poverty, the public began to recognize poverty as a consequence of inherent flaws in American political, economic, and social systems. Consequently, society began addressing poverty by building correctives (e.g., work programs, temporary public assistance, social work organizations) into the welfare system (Trattner 1994, 282).

By combining social insurance (entitlements) and public assistance (means-tested) relief, the Social Security Act also retained historical distinctions between worthy and unworthy poor. More specifically, the act expanded the concept of deserving poor to include working-class retirees and their survivors, even as it reinforced the categorization of unemployed males and some dependent-aged children and their poor single mothers as undeserving (Handler and Hasenfeld 1991, 105). Katz also commented on the distinctions between worthy and unworthy poor apparent in the Social Security Act: "By pointedly distinguishing social security from relief, they [the social security system's architects] froze the distinction between social insurance and public assistance into federal policy, where it has been stuck ever since" (1996, 242). Because social insurance operates under specific legal conditions that govern eligibility (without a means test and on the basis of worker contributions), it reaps the benefits of social acceptance as an earned and deserved form of relief. In contrast, the means-tested and non-work-related public assistance programs, such as ADC, became easy targets for social criticism, suspicion, and stigma as undeserving forms of aid, particularly in a nation that reveres the work ethic (Katz 1996, 244–46).

Indeed the means-tested, non-work-related, and low-benefit provisions of ADC reflected society's ambivalence about women's roles in society as both caretakers and laborers.

At the federal level, planners wanted to discourage mothers from earning and at times referred to them as "unemployables." At the state and local levels an entirely different scenario could exist. Administrators wanted to manage budgets by adjusting caseloads and maintaining work requirements. ADC perpetuated the ambiguity regarding women's dual roles which had existed in mothers' pensions. The entitlement framework of social insurance excluded them, yet they had great difficulty earning enough to support the family. (Goodwin 1997, 192)

As neither an entitlement nor a living wage, ADC benefits forced many women to seek alternative forms of employment. In doing so, ADC reinforced adherence to the work ethic and suggested that, at some level, direct relief (without work conditions) was undesirable.

Ultimately, however, and based on their belief that the family-wage model was normative and predominant, many reformers believed that ADC and other welfare programs would wither as old age insurance expanded to cover widows and orphans. In addition to reflecting social concerns about the work ethic and marriage, the presumed transient nature of ADC indicated the public's faith in the economic system and belief that social insurance programs would eventually make public assistance (e.g., ADC) unnecessry (Abramovitz 1996, 317–18; Axinn and Levin 1997, 195).[19] As ADC relief rolls began to grow throughout the next decades, however, transforming the temporary, small component of the Social Security Act into a major relief institution, the public once again began to change its views about welfare recipients; subsequent legislation validated these new depictions of the poor.

As demonstrated throughout this chapter, public assistance provision evolved from a familial and local obligation in colonial America to a state responsibility in industrial America. Following the onset of the Great Depression, the federal government assumed responsibility for welfare provision with the establishment of the first national welfare agencies and programs. These historic welfare reforms all were influenced by various societal perceptions of welfare recipients, the causes of poverty, and the goals of reform. As is evident in chapter 3, these historic representations of welfare recipients and their families make present certain views about who deserves aid and under what conditions (Perelman 1982). These views continued to shape welfare reform legislation from 1940 to the present. Indeed, themes from this period that have presence in contemporary debates include the idea that families (not government) should be the first source of support for their poorer relatives, the suspicion that poverty is genetic and welfare is an intergenerational phenomenon, the belief that Judeo-Christian values are linked with economic success, and an abiding faith in the power of individuals to overcome adversity through self-help.

NOTES

1. Several histories of welfare attend to the functions of welfare reform in American history. Cammisa identified four goals of welfare policies—assistance, prevention, deterrence, and rehabilitation (1998, 25–26). Koon also discussed competing theories about poverty, dependency, and the goals of public assistance (1997, 33–59).

2. For a thorough explanation of current welfare policy with regard to non-U.S. citizens, consult Michael Fix and Ron Haskins's "Welfare Benefits for Non-Citizens" (2002).

3. For additional information, consult Abramovitz 1996, 77; Axinn and Levin 1997, 8–12; Billingsley and Giovannoni 1972, 25; Cammisa 1998, 26–29; Coll 1971, 1–16; Corbett 1995, 43; Dolgoff, Feldstein, and Skolnik 1997, 52–55; Katz 1996, 14; and Koon 1997, 22.

4. For a more detailed account of women as wage-earners, as well as of societal perceptions of working women throughout history, consult Kessler-Harris (1982) and Tentler (1982).

5. As Julie Matthaei observed in her study of women's economic history in America, the "driving force behind the development of the putting-out system was capital expansion and not charity" (1982, 64) Matthaei did admit, however, that the system provided many impoverished women, particularly undeserving women, with a means of supporting their families.

6. In practice, however, voter prohibition laws against paupers were not enforced in most states where they existed. Thus, many paupers could amass influential voting power to elect persons who provided relief (Brown 1940, 16).

7. Andrew Billingsley and Jeanne M. Giovanni's *Children of the Storm* (1972) chronicles the effects of racism on child welfare institutions.

8. Axinn and Stern noted that, upon Dorothea Dix's request in an 1848 memorial to Congress for the allocation of 5 million acres of public land to be used for building institutions for the insane, Congress passed a measure allocating 10 million acres of public land on which to build institutions for the insane, blind, and deaf. President Franklin Pierce vetoed the bill, upholding state and private charity responsibility for welfare (2001, 51; Breckenridge 1927, 172–234; Coll 1971, 38). The federal government did take some tentative steps toward national welfare in the nineteenth century with pensions to disabled Civil War veterans; emergency relief to flood victims from 1867, 1874, 1882, and 1884 floods; and aid to farmers who suffered from a locust infestation in 1875 (Tanner 1996, 37).

9. The New York Association for Improving the Condition of the Poor (AICP) provides an excellent example of a charity organization typical of those arising in other major cities during the mid-1800s. The primary mission of such organizations was to "awaken the poor to the flaws of character that underlay their degradation" (Boyer 1978, 90). To do so, early social workers visited the dwellings of paupers, identified their flaws, offered moral guidance, and filed a report with the organization's main office, largely to prevent the paupers from trying to find charitable relief elsewhere (90–94).

10. Coll appropriately noted that almshouses cared for many people whom today we would not consider poor. For instance, a large component of almshouse residents comprised the mentally ill and mentally disabled (1971, 27).

11. Katz offered a critical analysis of the Hoyt Report (1993, 92–133, 164–65).

12. In his thorough critique of Hoyt's *Report*, Katz argues that the *Report*'s findings were skewed and "fabricated an image that suited the time" (1996, 90).

13. The Charity Organization Movement is credited with being one of the first moral welfare movements to use scientific methods extensively. By the mid-1890s, the Charity Organization Society of New York maintained data on 170,000 families (Boyer 1978, 143–61; Coll 1971, 44–62).

14. Workers and other citizens expressed their dissatisfaction with the economy and public policies in a variety of ways, including looting, rioting, and forming social protest movements such as the Townsend movement and Senator Huey Long's Share the Wealth movement (Axinn and Levin 1997, 169, 180–87; Katz 1996, 223–24, 243).

15. As mentioned earlier, the U.S. Constitution did not grant the federal government jurisdiction over relief. By default, such responsibilities fell to the states. Thus, national government involvement in social insurance posed some difficult issues. By funneling federal dollars through local and state agencies in a grant-in-aid system embodied in legislation, such as the Federal Emergency Relief Administration (FERA), the national government became involved in public welfare while skirting problematic constitutional issues (Bremner 1974, 520; Katz 1996, 224–27).

16. President Franklin Roosevelt modeled FERA on relief programs such as the Temporary Emergency Relief Association (TERA), which was initiated in New York State as part of the 1931 Wicks Act during Roosevelt's tenure as governor. Established on May 12, 1933, FERA appropriated $500 million of federal funds to

states in the form of grants in aid, with $250 million distributed solely on the basis of need and $250 million disbursed on a one-to-three (federal-to-state) matching basis (Katz 1996, 221–22, 226; Trattner 1994, 285).

17. Criticisms of the Social Security Act included its lack of health insurance, limited scope of unemployment insurance, and exclusion of many classes of people, including farmers, migrant workers, and domestic servants (Trattner 1994, 291–94).

18. Several scholars have argued that racist attitudes and classifications were a significant factor in the exclusion of agricultural and domestic workers from social insurance coverage (Gordon 1994, 276, 285; Lieberman 1995; Quadagno 1988; Skocpol 1995). For an alternative view, consult Davies and Derthick (1997).

19. The slashing of the WPA's budget and of welfare rolls in the latter part of the 1940s attests to public acceptance of the transient nature of relief programs as well as a general unshakable public faith in the power of the market to correct itself with jump starts, such as temporary relief programs (Piven and Cloward 1971, 111–14).

Chapter 3

American Social Welfare Policy in Context, 1936–2003

[I]llegitimacy is a moral problem and the Federal Government is not and indeed cannot be an effective moral teacher. Church-state separation requires the welfare bureaucracy to remain morally neutral and it cannot effectively promote sexual responsibility from a morally neutral pulpit. Rather than Federal solutions, I believe there is a principle that should guide any and all efforts toward welfare reform.... Those social functions that can be accomplished by a lower order of society should not be usurped by a higher order.... [T]he resources of first resort, of first resort, should be individuals, churches, neighborhoods, then towns and cities.

> Reverend Robert A. Sirico, president of the Acton Institute for the Study of Religion and Liberty and member of the Michigan Civil Rights Commission, House Committee on Ways and Means, 1995b, 209

In his testimony before Congress in 1996, Reverend Robert Sirico expressed what many witnesses and legislators had come to believe: that welfare was a problem of values, and thus, the federal government was not the best institution to enact welfare policies. Instead, Sirico, like many others, believed that states, localities, and families were better equipped to devise and enforce welfare policy. Such a belief has its roots in welfare legislation prior to the enactment of the Social Security Act and Aid to Dependent Children (ADC). Indeed, the period following the 1935 Social Security Act until the 1996 Personal Responsibility and Work Opportunity Reconciliation Act contained a number of landmark welfare initiatives, which quickly led to the devolution of welfare provision from the national level to state, local, and familial arenas.

Continuing the historical review outlined in chapter 2, this chapter contends that the historical context of welfare reform in America from 1940 to the present lends presence[1] to certain values (e.g., values about family, work, and religion) that exert an enormous influence on contemporary welfare debates. Specifically, this chapter reviews significant welfare reforms that occurred from 1940 to 1979, the Family Support Act of 1988, and PRWORA and its reauthorization discussions. As in the previous chapter, each section that addresses a period prior to PRWORA's passing begins with two quotations—the first from the period being discussed and the second from contemporary welfare legislation debates. The resemblance between the two quotations is striking and evinces the role of ideology in the policy-making process.

AMENDING PUBLIC WELFARE AS WE KNOW IT: 1936–1979

> The major line of defense against joblessness should be programs of training and retraining....Retraining programs should include retraining for new occupations as well as more limited goals, such as correcting poor work habits. (Report of the Ad Hoc Committee on Public Welfare to George K. Wyman, Secretary of Health, Education, and Welfare, September 1961, 84–85)

> And essentially it is a prescriptive contract.... It is a comprehensive assessment of each adult...to determine what education or training is necessary, and we have an individual plan for each adult delineating what they have to do to prepare for employment and the timeframes that they will be allowed to complete that in. Then they have to go to work. (South Carolina Governor Carroll Campbell, Senate Committee on Governmental Affairs, 1995, 37–38)

In the decades following the implementation of the Social Security Act, the United States experienced significant domestic and international conflict as well as major demographic shifts and notable economic prosperity. At the same time, ADC rolls continued to grow, resulting in increasing public criticism of welfare. As will become evident later, prevailing public opinions about welfare recipients, as well as critiques of the welfare system, heavily informed changes in welfare policy.

Between 1935 and 1970, the United States became involved with three overseas military actions, World War II, the Korean War, and the Vietnam War. Within the United States, the growth of the civil rights movement, the emergence of the women's rights movement, the advent of the War on Poverty, and the explosion of the sexual revolution signaled the public's heightened awareness of discrimination on the basis of race, ethnicity, sex, and economic class. The War on Poverty and other poverty movements helped to politicize the poor, who increasingly expressed their frustration over gross inequities in employment and living standards through protest in the form of marches, demonstrations, sit-ins, and riots (Handler and Hasenfeld 1991, 118–19; Piven and Cloward 1971, 222–39).

Also contributing to social upheaval during this period were significant shifts in demographic patterns as a result of changes in population growth and migration. The population of the United States grew from 132.1 million in 1940 to 204.8 million in 1970, in part due to increases in birthrates and life expectancy, a decrease in the death rate, and improvements in medical and health care. Increased industrialization and urbanization, spurred by World War II, encouraged many Americans to move from rural areas into urban centers: "By 1970, 72 percent of the white population and 81 percent of the nonwhite population lived in urban areas" (Axinn and Levin 1997, 222–24). Changes in agricultural production that favored larger, mechanized farms, as well as hiring practices that discriminated against nonwhites, encouraged black migration to northern cities (Axinn and Levin 1997, 225; Piven and Cloward 1971, 201–12; Wilson 1987).

As for economic growth, the gross national product (GNP) tripled, reaching $976 billion in 1970. In addition, the labor force expanded, while both unemployment and poverty rates declined. Despite general prosperity for all Americans regardless of race, ethnicity, or economic class, the dollar gap continued to widen between whites and nonwhites. Nonwhite Americans suffered disproportionately high poverty and unemployment rates. For many families, escaping poverty meant that both parents had to work (Axinn and Levin 1997, 220–21). The widening gap between the poor and the wealthy inspired many popular books, such as John Kenneth Galbraith's *The Affluent Society* and Michael Harrington's *The Other America,* which chronicled poverty conditions in the presence of prosperity.

Concurrent with this widening gap between the rich and poor during a time of general economic prosperity, ADC received mounting public criticism between World War II and the 1960s because of increasing caseloads, rising program costs, and changing recipient demographics. The ADC program served a growing number of families, from 372,000 in 1940 to 803,000 in 1960 (Handler and Hasenfeld 1991, 113). Although the number of welfare recipients increased by only 13 percent from 1950 to 1960, costs rose sharply by 92 percent to more than $1 billion (Abramovitz 1996, 319; Axinn and Levin 1997, 234). The demographic characteristics of recipients also changed: "The natural growth of the population along with rising rates of divorce, desertion, fertility, and births outside of marriage enlarged the pool of women eligible for ADC from all demographic groups" (Abramovitz 1996, 320).

A complex of racist practices also changed the demographic patterns of recipients. Discrimination in hiring practices led to low wages and high unemployment rates, particularly for black men and women. Those who did find work often did so in the most undesirable service and industrial jobs with low wages and few benefits. Furthermore, ADC supported more unmarried mothers and fewer widows. For example, whereas more than 80 percent of families received ADC in the 1930s because a father had died, more than 80 percent of families received AFDC in 1977 because a parent was divorced, separated, deserted, or unmarried (Abramovitz 1996, 320–21; Koon 1997, 23). In addition, many minority groups displaced from the labor market due to discriminatory practices became overrepresented in the ADC caseloads. "According to one estimate, black families accounted for two-thirds of the increase in ADC rolls between 1948 and 1961...[and]...the addition of non-white Hispanics to the rolls produced a non-white majority in the sixties, although nearly 42 percent of the ADC recipients nationwide were white" (Abramovitz 1996, 321; see also, Piven and Cloward 1971, 214–20). These changes in ADC rolls and costs occurred in a shifting political context of conservatism (McCarthyism), social aggravation (movements for women's and civil rights), and the expansion of the welfare state that challenged laissez-faire government. As a result, the social climate only fueled criticism of ADC (Abramovitz 1996, 327–28).

The reasons behind the expansion of ADC are complex and include changes in migration patterns, urbanization, population growth, rising program costs, and out-of-wedlock births. Nevertheless, the public focused attention on only three of those factors: rising costs, out-of-wedlock births, and migration patterns (specifically the migration of black Americans).[2] (Abramovitz 1996, 321; Axinn and Levin 1997, 235; Handler and Hasenfeld 1991, 120.) Public perception often characterized recipients as able-bodied and indolent (therefore unworthy) and attributed questionable motives to welfare recipients such as bearing children to avoid work. According to history professor James T. Patterson: "By the late 1930s, popular attitudes seemed harsher.... Majorities in polls said that most poor people could get off of relief if they tried hard enough. Respondents began to distinguish between the unemployed—perhaps deserving —and 'reliefers,' 'good-for-nothing loafers,' and 'pampered poverty rats'" (1994, 46). The results of a 1967 survey reveal that

42 percent of Americans thought that poverty resulted from "lack of effort"; only 19 percent blamed "circumstances beyond control." A poll two years later found that 58 percent of respondents thought poverty was caused by a "lack of thrift and proper money management by poor people;" 55 percent said it was the result of "lack of effort by poor people." A total of 84 percent agreed with the statement: "There are too many people receiving welfare who ought to be working," and 71 percent said, "Many people are not honest about their need." Only 34 percent agreed with the statement, "Generally speaking, we are spending too *little* money on welfare in this country." (171, emphasis in original)

Axinn and Levin added: "A picture of ADC as harboring, and even creating, families broken by illegitimacy, divorce, and desertion developed. This new picture was brought into even sharper focus by the program's continuing emphasis on the unemployable female parent in the home—the worthy-widow halo—at a time when the larger society was insistently labeling that parent 'unworthy' and employable" (1997, 237–38). Indeed, the increase of women into the labor force, especially during World War II, caused many to question a female parent's status as unemployable and worthy poor, especially when many non-welfare women with children worked to supplement their husband's wages (Koon 1997, 24). In addition, consistently low unemployment rates and economic prosperity in general suggested that poverty might not be systemic of political, economic, and social structures, but rather it was sporadic, situational, and individually based (Axinn and Levin 1997, 235–38).

From 1940 to 1979, welfare policies at local, state, and federal levels reflected changing public perceptions of welfare recipients and poverty. Legislation at the local and state levels centered on punitive actions designed to reduce welfare spending by deterring applicants from seeking aid and purging welfare rolls of fraudulent cases. Attempts to reduce welfare rolls consisted of enforcing residency requirements, initiating new application investigations, publicizing the names of recipients to prevent duplication of payments, conducting credit checks and home surveillance, threatening to remove children from the home, and enforcing suitable home and man-in-the-house provisions (Abramovitz 1996, 322–29; Handler and Hasenfeld 1991, 123).[3] Welfare experts Mary Jo Bane and David Ellwood[4] characterized this bureaucratic approach as an "eligibility and compliance" culture that actually deterred self-sufficiency. With the majority of welfare worker efforts directed at verifying an applicant's need or dependency and ensuring compliance, fewer resources remained to assist the applicant in learning skills or finding employment (1994, 1–19).

The increase in bureaucratic measures produced two important consequences, one of which was to overburden staff with verification requirements. "With staff under great pressure to get the work out correctly, clients with problems became problems" (Handler and Hasenfeld 1991, 121). As a result, the burden of proof to demonstrate need shifted to recipients, who had to undergo a lengthy interview, produce proper documentation, and spot errors in their application to avoid losing benefits. Bane and Ellwood illustrated just one part of the complicated and burdensome application process in a passage worth quoting at length:

Many applicants know to bring birth certificates to their initial interview. But the worker will list additional verifications needed.... For instance, depending upon the programs for which she is applying, the applicant may be instructed to bring in birth certificates for the children...; utility bills; rent receipts or letters from past and present landlords verifying residence...; copies of past and present bank

account statements, from as long as two years previous; social security cards for
everyone in the family; if anyone in the family has life insurance, a letter from the
company naming the beneficiary and the cash surrender value; verification of
school attendance from the children's schools; copies of car registrations and titles;
pay stubs; if pregnant, a letter from the doctor stating estimated due date; marriage
or divorce papers. Depending upon the case, there may be fifteen to twenty verifications that the applicant will have to furnish before being termed eligible. (1994, 4)

To acquire these multiple verifications, applicants visited numerous government agencies, such as the Bureau of Vital Statistics, the Social Security
Administration, the Department of Motor Vehicles, and the Unemployment Office. After supplying the required documents, applicants waited
while social workers cross-checked the information and determined eligibility. If eligible, recipients were subjected to reverification at least once
every six months. Clearly, for welfare recipients and social workers with
caseloads of around two hundred or more, this eligibility-compliance
model consumed significant time and did not move the recipient in the
direction of self-sufficiency (Bane and Ellwood 1994, 2–7).

A second important consequence of tightened eligibility requirements
was the use of moral standards (e.g., suitable home, man-in-the-house, and
substitute father provisions) rather than financial need to determine ADC
benefits. "Using vaguely defined rules, state welfare departments denied
aid to single mothers who took in male boarders, who cohabited with men,
who refused to identify the fathers of out-of-wedlock children, or whose
homes and behaviors simply did not look right to the investigating worker"
(Abramovitz 1996, 324). In short, these rules discriminated against women
who did not conform to social ideals of womanhood. Taken together, these
disciplinary measures revealed public opinion about welfare recipients by
depicting beneficiaries as immoral, incapable of providing adequate homes
for their children, and persistent in their efforts to cheat the welfare system.

At the federal level, several important pieces of legislation emerged to
address situation-specific poverty and discrimination as causes of
poverty. For instance, the Area Redevelopment Act of 1961 ameliorated
poverty in specific depraved geographic regions, and the Civil Rights Act
of 1964 prevented employment discrimination on the basis of sex, ethnicity, and race (Axinn and Levin 1997, 236–37). Of particular interest here are
the Public Welfare amendments of 1962, the Economic Opportunity Act of
1964, and the Social Security amendments of 1967, all of which significantly changed the nature of the ADC program.[5] Common to all three
pieces of legislation, in varying degrees of importance, was an emphasis
on strengthening family life through employment training, work incentives, and social services. For instance, key components of the Public Welfare amendments reflected the recommendations of the 1961 Ad Hoc
Committee on Public Welfare to eliminate the abuses of welfare programs

and groom people for productive roles in society. The amendments provided for community work and training programs for able-bodied workers, social service programs (e.g., counseling for recipient rehabilitation), and public child welfare services (e.g., day care for children of working parents). In the first presidential message entirely devoted to public welfare on February 1, 1962, President John F. Kennedy explained to Congress the reasons behind social service provision:

But merely responding with a "relief check" to complicated social or personal problems—such as ill health, faulty education, domestic discord, racial discrimination, or inadequate skills—is not likely to provide a lasting solution. Such a check must be supplemented, or in some cases made unnecessary, by positive service and solutions, offering the total resources of the community to meet the total needs of the family to help our less fortunate citizens help themselves. (99; see also Axinn and Levin, 1997, 206)

The call to self-help and implicit suspicion of outdoor or cash relief as a solution to poverty reflected a long-standing tradition of independence, responsibility, and morality through work, dating back to the Elizabethan Poor Laws of 1601. Subsequent legislation codified these traditional values of work and responsibility at the national level in programs such as the Community Work and Training Programs (CWTP), which required adult recipients to work in exchange for their relief payments (Abramovitz 1996, 333). To further stimulate production, the 1962 amendments also obligated states to disregard expenses, within reason, associated with wage earning prior to calculating AFDC benefits (Handler and Hasenfeld 1991, 142). The emphasis on aiding families was also reinforced in the five-year extension of AFDC-UP (Unemployed Parent), an optional welfare program for two-parent families that was approved by Congress in 1961 (Patterson 1994, 130–32). Also reflecting the importance of families, the 1962 amendments provided for a federal matching fund bonus to states that developed a social study profile on the physical condition and educational progress of all AFDC children recipients (Bane and Ellwood 1994, 8). Finally, as a result of the 1962 Public Welfare amendments, Aid to Dependent Children was changed to Aid and Services to Needy Families with Children, henceforth known as Aid to Families with Dependent Children, and the Bureau of Public Assistance was renamed the Bureau of Family Services, further illustrating this heightened focus on family.

President Lyndon B. Johnson continued many of the public welfare policies initiated in the Kennedy administration. When Johnson launched his Great Society reforms and War on Poverty program in 1964, he continued to emphasize family, work, training programs, and social services as keys to alleviating poverty. Passed on August 20, 1964, the Economic Opportunity Act asserted:

The United States can achieve its full economic and social potential as a nation only if every individual has the opportunity to contribute to the full extent of his capabilities and to participate in the workings of our society. It is, therefore, the policy of the United States to eliminate the paradox of poverty in the midst of plenty in this Nation by opening to everyone the opportunity for education and training, the opportunity to work, and the opportunity to live in decency and dignity. (Pub. L. 88–452, Sec. 2)

Essentially, the Economic Opportunity Act established youth programs, employment and investment incentives, and community action programs designed to provide individuals with the skills, training, attitudes, and education necessary to succeed. Underlying the program's efforts was a persistent public view that a culture of poverty existed in America that prevented certain individuals from moving out of impoverished conditions. Because prevailing social beliefs supported a correlation among individual improvement, family stability, employment, and educational opportunities, the Great Society legislation responded with programs designed to integrate work, family, and education.

Despite a prosperous economy and attempts to reduce welfare rolls, AFDC costs and recipients continued to rise at an alarming rate. From 1961 to 1967, welfare rolls increased from 3.5 million recipients to nearly 5 million people, while costs rose from $994 million to $2.2 billion during that same time (Abramovitz 1996, 334). By 1970, AFDC served an estimated 9 million recipients, with costs nearing $5 billion (Handler and Hasenfeld 1991, 113). Simultaneously the percentage of AFDC families headed by nonwhite, unwed, divorced, separated, or deserted women continued to rise. Divorce and illegitimacy rate increases, welfare state expansion, and Supreme Court rulings that removed barriers to welfare eligibility all contributed to the swelling of welfare rolls (Bane and Ellwood 1994, 13; Handler and Hasenfeld 1991, 113–14).

The federal government responded to this welfare crisis with additional reforms in the form of the Social Security amendments of 1967. These new reforms established a Work Incentive Program (Eventually, the unfortunate acronym of the Work Incentive Program [WIP] became WIN.),[6] which included an earnings disregard that allowed working recipients to retain the first $30 and subsequent one-third of their earnings before experiencing any benefit reduction. Departing from previous welfare legislation, the 1967 reforms separated social services from cash benefits, no longer making recipient receipt of cash payments contingent on recipient use of social worker services (Bane and Ellwood 1994, 14–15). Such a change was consistent with the rights-based discourses of the era as well as with movements, legislation, and public opinion touting the rights of women, minorities, elderly, and the mentally ill. Similarly, by making social services a choice, the 1967 welfare reforms affirmed the rights of poor people to choose assistance, even as the reforms allowed social workers to target social services to those most in need (Axinn and Levin 1997, 247–48). The growth of such welfare rights organizations as Aid to Needy Children Mothers' Organization, National Welfare Rights Organization, and the Poverty Rights Action Center provided further evidence of growing concern with welfare recipients' rights in the 1960s (Abramovitz 1996, 336; Handler and Hasenfeld 1991, 118–20).

In addition to the three pieces of legislation discussed above, the Family Assistance Plan (FAP), proposed in 1969 by President Richard M. Nixon to Congress, deserves mention. Effectively, FAP aimed to make welfare and the Great Society programs unnecessary by providing every working American family with a minimum annual income through a negative income tax. In other words, if a family earned less than the specified amount of $1,600, the government would make up the difference. The controversy surrounding FAP illuminates the crux of the welfare debate.

The heart of the debate was precisely the daring attempt of FAP to blur the distinctions between able-bodied and disabled poor, and between the welfare and the working poor. By softening these distinctions, especially through the inclusion of the working poor, FAP produced an irreconcilable tension between the provision of a guaranteed minimum income to all citizens and the preservation of the incentive to work, while trying to contain the fiscal burden of welfare. That is, FAP heightened the conflict between the relief of misery and the maintenance of the work ethic, in a context of a capitalist economy that abhors raising the overall costs of welfare. (Handler and Hasenfeld 1991, 149)

Despite some congressional support and presidential backing, Nixon's FAP proposal failed to pass through Congress. FAP's death in Congress cemented the public's preference for work-related assistance and distinctions between classes of worthy and unworthy poor.

Emergent in the three legislative reforms that gained congressional and presidential approval—the Public Welfare amendments, the Economic Opportunity Act, and the Social Security amendments—are several common themes that provide clues into the prevailing social conceptions of welfare. First, through an emphasis on counseling and worker training programs, the legislation marked a return to seeking causes of poverty within individuals, reminiscent of sentiments in the mid to late nineteenth century, with one major exception. Unlike nineteenth-century philosophies, the legislation of the 1960s and 1970s did not hold individuals accountable for their failings; instead the legislation focused on providing opportunity to individuals. In other words, although people generally believed that the causes of poverty were inherent in individual lifestyles and actions, they also thought that individuals were not responsible for their poverty; such individuals, through no real fault of their own, simply did not have the skills or opportunities to climb out of depraved conditions. Legislative reforms combined this curious contradictory blend of blaming individuals and recognizing institutional shortcomings in a fashion that clearly departed from the spirit of early twentieth-century legislation, which had focused largely on institutional structures as causes of poverty.

Second, the goals of state and federal welfare policy differed significantly, reflecting a distinction between the worthy and unworthy poor established in the 1935 Social Security Act, which allocated federal dollars to support the worthy poor, including the able-bodied poor, through social insurance (social security and unemployment compensation). This left states to care for those unemployables not covered by federal programs. Care for the unworthy poor thus devolved to the states. As a joint federal-state program, AFDC seemed to straddle the line between the worthy and the unworthy poor. Unlike social insurance, however, AFDC was not based on prior earnings or earmarked taxes. In other words, a tacit distinction between work and nonwork marked AFDC recipients as less-deserving recipients. "The popular perception has been that social insurance pays people for working, whereas categorical programs pay people for not working" (Cammisa 1998, 44). Reflecting a growing perception of AFDC recipients as less-deserving poor, states instituted strict eligibility-compliance welfare policies aimed at deterring the unworthy poor from applying for and relying on assistance.

In contrast, federal policies approached AFDC recipients as part of the deserving poor. As suggested by the names of legislation and welfare bureaus, such as the Employment Opportunity Act, Worker Incentive Program, and Social and Rehabilitation Services, the focus of federal reforms was on training and rehabilitating welfare recipients to ensure their employment success. In an important shift, these amendments promoted the work ethic by joining welfare and work together, as they remain linked today. Further, WIN represented a moral position, best articulated by Handler and Hasenfeld: "The work requirement has both symbolic and social regulation functions. As a symbol, it reinforces for the poor and nonpoor alike the moral superiority of those who work, even if the work is menial, low paying, or degrading. The work requirement casts welfare recipients as morally depraved because it assumes that they lack the inner motivation to work, which must, therefore, be forced upon them" (1991, 38–39).

One major consequence of relief as contingent on work was that welfare recipients lost the right to exchange freely their labor for wages. Forcing people to accept any job offer, as was the case with WIN legislation, promoted a cheap supply of low-wage labor (Abramovitz 1996, 339). Particularly in a capitalist nation that lauds individual control over labor, this shift in labor, from a private commodity to a public commodity subject to federal regulation, seemed to contradict time-honored values (Handler and Hasenfeld 1991, 39).

Finally, distinctions between the worthy and unworthy poor sustained racial and gender biases, particularly at the state level. For instance, many critics argued that man-in-the-house, suitable home, and substitute father rules were targeted toward black women, who had higher divorce and illegitimacy rates than white women (Cammisa 1998, 47). Even at the federal level, gender biases pervaded the legislation. More specifically, the welfare legislation reflected growing public ambivalence about women's roles and the relationship between family and work. In the tradition of mothers' pensions, many individuals still supported the notion that a woman's place was in the home. National Association of Social Work President Charles Schottland commented on women's responsibilities: "We cannot...accept compelling mothers with children to take jobs without due regard to the welfare of children and limitations on AFDC families where the father is absent from the home. Forcing mothers with young children into a job goes against a universally held conviction that a mother's first responsibility is to her home and children" (quoted in Bremner 1974, 563–64).

Despite the popularity of such views, the welfare legislation, informed by another strong segment of society, advocated the strengthening of family life through employment to encourage responsibility and self-support. Although programs targeted to youth (e.g., day care, Head Start, Upward Bound) and programs tailored to adults (e.g., job counseling and skills training) encouraged work and self-support, they masked a policy seemingly counterproductive to traditional family life. In effect, these policies removed children and parents from their homes and separated parents from their children. Not unlike the philosophies of the Charity Organization and Sunday School movements of the late nineteenth century, implicit in the entire day-care outlook was the notion that children were at least as well-off outside of the home. Such a view marked a radical departure in public perceptions of welfare from the mothers' pensions and ADC programs originally designed to allow deserving women to care for their children at home.

FURTHER REFINING WELFARE AS WE KNOW IT: 1980 TO 1996

> No Individual Entitlement: This part shall not be interpreted to entitle any individual or family to assistance under any State program funded under this part. (*PRWORA of 1996*, 2113)

The economic and social climate of the 1980s and 1990s resulted in further changes to welfare policy. More specifically, high unemployment and poverty rates, public dissatisfaction with previous welfare reforms, and public hostility toward welfare recipients spurred stricter welfare policies.

First, as they had in previous decades, high unemployment and inflation rates continued to plague the economy, further widening the gap between the rich and poor. High poverty rates also continued; by 1994, an estimated 16.2 percent of families with a worker employed year-round and full-time lived below the poverty line. As in previous years, high unemployment rates and poverty levels disproportionately affected female-headed families and minority groups, including African Americans, Native Americans, and Hispanics (Axinn and Levin 1997, 168–80, 308; Wilson 1996).

Throughout this time, the profile of AFDC recipients also changed. Between 1975 and 1994, AFDC families headed by never-married mothers doubled from 33 percent to 66 percent. Divorced and separated female-headed families also consumed a considerable part of the 1994 AFDC caseload, at 30 percent, while widows represented only 2 percent of the caseload (Besharov 1996; Cammisa 1998, 16). As a result, the public's "view of program recipients had become increasingly hostile" (Axinn and Levin 1997, 285). Characterizing welfare recipients as able-bodied and therefore unworthy of public assistance, many Americans felt that welfare encouraged a lifestyle of indolence, unfairly supporting some people at the expense of hardworking others.

Racial overtones also influenced social perceptions of welfare. For instance, data show that black women are disproportionately represented on the welfare rolls relative to their population, and they are more likely to rely on welfare for long-term spells. Black welfare recipients, however, also represent a smaller percentage of total welfare recipients and the poor than whites (Bane and Ellwood 1994, 45–49; Gilens 1999, 102; Weaver 2000, 20–21). Even so, prevailing public opinion endorsed a depiction of welfare recipients as African American or Hispanic (Axinn and Levin 1997, 285). As a result, some concluded that "racial stereotypes played a central role in generating opposition to welfare in America" and "racial stereotypes constituted an obstacle to public support for anti-poverty programs" (Gilens 1999, 3).[7]

Together, changing demographics of welfare recipients and perceptions of the significance of those changes encouraged the public to circumscribe even more narrowly their conception of the worthy poor. The mere mention of welfare reform stirred up myriad public frustrations and resentments, and "welfare reform" achieved status as a "code word for racial stereotyping, or for excessive government spending, or for bloated government bureaucracies, or for misguided liberal attempts to engineer society" (Cammisa 1998, 71). Public opinion foreshadowed critiques of the current system and more restrictive welfare policies.

As growing numbers of unmarried mothers applied for welfare assistance, critics attacked the welfare system and casework model reforms, such as WIN, for failing to encourage work and marriage (Abramovitz 1996, 351). With the apparent failure of the casework approach to decrease welfare rolls or to encourage the work ethic and promote stable families, "many came to see welfare as a dependency trap, in which clients received income maintenance for long periods with little hope of moving off welfare" (Bane and Ellwood 1994, 19). Such views seemed to warrant imposing sanctions on recipients who failed to become self-sufficient in a specified amount of time. Reformers hoped such strict requirements would also lead to decreased welfare spending and decreased federal involvement in public welfare.

One main reason for WIN's failure was that it only required welfare recipients to *register,* not *participate,* in state employment programs. Although by 1986, 1.6 million AFDC recipients had registered for WIN programs, only about 220,000 received services. In addition, "[By 1986,] only 130,000 WIN registrants left welfare by 'working their way' off the rolls, most of them without any help from the WIN program. In most welfare offices WIN quickly became a paper compliance process, with clients and workers going through the motions of WIN registration, followed by a tacit understanding that neither the client nor the employment service was required to do much more" (Bane and Ellwood 1994, 21).

Clearly, forced registration did not lead to increased participation in work-related programs. As a result, critics urged for welfare reforms that imposed mandatory work requirements on recipients as a condition for aid.

The perceived failure of WIN in light of the still growing caseloads dampened the public's faith in the national welfare state. The federal government responded with reforms designed to reduce welfare expenditures and, by association, big government. In addition, the reforms aimed to strengthen work and family ethics through support of education, employment opportunities, and training programs. Because they had a significant impact on AFDC, the most important welfare policies for the purposes of this discussion are the Omnibus Budget Reconciliation Act of 1981 (OBRA), the Family Support Act of 1988 (FSA), and the Personal Responsibility and Work Opportunity Reconciliation Act (PRWGRA) of 1996.[8]

Both OBRA and FSA, passed under the Reagan administration, marked a major shift in welfare policy. These two acts decreased federal government involvement in public welfare and moved public welfare programs into the private and state sectors. A comparison of the Johnson and Reagan administrations' policies illustrates the magnitude of this change: "Whereas the Great Society created programs to rehabilitate the poor, the Reagan Revolution sought to reduce dependency on those programs. Whereas the Great Society expanded the role of the federal government in providing welfare under 'creative federalism,' the Reagan Revolution sought to give authority back to the states under "new federalism" (Cammisa 1998, 56).

The Reagan administration's policy of increased state responsibility for welfare reform is most clear in the government's support of state waivers. In an attempt to encourage state initiatives in welfare reform, Reagan allowed states to apply for waivers from welfare requirements to create their own programs. Many states responded with several innovative programs, such as Massachusetts's Employment and Training (ET) Choices program, Baltimore's Options program, and California's Greater Avenues to Independence (GAIN) program. Frequently, however, these programs achieved only modest successes (Bane and Ellwood 1994, 22–23).

The Omnibus Budget Reconciliation Act had profound implications for AFDC. Because AFDC was an entitlement, all states were legally bound to pay benefits to all eligible applicants. Moreover, "the entitlements [could not] be cut back simply by reducing authorizations or capping federal funds" (Abramovitz 1996, 355). The federal and state governments could, however, limit eligibility, and Reagan's OBRA proposed to do just that. In an effort to cut costs, reduce welfare rolls, and decrease government intervention, OBRA departed from previous work incentive programs by reducing recipient benefits, tightening eligibility requirements, and eliminating public-service jobs programs (Bane and Ellwood 1994, 20; Koon 1997, 25). It is estimated that, as a result of OBRA, federal and state governments saved more than $1.1 billion, that 400,000 working welfare mothers lost their AFDC grant, and that many more female-headed households became further impoverished (Abramovitz 1996, 356).

The late 1980s witnessed a growing concern with out-of-wedlock births and long-term dependency on public aid. Moreover, "the increase in the number of middle-class mothers with young children who are in the paid labor force increased political support for requiring AFDC mothers to work" (Weaver 2000, 70). In addition, there was a growing bipartisan consensus that requiring fathers to pay owed child support would lessen dependency. To research these views, President Reagan commissioned the White House Working Group on the Family, which issued a report in 1986 that reflected these concerns.

Raised in an environment in which fathers don't provide for their young and [in which] dependency on the government is assumed, few children will develop the skills of self-sufficiency or even the concept of personal responsibility. Young men will not strive to be good providers and young women will not expect it from their men. Family breakdown becomes cyclical, out-of-wedlock births become cyclical, and poverty and dependency become cyclical. (23)

Underscoring traditional family values, the report condemned out-of-wedlock births and stressed individual responsibility. The report failed to consider, however, the significant number of welfare recipients who were already making efforts at self-sufficiency: "Contrary to popular opinion, the perception of critics of welfare programs, and the imperatives of the family ethic, AFDC program statistics showed that many women on welfare already worked, actively sought a job, or became enrolled in an educational or training program" (Abramovitz 1996, 352). In fact, by the mid-1970s, almost 40 percent of the AFDC caseload was working, actively seeking employment, or participating in an educational program.

Consistent with the findings of the White House Working Group on the Family, President Reagan signed the Family Support Act of 1988, which was a more centrist welfare reform bill representing a compromise between liberals and conservatives. The goal of FSA was "to revise the AFDC program to emphasize work, child support and family benefits…[and] to encourage and assist needy children and parents under the new program to obtain the education, training and employment needed to avoid long-term welfare dependence" (Pub. L. 100–485). In contrast to previous legislation, FSA focused on providing people with the opportunity to succeed through an emphasis on training programs. Essentially, FSA reflected previous distrust with the eligibility-compliance model and support for encouraging welfare recipient self-sufficiency.

The major thrust of FSA was the Job Opportunities and Basic Skills (JOBS) program. JOBS included federal funds for child-care programs, employment and training programs, and mandatory work requirements. In contrast to WIN, which required AFDC recipients to *register* for a work-related program, the FSA mandated that states require a certain percentage of AFDC recipients with children age 6 or older to *participate* in the workforce, job-training programs, or educational programs. Some states required mothers with children as young as one year old to participate (Bane and Ellwood 1994, 23). Failure to comply could result in a loss or reduction of welfare grants (Abramovitz 1996, 358). Combining sanctions with incentives, the JOBS program also added transitional child care and Medicaid benefits during the period when families left AFDC and attempted to find work. Although FSA did contain work requirements similar to previous legislation like WIN, the shift in ideology was profound. "The distinction is more than a matter of semantics. Whether a work requirement is understood as a route out of welfare or as just another prerequisite for continued eligibility is a subtle but crucial difference for the behavior of both clients and front-line workers" (Bane and Ellwood 1994, 2).

Despite its popular goal of moving people off welfare and into work, the JOBS program received significant criticism for a variety of reasons. First, opponents feared that JOBS would force welfare recipients into the labor force, resulting in decreased wages far below the federal minimum.

Others critiqued the program for failing to meet the needs of recipients. Implicit in the JOBS philosophy was the notion that only through mandatory work requirements could welfare recipients break the cycle of dependency and move off welfare. Although consistent with prevailing public opinion, such a philosophy was inconsistent with reality; most people already used welfare as a transitional program (Abramovitz 1996, 359–63; Cammisa 1998, 10–11).

In the end, the JOBS program experienced limited success, chiefly due to program implementation problems and economic difficulties. Because the program was instituted during an economic recession, many states had trouble amassing the financial resources necessary to create the programs. Moreover, FSA never received proposed funding amounts, which imposed additional constraints on state programs (Cammisa 1998, 70). According to Bane and Ellwood: "Providing the education, employment, and training services mandated by FSA required state money (the federal government paid only about 60 percent of the cost), and the states did not have it. In 1991, the states claimed only about 60 percent of the $1 billion that the federal government had authorized for the JOBS program" (1994, 24). By 1992, only 16 percent of nonexempt AFDC recipients, which correlates to about 7 percent of all adult AFDC recipients, were participating in the JOBS program (24–25). Beyond that, participation in job programs did not guarantee that welfare recipients would be hired. Indeed, many trained program recipients remained unemployed.

THE PERSONAL RESPONSIBILITY AND WORK OPPORTUNITY RECONCILIATION ACT OF 1996: THE END OF WELFARE AS WE KNOW IT?

By the 1990s, legislators expressed a growing desire to reform welfare yet again. A number of factors fueled this interest, including implementation difficulties with the JOBS program. In addition, many social scientists and welfare scholars were frustrated with a system that did not seem to support work. As evidence, these scholars cited that working mothers were often not much better off financially than mothers who relied on public assistance. Still others noted that if the welfare system enforced child-support payments from noncustodial parents, many families currently on welfare could escape poverty and welfare dependence. In short, scholars, community leaders, and legislators charged that the current welfare system was incompatible with core mainstream American values of work, family, and personal responsibility.

Political interests also sparked hearings and debates that led to the passage of the 1996 Personal Responsibility and Work Opportunity Reconciliation Act. In an interview with the author on March 19, 1999, Ron

Haskins, staff director for the Subcommittee on Human Resources of the House Committee on Ways and Means, revealed that Republican leaders were mindful of welfare's paramount importance as a key political issue, and they carefully planned a strategy to ensure a conservative policy victory. The seeds for the Republican position can be found in what Haskins referred to as a Republican educational document on welfare, a paper entitled "Moving Ahead: How America Can Reduce Poverty through Work." Produced in July 1992 by Republican members of the Human Resources Subcommittee, including Representatives E. Clay Shaw (R-Fla.), Nancy L. Johnson (R-Conn.), and Fred Grandy (R-Iowa), this document served as the basis for a systematic education campaign to inform key legislators about welfare reform issues and concerns. Haskins explained that a major key to winning the welfare reform debate was to ensure that a core "A-team" of Republicans knew the arguments and research that informed the Republican welfare philosophy. In addition to the authors of "Moving Ahead," key Republican leaders included, among others, Missouri Representative James Talent, Pennsylvania Senator Rick Santorum, Texas Representative Tom DeLay, and Arkansas Representative Y. Tim Hutchinson.

As they prepared to control the House of Representatives, Republicans organized several welfare reform task forces and devised several welfare reform proposals grounded in the 1992 "Moving Ahead" document. Similar in many respects, all of the proposals continued a trend of decreased federal involvement and increased state control over public welfare. Reflecting growing public hostility toward welfare, the proposals further stressed work requirements (rather than social services or education) as the principal vehicle for leaving welfare and instituted strict regulatory measures designed to reform welfare recipients. What was significant about these proposals and task force efforts, noted Haskins, was that they allowed the Republican party to build solid relationships with various constituencies and to test carefully the conservative and moderate limits of welfare policy, thereby ensuring support from the greatest number of both Democrats and Republicans.

Meanwhile, in an attempt to keep his campaign promise to "end welfare as we know it," President Clinton introduced the Work and Responsibility Act of 1994, consisting of four main goals: (1) limit welfare receipt to two years, after which time recipients would be required to work; (2) increase enforcement of child support; (3) reduce teenage pregnancy; and (4) assist welfare recipients in finding employment through provision of education, child care, and job training (Abramovitz 1996, 361; Cammisa 1998, 64–65, 72).[9] In retaining support services and job skills training, Clinton's Work and Responsibility Act was actually a logical extension of the FSA, which Clinton had helped negotiate during his tenure as Arkansas governor and head of the National Governors Association (NGA), an interest group comprising the 50 state governors (Cammisa 1998, 57, 72). The main difference between Clinton's proposal and FSA was that in addition to the reform goals characteristic of FSA, the Work and Responsibility Act included a deterrent in the form of a welfare time limit.

When Clinton's proposal reached the Republican-dominated Congress, it was rejected. Instead, the Congress offered another proposal, which extended and incorporated some elements from Clinton's plan. Republicans outlined this proposal in their Contract with America, promising to balance the budget, reduce taxes, and cut social welfare programs (Axinn and Levin 1997, 305; Cammisa 1998, 65).[10] The Contract with America, a group of initiatives endorsed by the Republican party prior to the 1994 November congressional elections, was just one in a series of welfare reform proposals that informed PRWORA. The contract proposed a five-year lifetime limit of welfare benefits. In addition, the Republican Congress offered states the option of taking welfare as a block grant. Theoretically, a block grant gives states greater control over welfare spending and, therefore, narrows the role of federal government in public welfare as well as shifts the burden of program administration and responsibility to the states. The Republican's two proposals, both vetoed by President Clinton on December 6, 1995, and January 9, 1996, called for a number of controversial work and family regulations.[11] These requirements included a ban on the use of federal funds for unmarried mothers under age 18, strict paternity penalties, and a family cap (i.e., cutting off AFDC benefits to families who gave birth to more children while on welfare) (Abramovitz 1996, 363; Axinn and Levin 1997, 314; Cammisa 1998, 73). A key difference between the Republican bills and Clinton's 1994 proposal was that the Republican versions ended entitlements through the block grant. Under AFDC, any family that met eligibility requirements was entitled to receive benefits. In contrast, block grants capped federal spending and allowed states to deny aid to individuals who otherwise met eligibility requirements.

While the Congress and President Clinton debated national welfare policy, President Clinton continued a practice begun under the Reagan administration of allowing states to experiment with welfare policy. In so doing, Clinton implicitly supported the increasing public dissatisfaction with big government and the welfare state and growing public support for greater state control of welfare programs. By March 1996, 37 states had applied for and received waivers from the federal government to experiment with family caps, work requirements, and time limits (Cammisa 1998, 70). According to Axinn and Levin, "Many of the state 'experiments' include[d] provisions such as mandating that teenage beneficiaries stay in school and live with a parent, cutting benefits for any child born while the mother was receiving welfare, cutting the grant to the family if a child had too many unexcused absences ('learnfare'), and proposals to reduce grants if the children miss their vaccinations or if women miss rent payments" (1997, 314). Inherent in these policies were myriad assumptions about welfare recipients. Sanctions on reproduction and learnfare policies implied that welfare mothers needed guidance in making reproductive choices and in raising their children appropriately. Guided by prevailing public opinion, the proposals responded to perceptions that welfare families had children simply to stay on welfare, a conception that contradicted reported data: Approximating the national average, most welfare families had two children (Abramovitz 1996, 364; Cammisa 1998, 16–17).

In addition to suggestions from President Clinton, congressional members, and state representatives, the NGA offered its own suggestions on welfare reform. The NGA, which convened in February 1996, endorsed block grants and proposed welfare reforms, including cuts in food stamp, child nutrition, and job programs. The NGA proposal was highly influential because it represented a bipartisan effort. In addition, the NGA proposal reflected the views of the governors who would be responsible for running any state-controlled welfare block grants.

Legislators debated each of these proposals to varying degrees in a series of hearings and debates held from 1992 to 1996, the majority of which occurred during the Republican-dominated 104th Congress. Haskins explained that several benefits accrued to the Republicans during the hearings because of their majority status. For example, Republican leaders were able to hand select the majority of the witnesses and determine the order and structure of the hearings panels. Not surprisingly, then, a large number of witnesses within the hearings and debates were affiliated with groups supportive of the Republican platform, including such religious organizations and conservative institutions as the American Enterprise Institute (Douglas Besharov, Marvin H. Kosters, Charles Murray), Heritage Foundation (Robert Rector, Kate Walsh O'Beirne), Christian Coalition (Heidi Stirrup), Traditional Values Coalition (Andrea Sheldon), American Fathers Coalition (David Burgess, Bill Harrington, Murray Steinberg), and Hudson Institute (Anna Kondratas, Michael Horowitz).[12] Commenting on the force of conservative scholars in the hearings process, Michigan Representative Dave Camp (R) observed: "With the help of prominent conservative thinkers, several of whom will testify today, Republicans have succeeded in drawing the Nation's attention to the magnitude of the illegitimacy crisis. Millions of Americans now understand that out-of-wedlock births are at the center of a tangle of social pathologies, including school dropout, welfare use, unemployment, drug addictions and crime" (House Committee on Ways and Means 1995b, 134; see also Weaver 2000, 142–43). Three important consequences resulted from Republican structuring of the hearings. First, in selecting witnesses whom they knew would support the Republican welfare reforms, Republicans created a group of texts with constitutive force. Specifically, these texts invited legislators to act on evidence presented in the hearings and debates in ways that benefited both the legislator's and the party's public record. Second, Republicans were able to mitigate the force of opposing testimony that threatened to damage the Republican position. As Haskins pointed out, Republicans could bury strong Democratic witnesses in panels that Republicans perceived had less significant testimony and during unfavorable times. Third, witness selection and panel structuring clearly facilitated Republican leadership's use of the hearings as a critical venue for presenting their views and educating other Republican members on the party policy platform.

The consistency of viewpoints and statements expressed in the hearings by Republican representatives indicates the success of this campaign in forging a Republican welfare reform policy. For example, the statements of Representative Tom DeLay, Connecticut Representative Christopher Shays (R), and Maine Senator Olympia J. Snowe (R) bear unmistakable resemblance to one another. Early in the hearing process, DeLay remarked:

I know time is fleeting, so let me just quote our minority whip, Newt Gingrich, who is often known to say, when we are having 12-year-olds having babies, and 15-year-olds shooting each other, and 17-year-olds dying of AIDS, and 18-year-olds graduating with diplomas they can't read, it is time to say farewell to welfare as we know it. (House Committee on Ways and Means, 1994a, 448)

Six months later, Congressman Shays wrote:

When you have 12-year-olds having babies, 14-year-olds selling drugs, 15-year-olds killing each other, 18-year-olds who can't even read their own diplomas, and 30-year-olds who have never held a job, you see that measures such as orphanages and foster homes must be considered as possible solutions in reforming the existing welfare system. (House Committee on Ways and Means, January 1995a, 734)

Nearly eight months later, Senator Snowe observed:

In today's society, it is hardly uncommon for an individual to be smoking or drinking by the time they are 10; to be caught stealing by the time they are 11; to be hooked on drugs by the time they are 12; to be sexually active by 13 years of age; to be pregnant by the time of their 14th birthday; to be on welfare at 15; to be a high school drop-out at 16; and to have the American dream be nothing more than a pipe dream at 15. (*Cong. Rec.* 1995, S13790)

Notably, all three comments draw on information in the *Moving Ahead* document, in which welfare and single-parenthood are explicitly tied to "poor school attendance and achievement, dropping out of school, committing crimes, having illegitimate children, being without a job" (ii–iii).[13] Such similarities that link welfare to social ills are evidence of a carefully orchestrated strategy to ensure incorporation of Republican ideas into public policy.

With such strong evidence of a partisan hearing and debate process, it might be easy to conclude that the resulting legislation codified a Republican and conservative agenda with little Democratic or liberal influence. Despite the emphasis on conservative witnesses, however, the proposals submitted by both Democratic and Republican leaders, as well as the resulting legislation, actually demonstrate remarkable ideological consistency.[14] An exchange of political position papers between Secretary of Health and Human Services Donna E. Shalala, who represented the Clinton administration's views, and the House Republican conferees over welfare bill H.R. 4 provides an illustrative example. In an October 26, 1995, letter to Senate Majority Leader Bob Dole (R-Kans.), Shalala outlined the administration's views on H.R. 4. In a December 5, 1995, document, entitled "Comparison of Administration Positions on Welfare Issues Raised by HHS with Final Bill Resulting from House-Senate Conference," the Republicans responded to Shalala's letter. In these exchanges, both parties were in substantive agreement with all major welfare reform issues, including child-support enforcement, child-care provision, teenage residency requirements, and time limits. As the Republican conferees noted, overall, the administration's and the Republican's bill were in full or almost complete agreement on 85 percent of all welfare issues and strategies for reform. Most differences between the Democratic and Republican bills were not ideological or substantive, but rather technical. In other words, the bills differed on implementation details, such as the percentage of people who should be exempt from the time limit and whether a requirement should be federally mandated or included as a state option.

The result of the hearings and debates over the NGA proposals, state initiatives, the Contract with America, and Clinton's 1994 proposal was the Personal Responsibility and Work Opportunity Reconciliation Act of 1996. PRWORA promised to decrease welfare spending by $55 billion over five years; limit welfare receipt to two years, after which recipients must work; establish a lifetime limit of five years on the use of federal dollars for welfare; and allocate a lump-sum payment (block grant) to states to create state-based welfare programs. This block grant became known as Temporary Assistance for Needy Families (TANF) and replaced AFDC. PRWORA was highly controversial and sparked heated debates among government officials, welfare advocates, welfare recipients, and the public. PRWORA advocates argued that the new legislation would decrease welfare rolls, allow states to tailor programs to their regional needs, and put the able-bodied to work. In contrast, opponents expressed concern over increased state flexibility, with some asserting that state welfare control would result in pronounced hardship and poverty for poor people and their families (Cozic 1997, 8; Sawhill, Weaver, Harkins, and Kane 2002, 3–29).

With the passage of PRWORA, the cycle of responsibility for welfare provision moved back toward the states. From local welfare efforts characteristic of colonial times, responsibility for supplying welfare gradually had moved to the states and then to the federal government. Although it was a state-federal program in many ways, the Social Security Act of 1935 strongly favored the federal government's involvement in public welfare. This federal emphasis prevailed throughout the 1960s. More recently, however, as evident by state waiver experimentation, welfare reforms have indicated a trend toward reducing federal government and increasing state involvement in public welfare. Although PRWORA provides federal funding for welfare and establishes general guidelines for state maintenance of welfare programs, it also allows states much more flexibility in creating rules and administering the programs.

Another major consequence of PRWORA is the return to locating the source of poverty within individuals. As its name suggests, the focus of the Personal Responsibility and Work Opportunity Reconciliation Act is on individual self-sufficiency and independence. Nowhere is the focus on individual responsibility for success more clear than in the time limit and work requirement provisions of the law, which officially ended entitlements and mandated self-support. Simply stated, no longer are poor people guaranteed government assistance. Explaining the significance of entitlement termination, Cammisa commented:

As an entitlement, anyone who was eligible for AFDC could sue the government if they were denied benefits, and by law, funding would have to increase commensurately with the number of people eligible. The only way to change this entitlement to welfare benefits was to change the statutory law—which Congress did when it established TANF. Eliminating the welfare entitlement was the most fundamental change to the welfare law.... It signaled a change in attitude about the causes of poverty. By saying that recipients are no longer entitled to welfare, Congress was also saying that individual lack of initiative is the root problem of poverty. Ending the entitlement status of welfare marked the end of an era. (1998, 119)

Consistent with placing responsibility on individuals, PRWORA states that the route off of welfare is through hard work. Mandatory work requirements and significant cuts or elimination of social services, for example, imply that most welfare recipients are capable of and obligated to work their way off of assistance through their own efforts.

In promoting work and self-responsibility, PRWORA further narrows the number of people considered to be the worthy poor. In fact, with the end of entitlements came the end of the notion of deserving poor. Implicitly, no longer does one *deserve* aid; rather one merely *needs* temporary assistance. A recent trend toward referring to welfare recipients as clients and the emphasis on welfare as a social contract in which the client is obligated to perform services (work) in return for government assistance illustrate the end of rights-based aid (Cammisa 1998, 114). In addition, PRWORA codifies increased public hostility toward welfare recipients, largely a result of the increasing numbers of never-married mothers on welfare, whom many people perceive to be able-bodied but not employed outside of the home and, therefore, unworthy of sustained public aid. If welfare expenditures are any indicator of public perceptions of poverty, the 1990 welfare outlays clearly illustrate growing public disdain of the nonworking poor. In 1990, approximately half of the $1,045 billion spent on social welfare went toward non-means-tested, work-related social insurance and government retirement programs, and 25 percent went toward education. In contrast, less than 16 percent of this money went to categorical, means-tested, non-work-related programs, such as AFDC, Medicaid, and food stamps (Axinn and Levin 1997, 180). By placing caps on federal funding in the form of lump-sum block grants, PRWORA continues the trend of reducing federal welfare funds. Moreover, PRWORA excludes legal immigrants from receiving assistance (illegal immigrants have always been ineligible). Although PRWORA does allow states to make exceptions in particular cases, the focus of the law indicates a public perception of welfare recipients as able-bodied individuals (unworthy of public assistance) responsible for moving off of welfare and into paid employment.

To aid welfare recipients in making the right choice of finding work, PRWORA includes stipulations that perform the dual function of reform and deterrence. Embedded within President Clinton's August 1, 1996, statement in support of legislation are the seeds of these reform and deterrence functions. Clinton praised the legislation for its promise: "To transform a broken system that traps too many people in a cycle of dependence, to one that emphasizes work and independence, to give people on welfare a chance to draw a paycheck, not a welfare check. It gives us a better chance to give those on welfare what we want for all families in America, the opportunity to succeed at home and at work" (*New York Times* 1996, A24).

In this passage, individuals are responsible for their own success. Implicit in any failure, marked by receipt of a welfare check, is a stigma associated with welfare receipt. Stigma, along with strict work requirements and lifetime limits on welfare receipt associated with PRWORA legislation, is theoretically supposed to deter applicants from applying for aid and to reform welfare recipients by forcing them into the labor market. Moreover, the twin goals of deterrence and reform mask a new welfare strategy. Whereas previous legislation aimed to improve people's lives and reduce poverty, current policies intend for people to work without necessarily decreasing hardship. As public affairs and economics professor Robert Haveman contended: "[W]elfare reform policy is no longer antipoverty policy. The ultimate goal of all of this activity is not to make poor people's lives better than they are now. Getting poor people to *work* is equated with making their lives better" (1995, 199, emphasis in original).

In sum, PRWORA is informed by many of the same themes and arguments that influenced previous welfare legislation, from colonial times to the present. Colonial emphasis on a family ethic in which relatives are primarily responsible for caring for their less fortunate and destitute family members is reflected in PRWORA's kinship laws. In addition, colonial efforts to enforce stringent work requirements and emphasize personal responsibility are clearly evident in contemporary reforms. Indeed, as stated earlier, the very name of the Personal Responsibility and Work Opportunity Reconciliation Act underscores the importance of self-help and hard work.

A significant portion of PRWORA has its ideological roots in nineteenth-century welfare reforms, as well. Officials in the nineteenth century accused paupers of being intimately connected with indolence, intemperance, moral degeneracy, and criminality. Such perceptions are found in PRWORA, with its provisions to address the immorality, substance abuse, and fraudulent behavior of welfare recipients. PRWORA also codifies legislation reflective of nineteenth-century suspicions of the pauper's family ethic. For example, several representatives and witnesses in the contemporary debate promoted religious schools, orphanages, foster care, and charitable organizations as welfare reform strategies. Following these suggestions, PRWORA eases restrictions on adoption and foster care policies and allows states to establish second-chance homes for young mothers to "learn parenting skills, including child development, family budgeting, health and nutrition" (*PRWORA of 1996*, 2137). PRWORA also funnels federal money to religious charities that wish to address welfare-related issues. In a manner reminiscent of the nineteenth-century Sunday school movement, these contemporary strategies aim to separate children from the perceived negative influences of their parents. Similarly, the strategies also imply that public programs best provide welfare children with proper moral instruction.

As with mothers' pensions, several provisions of PRWORA emphasize the importance of women as caretakers. For example, the act reduces work hour requirements for women who have small children under the age of six and, as a state option, excuses mothers from all work activities if they have a child under the age of one. In addition, states cannot terminate assistance to single parents who fail to meet work requirements if child care is unavailable, unsuitable, or unaffordable. PRWORA also counts "the provision of child care services to an individual who is participating in a community service program" as an accepted work activity (*PRWORA of 1996*, 2133). These provisions all reinforce the perception that the federal government should safeguard a mother's responsibility to her children.

Vestiges of the 1935 Social Security Act and Aid to Dependent Children welfare reforms remain in PRWORA. Most notably, the idea prevails that public assistance renders recipients incapable of self-help through hard work and dedication to family. PRWORA's support for temporary assistance only and condemnation of individual entitlements reflect a continued suspicion of the power of long-term aid to debilitate individuals. In addition, some aspects of PRWORA embody social perceptions of welfare recipients as similar to all Americans who are subject to temporary misfortune. Economic provisions of PRWORA, such as Individual Development Accounts (IDAs), are geared toward capable talented individuals who simply need temporary aid to overcome hardship.

Themes of welfare reform legislation from 1936 to 1979 are also evident in PRWORA. For example, PRWORA provides recipients with some opportunities for skills training and community service. Reflecting the belief that welfare dependence and out-of-wedlock births are linked, PRWORA aims to reduce the incidence of out-of-wedlock births by promoting two parent families and ensuring parental responsibility for and financial support of children. PRWORA's emphasis on work requirements also has its ideological roots in the work requirements of the 1940s through the 1970s. The act specifies, for instance, that "if an individual in a family receiving assistance under the State program funded under this part refuses to engage in work required in accordance with this section, the State shall (A) reduce the amount of assistance otherwise payable to the family...(B) terminate such assistance, subject to good cause" (*PRWORA of 1996*, 2133). Later the act specifies that recipients who fail to register for employment activities will also be ineligible for the food stamp program (2315–16). Like views of welfare recipients prevalent in the 1940s to the 1970s, these provisions support a perception of welfare recipients as unskilled and able to work only in conjunction with strict guidelines and sanctions.

Despite criticism and limited success, OBRA and FSA also have informed PRWORA in important ways. PRWORA continues a practice from the 1980s of supporting increased state responsibility for legislating welfare. PRWORA's incorporation of block grants and support of state waivers all theoretically give states the option for greater control over welfare. In addition, PRWORA persists in the 1980s trend of valuing work, over training and education, as a strategy to independence, with greater attention to work requirements.

After the Reforms: Some Mixed Reviews

Set to expire six years after its implementation, PRWORA's October 1, 2002, reauthorization prompted congressional discussion of several proposals. Based on the assumption that the 1996 Act had been a success, many of these proposals retain much of the substance of PRWORA, with a greater emphasis on marriage promotion, responsible fatherhood, and stricter work requirements. Nevertheless, for a variety of reasons, including the primacy of foreign affairs and terrorism, welfare reform has become a lower policy priority. Not surprisingly then, PRWORA has not been reauthorized.

Judging the effectiveness of the 1996 reforms has been somewhat difficult. The passage of the Act occurred during a time of relative economic prosperity and followed other benefit changes, such as an increase in the Earned Income Tax Credit. Consequently, it is difficult to attribute any success directly to the 1996 reforms. Nevertheless, many scholars agree that the 1996 reforms have produced some positive results. Cofounders of Empower America, William J. Bennett (former secretary of education) and Jack Kemp (former secretary of housing and urban development) reported in an August 1, 2002, *Wall Street Journal* article, entitled "Keep Reforming Welfare," that the 1996 bill was "one of the most significant and successful pieces of social policy enacted in the last half century. Since it was signed, welfare rolls have plummeted by more than 50%. Child poverty is at its lowest point in more than 20 years, and poverty levels for black children are at their lowest recorded level ever." A Health and Human Services (HHS) September 3, 2003 press release pointed out that the "number of recipients (defined as individuals) in March 2003 was 4,963,771, a decline of 4.3 percent since March of 2002 and 59.5 percent since August 1996, when the TANF law was signed into law." Other scholars pointed to different promising trends, such as stabilizing or declining rates for teenage pregnancy, increased employment among single mothers, and higher earnings and a decline in welfare payments for lower-income families (Sawhill, Weaver, Haskins, and Kane 2002, 8–19; Sawhill 2002, 160). Ron Haskins, a senior consultant at the Annie E. Casey Foundation and a guest scholar in economic studies at the Brookings Institution, noted that, since the 1996 act, "cash welfare rolls are in the first sustained period of decline in history." He added that there has been an "unprecedented rise in employment by single mothers" since 1996 and that there have been "large increases in the income of mother-headed families" (2002, 17). Consequently, in a September 23, 2003 HHS press release, HHS Secretary Tommy G. Thompson announced that "TANF has been a tremendous success because of its central focus on helping families find and succeed at work so they can leave welfare dependency behind."

Other supporters have argued that the act's commitment to marriage and two-parent families signals an important and long-overdue change in America's family values. According to David Popenoe, professor of sociology at Rutgers University, "1996 proved to be a pivotal year for family issues.... [M]ost importantly, a bipartisan welfare reform bill was passed which for the first time took seriously the need to change family structure among the poor. Three out of the four legal goals of the welfare reform law were marriage related: promote 'marriage, encourage...two-parent families, and reduce...out-of-wedlock birth" (2002, 17–18). Preliminary data, such as an increase in the number of women who received child support payments owed to them and a decline in the number of children living in single-parent households, seems to justify the success of the 1996 act. Not surprisingly, some scholars, including Wade F. Horn, founder of the National Fatherhood Initiative and current assistant secretary of health and human services for children and families under the Bush administration, have urged reformers to "build on the successes we've seen over the last five or ten years in terms of increasing the public's awareness of the consequences of fatherlessness and the importance of marriage to children, adults, and communities" (2002, 11). Clearly, much evidence appears to affirm the 1996 reforms as successful.

Other factors, in contrast, suggest that the 1996 Act has had a more negative impact on welfare recipients and poor working families. For example, critics of PRWORA argue that many groups of people such as the hard-to-employ, legal immigrants, and some working families are now worse off following the 1996 reforms. Some recipients have been subject to sanctions and many of those sanctioned already face more barriers to employment than other recipients. In addition, some recipients and low-income working families, who are entitled to benefits such as food stamps and Medicaid have lost those benefits because of difficulties associated with eligibility procedures. "In 2000, only about half of eligible families— that is, families that were poor enough to qualify for TANF cash benefits— received TANF assistance" (Fremstad 2003). Furthermore, legal immigrants have lost eligibility to many benefits, resulting in increased hardship among this population (Fix and Haskins 2002). Although it is true that many mothers have left welfare and found jobs, it is also true that low earnings, lack of health-care insurance, transportation barriers, and child-care issues pose significant obstacles to economic self-sufficiency (Sawhill, Weaver, and Kane 2002c, 4–5; Moffitt 2002, 79–86). Arguing that many of the Bush Administration's reauthorization proposals would have a negative impact on families, Brookings scholar Margy Waller shared the results of her 2002 survey of states where the 50 largest cities are located. Investigating the cash assistance caseloads in the counties where the cities are located and the number of cases facing the time limit on federally funded assistance, Waller reported: "We learned that while only 33 percent of the state residents live in the urban counties we surveyed, those counties were home to over half of their state's welfare cases facing a federal time limit, and an astounding 71 percent of their long-term cases facing the time limit." She added that "welfare rolls in almost half of the cities increased," and "two-thirds of cities saw an increase in the proportion of welfare recipients facing substantial barriers to work" (e.g. lack of skills training and health problems) with "layoffs due to the economy" as the top reason for welfare recidivism.

Most mayors reported that they would have to reduce benefits and services to TANF families and poor working families in the coming year. According to Waller, the mayors' responses to the survey and concerns over reauthorization proposals are consistent with other research findings. (Waller's remarks made at the American Public Human Services Association Summer Meeting, July 21, 2003.)

Indeed, many supporters of the 1996 act have acknowledged the central role of a strong economy in welfare reform success. For example, Bennett and Kemp wrote: "There is no doubt a growing economy is essential to the continued success of welfare reform" (2002; Blank 2002, 103). Some indicators of economic health, however, are especially troubling. Although poverty rates generally have not increased significantly, measures of the severity of poverty increased so that "In 2002, the average amount by which people who were poor fell below the poverty line was greater than in any other year since 1979, the first year for which these data are available" (Center on Budget and Policy Priorities 2003). *New York Times* reporter John W. Fountain remarked on this disturbing trend in a September 29, 2002, article: "[T]he number of Americans in poverty has risen again, for the first time in eight years." At the same time, over the past couple years, unemployment rates have declined and the number of long-term unemployed (those out of work for more than six months) has risen dramatically from 650,000 a month in 2000 to 810,000 in 2001, 1.55 million in 2002, and an average of 1.89 million so far in 2003 (Center on Budget and Policy Priorities 2003). Recent economic turbulence that seems unlikely to improve imminently certainly raises serious concerns about the effectiveness of reform proposals that, like PRWORA, are dependent on a strong economy.

In light of economic challenges and because reauthorization proposals include increased work requirements, some welfare policy experts like Mark Greenberg of the Center for Law and Social Policy do not believe states are prepared to meet reauthorization requirements. Greenberg observed, for example, that "A new analysis by the Congressional Research Service (CRS) concludes that if the participation requirements of H.R. 4 (the House TANF reauthorization bill) had been in effect in 2001, the national average participation rate would have been 32 percent. Under H.R. 4, when the requirements are fully phased in, most states would be required to meet a 70 percent participation rate" (Greenberg 2003). Already, most mayors reported that they would have to reduce benefits and services to TANF families and poor working families in the coming year ((Margy Waller 2003a). Robert Greenstein, executive director for the Center on Budget and Policy Priorities pointed out that due to budget crises, "more than 35 states either have made or are now actively considering cuts in programs funded through TANF or the child care block grant" (remarks presented at the Brookings Institute Forum entitled "Ending the Safety Net as We Know it?: Assessing the New Federal Block Grant Proposals" on 13 June 2003).

Block grants, like TANF, are especially susceptible to budget cuts because the identity of the people who are being affected is more obscured in a block grant program than a categorical assistance program (Waller 2003b; Greenstein 2003). "The [Bush] administration has clearly understood from day one that if it publishes deep cuts in specific programs in its budget—with the potential to harm identifiable groups of families, children, elderly, and people with disabilities—this would reduce its ability to get its tax cuts enacted. It has pursued a different strategy.... [T]he block grants are a fundamental part of that strategy. It is a strategy to reduce very gradually, over time, the federal government's financing role in an array of programs" (Greenstein 2003). Superwaivers which give states considerable power to combine and integrate TANF social services block grants and child care programs are one such measure included in both the House and Senate bills to reduce the federal government role in assistance provision. Some organizations worry that if superwaivers are included in reauthorization legislation, states will eliminate standards, protection, and services for low-income families (Coalition on Human Needs 2003).

Data on recent demographic trends also cast doubt on the act's success. Observed *New York Times* reporter Nina Bernstein in a July 29, 2002, article:

When studies last year showed that the share of the nation's children living in single-parent households had declined in the late 1990s, many welcomed the results as signs that the 1996 welfare overhaul was working. But new research underscores a smaller, unwelcome trend: a rising share of children, particularly black children in cities, are turning up in no-parent households, left with relatives, friends or foster families without either their mother or their father.

Despite the efforts of the fatherhood and marriage movements, the nuclear family and marriage do not seem to be making a strong comeback, especially in lower-income families likely to be affected most by welfare reform changes. "For the First Time, Nuclear Families Drop Below 25% of Households" was the headline gracing the front page of the May 15, 2001, edition of the *New York Times*. Relying on census data, this same article noted a rise in unmarried couples living together and an increase in households with children headed by single mothers. These trends correlate with the findings of the Fragile Families Study, an impressive nationwide study of 5,000 low- to middle-income couples who are new parents. In an August 1, 2002 Brookings Institution briefing, Christina M. Gibson, assistant professor of public policy studies at the Terry Sanford Institute of Public Policy at Duke University, reported on the results of the Fragile Families Study. According to Gibson, although 80 percent of the 5,000 couples had "pro-marriage attitudes" (saying that they wanted to marry), only 10 percent had done so a year later. Indeed, these statistics and trends pose challenges and concerns for social policy makers and scholars.

This brief thumbnail sketch of American welfare history characterizes the competing depictions and themes that have informed contemporary welfare policy and public perceptions of the welfare system. These competing depictions and arguments of welfare recipients and the welfare system that led to the passage of PRWORA all warrant different responses to questions of Who is responsible for welfare provision? Who deserves aid? What are the functions of public assistance? and Who or what are the causes of poverty? This historical overview also serves to clarify present values and ideas that continue to guide welfare policy today. For example, throughout history, undeserving welfare receipt is frequently characterized in racial and ethnic terms, connected to poor morals and upbringing, and associated with out-of-wedlock births. In contrast, deserving welfare recipients are often classified as morally upright citizens who experience a misfortune beyond their control. Racial and ethnic qualifiers are largely absent in characterizations of deserving welfare recipients, although whiteness is implied. The nuclear family, hard work, individual responsibility, and Judeo-Christian values emerge as normative. Finally, the focus remains largely on women, whereas men are noticeably absent.

As we shall see in the next chapters, and building on Perelman and Olbrecht-Tyteca's (1971) concept of presence, the themes embedded in this historical framework lend primacy to values that shape and guide contemporary discussions. Recognition of the multiplicity of competing themes and the ability of legislation to legitimate and codify select accounts provide the context for an in-depth analysis of the hearings and debates surrounding PRWORA's passage and its impending reauthorization.

NOTES

1. Chaim Perelman defined the concept of presence in his book *The Realm of Rhetoric*: "Every argument implies a preliminary selection of facts and values, their specific description in a given language, and an emphasis which varies with the importance given them.... Choosing to single out certain things for presentation in a speech draws the attention of the audience to them and thereby gives them a *presence* that prevents them from being neglected.... Presence acts directly upon our sensibility" (1982, 34–35).

2. Although public opinion sustained societal perceptions that black migrants to northern cities were disproportionately taking advantage of welfare benefits, the settlement laws (residency requirements) largely prevented migrants from appearing on welfare rolls.

3. As during the nineteenth century, suitable home provisions persisted, and these provisions, along with man-in-the-house and suitable father rules, mandated that the presence of any man, even one who was unrelated to the child, excluded the family from aid. Of course, the underlying assumption was that any man in the house was a suitable father and, therefore, a financial provider for the child or children. Officials conducted midnight raids to identify the presence of such unrelated men, claiming that their presence was evidence that the family in question had a breadwinner and did not need financial aid. Man-in-the-house rules and durational residence requirements were eventually eliminated by U.S. Supreme Court judgments in 1968 and 1969 (Axinn and Levin 1997, 234–35; Cammisa 1998, 47).

4. Mary Jo Bane later became the assistant secretary of Children and Families in the U.S. Department of Health and Human Services. David Ellwood became the assistant secretary for Planning and Evaluation at the U.S. Department of Health and Human Services.

5. The Public Welfare amendments of 1962, Economic Opportunity Act of 1964, and Social Security amendments of 1967 all suffered delayed and partial implementation for a variety of reasons (Abramovitz 1996, 331–32, 341; Bane and Ellwood 1994, 10–11; Cammisa 1998, 53–54). Additional information on the Public Welfare and Social Security amendments and related historical context can be found in Axinn and Levin (1997, 236–49). Zarefsky's (1986) *President Johnson's War on Poverty* provides extensive analysis of the Economic Opportunity Act of 1964, the War on Poverty, and the Great Society. Charles Murray's (1984) *Losing Ground* critiques the Great Society programs for creating dependence and impoverishing the poor.

6. Presidents Lyndon B. Johnson and Richard M. Nixon both delayed implementation of the welfare freeze, which Congress repealed in 1969 (Axinn and Levin 1997, 247).

7. In an earlier study, Gilens concluded that public "racial attitudes are the single most important influence on whites' welfare views," and that these "negative views of black welfare mothers are more politically potent, generating greater opposition to welfare than comparable views of white mothers" (1996, 53).

8. Weaver provides a balanced discussion of the political forces that stalled, thwarted, and propelled these legislative measures (2000, 54–101).

9. Two recent books provide in-depth analyses of work and welfare alternatives from the perspectives of welfare recipients, economists, and public policy officials. In *Making Ends Meet,* Kathryn Edin and Laura Lein (1997) discuss the findings of interviews with low-skilled single mothers in Boston, Charleston, Chicago, and San Antonio. The authors explored the sources of the mothers' income, the types of hardships the mothers and their children endured, and the ways in which mothers assessed the economic and noneconomic choices of work or welfare. Based on their findings, Edin and Lein concluded that neither welfare nor low-wage work provide a living wage. Essays in *The Work Alternative,* edited by Demetra Nightingale and Robert Haveman (1995), examine welfare reform in relation to the labor market by discussing work as an alternative to welfare, questioning the availability of living-wage jobs, and suggesting alternative welfare policies.

10. On Election Day, November 8, 1994, the Republicans gained control of the U.S. Senate and House of Representatives. Led by Representatives Newt Gingrich (R-Ga.) and Dick Armey (R-Tex.), Republicans outlined basic values and principles guiding their platform. "Based on these principles House Republicans outlined a vision for America's future and the role of government. That vision seeks to renew the American dream by promoting individual liberty, economic opportunity, and personal responsibility, through limited and effective government" (Gillespie and Schellhas 1994, 5).

11. The first Republican welfare reform bill was tied to budget reconciliation legislation. When Clinton vetoed this bill on December 6, 1995, he justified his opposition on the grounds that the deficit reduction provisions were unsatisfactory. Attempting to get President Clinton to veto welfare reform specifically and thereby renege on his campaign promise to "end welfare as we know it," Republicans separated the welfare reform bill from the budget legislation and sent the welfare bill to the president as a stand-alone bill. President Clinton vetoed this welfare reform bill on January 6, 1996 (Cammisa 1998, 75).

12. Haskins also indicated that the testimony of African American witnesses was extremely important for the Republican case because it highlighted the party's awareness of racial and gender issues in welfare. Haskins mentioned, in particular, the utility of testimony from Boston University economics professor Glenn Loury, University of California public policy professor James Q. Wilson, and Kellogg Stress Institute owner Virginia Kellogg.

13. Other representatives made similar comments, including Greg Ganske (R-Iowa): "To take a chapter from our Speaker, my wife has helped 13-year-old girls deliver their babies. I have taken care of 15-year-olds with gunshot wounds to the head. I have taken care of 17-year-olds with needle track infections up and down their arms and who probably have AIDS because of it. And my wife and I have personally seen violence in our daughter's public school" (House Committee on Ways and Means 1995c, 796–97); Charles B. Rangel (D-N.Y.) said in January 1995: "They [welfare recipients] come from communities with the highest unemployment...the highest number of high school dropouts, the highest number addicted to drugs, the highest incidence of violence, the highest crime rates, the highest number of AIDS cases in these areas...the babies keep coming, the crack keeps

coming, the violence and crime keep coming, and the jails are now exploding" (House Committee on Ways and Means 1995b, 294; 1995a, 22).

14. Welfare scholar Mimi Abramovitz supported this finding, noting that liberals offered little resistance to conservative efforts: "[T]he conservatives' anti-government rhetoric and the liberals' failure to adamantly oppose increasingly punitive welfare reforms had paved the way for the Contract with America" (1996, 351–52).

Part II

Rhetorical Constructions of Welfare Recipients and Welfare Families in U.S. Congressional Hearings, Debates, and Legislation

Chapter 4

"Are We Going to Now Govern by Anecdote?": A Portrait of the Misfortunate, the Feckless, the Young, and the Fathers

THE MISFORTUNATE

[T]he vast majority of the American people and even the welfare population itself would like to be connected and go to work and be placed in a job.... Our job is to look at the individuals as real people who are on welfare today and to recognize that at least half of them come into their situation with adequate education, more than high school in many cases, and with work experience. The problem with our system right now is...they are sort of left on their own.

Harold E. Ford (D-Tenn.), House Committee on Ways and Means 1994a, 492–93

THE FECKLESS

[S]he is irresponsible...she is a high school dropout...she probably comes from a family that has had no male in the house...she [is] a second, third, or fourth generation welfare [recipient]...she comes from a community with very high unemployment...she doesn't really find a stigma to getting pregnant, she doesn't really have a hope that there is some fellow in the community that she would fall in love with and marry and raise a family because...he is shooting somebody or shooting up drugs. This person has very little self-esteem, but more impor-

---

Portions of this chapter are reprinted with permission from *The Quarterly Journal of Speech.*

tantly, very little hope that her life is going to be a part of the American dream and lacks that motivation to try to do any better.
Charles B. Rangel (D-N.Y.), House Committee on Ways and Means 1995a, 354

THE YOUNG

Are we not talking about young children getting pregnant?
Fred Grandy (R-Iowa), House Committee on Ways and Means 1993a, 49

THE FATHERS

[W]hy isn't anyone talking about the father that was involved in this, and the fathers that are involved in all these children's lives?
Penny Young, director of legislation and public policy for the Concerned Women of America, Senate Committee on Finance 1995g, 29

The misfortunate, the feckless, the young, and the fathers—these are the central characters in the welfare debate. Interestingly, the first three representations, used largely to describe female welfare recipients, are the predominant representations that surface in the transcripts of hearings and debates. As suggested by the testimony at the start of this chapter, the fourth characterization of fathers receives much less discussion. These four distinct depictions grow out of a public need to reconcile an apparent contradiction between cherished values (e.g., work ethic and family ethic) as keys to success with the harsh reality of high poverty rates, historically high levels of AFDC receipt, and growing numbers of female-headed, single-parent families. One may wonder, If the American dream is a reality, then why do so many people rely on welfare? To answer this question, legislators and witnesses collectively construct several distinct depictions of welfare recipients.

As the following discussion illustrates, these depictions—the misfortunate, the feckless, the young, and the fathers—represent main characters in a larger welfare narrative. Each narrative offers an explanation of who is poor, who deserves assistance, what the goals of assistance are, and who should provide assistance if any is offered. These narratives, in turn, exerted a surprising influence on the resulting PRWORA of 1996.

Ultimately, through an analysis of the congressional hearings and debates from the 102nd, 103rd, and 104th Congresses, this chapter demonstrates how representations of welfare recipients and their families influenced the construction of PRWORA. Although communication theorist

Walter Fisher contended that legislator reliance on narratives frees policy makers to evaluate the validity of the stories in an environment "inimical to elitist politics" (1984, 9), this chapter suggests otherwise. In contrast, the narrative forms facilitate elite discourse, discourage the inclusion of alternative public views, and delegitimate some important public voices. Building on the historical context examined in the previous chapters, this chapter first briefly reviews the theoretical approaches that informed this study. Next, the chapter explores how those who testified depicted the welfare population. After examining the depictions, and in an attempt to add to our developing knowledge of deliberative hearings as a precursor to the legislation, the chapter shows how the depictions influenced the resulting legislation. The chapter concludes with a discussion of rhetorical implications.

DEPICTION AND NARRATIVE: THEORETICAL CONTEXT

Michael Osborn's work on depiction is especially useful in identifying significant representations emergent in the legislative hearings and debates surrounding the passage of PRWORA. As mentioned previously, an emphasis on depiction "seeks those moments in which audiences encounter significant presentations of reality, and it strives to illuminate the rhetorical implications of such encounters" (97). This chapter analyzes significant presentations of reality concerning welfare recipients and their families as constructed in hearings and debates. Taken together, these depictive forms create a vivid portrait of the typical welfare recipient, a portrait that serves as the basis for policy formation in the context of a public moral argument.

In his work on the narrative paradigm, rhetorical theorist Walter Fisher (1984; 1985) explored the role and function of one form of depictive rhetoric—narratives. Fisher contrasted this narrative approach with what he termed "the rational world paradigm," or traditional logic associated with public deliberation. Reliance on technical expertise and formal logic excludes the general public from actively participating in the decision-making process. "Traditional rationality implies some sort of hierarchical system, a community in which some persons are qualified to judge and to lead and some other persons are to follow" (Fisher 1984, 9). Fisher proposed the concept of narrative rationality to capture the role of the general public in making and assessing public moral arguments without the aid of technical experts and training in formal logic. Because all humans have an innate ability for narrative rationality, the narrative paradigm is "inimical to elitist politics," because it insists that the "'people' do judge the stories that are told for and about them" (9). Although Fisher did not claim that such rationality guarantees that audiences will not adopt bad stories, he did argue that narrative rationality "does mitigate this tendency" (1985, 349). Moreover, Fisher contended, the narrative paradigm allows for the natural tendency of the people to "prefer the true and the just" (1984, 9) and narrative rationality "engenders critical self-awareness and conscious choice" (1985, 349).

Fisher offered two ways in which people evaluate stories: narrative probability (what constitutes a coherent story) and narrative fidelity (whether or not the story rings true to experience). In particular, Fisher believed that character is essential to evaluating the narrative probability of a story: "Central to all stories is character. Whether or not a story is believable depends on the reliability of the characters, both as narrators and as actors. Determination of one's character is made by interpretations of a person's decisions and actions that reflect values" (1987, 16). People judge fidelity by assessing the merits of the good reasons that all narratives contain. As "elements that give warrants for believing or acting in accord with the message fostered by that text," these value-laden reasons are expressed in a variety of forms, including argument, metaphor, and myth (1985, 357).

In essence, as this chapter demonstrates, depictions serve as evidence for audiences to determine both narrative probability and narrative fidelity. Because they assess character, depictions provide insight into the attitudes, values, and behaviors of welfare recipients. The consistency and volume of the repetitive depictions encourage legislators to judge them as coherent. Because legislators use the depictions to warrant policy reforms, the depictions also serve as the good reasons that legislators use to make decisions and assess the fidelity of welfare narratives. In contrast to Fisher's theory, however, this case study questions the democratic and participatory nature of narratives, arguing that some narrative forms foster elitism and discourage critical, self-reflexive analysis.

DEPICTIONS OF WELFARE RECIPIENTS IN THE HEARINGS AND DEBATES

As stated earlier in this chapter, four predominant characterizations of welfare recipients emerge in the hearings and debates: the misfortunate, the feckless, the young, and the fathers. Describing these characterizations in detail is necessary to understand how these rhetorical depictions have influenced the construction of the PRWORA of 1996.

The Misfortunate

The typical narrative of the misfortunate welfare recipient constructed in the hearings and debates is of a competent, able-bodied individual who expresses a strong desire to work, but who is unable to achieve the American dream of working for wages, largely due to the lack of living-wage job opportunities. The misfortunate poor, then, are those individuals who experience an unexpected misfortune or circumstance and require short-term assistance to stabilize their lives.

During the hearings, many legislators and witnesses praised the abilities and talents of the misfortunate welfare recipient. For example, Robert Friedman, chair and founder of the Corporation for Enterprise Development, argued, "Among the poor are people of considerable talent and energy whose futures are limited by lack of opportunity, not lack of capacity" (Senate Committee on Finance 1995e, 47; House Committee on Ways and Means 1995c, 1191). Attesting to the hardworking entrepreneurial spirit of welfare recipients, John Else, president of the Institute for Social and Economic Development, explained, "Welfare recipients have demonstrated their ability to achieve what everybody considers the American dream, owning a business, sustaining their own lives through that business." As support for his claim, Else offered several powerful anecdotes, including one about a welfare recipient who could do profit-and-loss statements that an MBA graduate could not do (Senate Committee on Appropriations, 1994b, 36–38). As these passages demonstrate, many participants in the hearings and debates believed that some welfare recipients are intelligent, industrious, responsible individuals capable of professional achievements.

To affirm the values and abilities of welfare recipients, however, is to place the American dream at risk. As evident in the preceding chapters on welfare reform history, hard work and dedication to family have gained presence as keys to success (Perelman and Olbrechts-Tyteca 1971). Theoretically, individuals who enact these values should succeed. To explain the apparent contradiction between the American dream and the lived experiences of the misfortunate welfare recipient, those who testified looked to external extenuating circumstances. In particular, legislators and witnesses explained that misfortunate welfare recipients encounter difficulties due to unanticipated circumstances outside of their control, such as personal tragedy (e.g., serious illness or disability) or poor economic conditions (e.g., job layoffs, unemployment rates, unequal job distribution). For example, according to Senator Patrick G. Leahy (D-Vt.), chair of the Committee on Agriculture, Nutrition, and Forestry: "There are too many Americans today that are just a step away from government assistance. You are suddenly unemployed; you have a serious illness; or you are faced with a natural disaster . . . That is all it takes. Americans cannot anticipate the emergency situations where their families will suddenly be in need" (Senate Committee on Agriculture, Nutrition, and Forestry 1994, 2). Carroll Campbell, former governor of South Carolina, added later in the hearing process:

My mother grew up in Youngstown, Ohio, which for generations was a thriving community. People had good jobs in the steel mills. Then in the early 1980s, the auto industry went through terrible circumstances. There is now no functioning steel mill in Youngstown, Ohio. There are families who, for a couple of generations, relied on those steel mills for their livelihood and could have good jobs without college education, sometimes without even a high school education, and could support their families. Those kind of folks need our help, as well, when we are looking at a welfare reform measure. (Senate Committee on Governmental Affairs 1995, 53–54)

In this instance, legislators noted that all American families, even hard-working, law-abiding families, experience adversity and may need aid. Because these passages all blame the welfare recipient's current poverty state on unanticipated circumstances, the statements preserve faith in the power of the American dream. In other words, all able-bodied people who work hard can succeed with limited temporary public assistance to alleviate short-term need.

The legislators' emphasis on equal opportunity and the similarities between all Americans frequently overlooked the importance of racial, ethnic, class, or gender differences. For example, in one hearing, Vermont Governor Howard Dean concluded his remarks by claiming, "The colors of peoples' skins may be a little bit different, but poverty is poverty wherever it is, and we have the same kinds of problems that everybody else does" (Senate Committee on Finance 1994b, 22). One year later, Representative John Ensign (R-Nev.) remarked: "We have to eliminate looking at race or religion, for example, and provide for all people that are economically disadvantaged the incentives for getting off welfare. This may affect one race more than another, but it certainly affects everyone. You know, poverty knows no creed or race" (House Committee on Ways and Means 1995c, 985–86). Given evidence that suggests welfare recipients are just like other hardworking Americans, it would be easy to conclude, along with Representative E. Clay Shaw (R-Fla.), that "the problem with welfare is not the people who are in it.... The problem is a failed system that we risk leaving in place" (House Committee on Ways and Means 1996a, 5).

In fact, however, most witnesses and legislators adamantly maintained that in the United States, self-improvement is possible without any public assistance through initiative, perseverance, and hard work. This idea casts suspicion on the misfortunate welfare recipient paradigm. Expressing widespread skepticism about the misfortunate welfare recipients, New Mexico Representative Steven Schiff (R) remarked in March 1994: "People today find themselves in that circumstance [single-parenthood], for whatever reason. Quite a number of those people—mostly women, not entirely women, have been able to overcome those problems without the assistance of government" (House Committee on Government Operations 1994, 60).

An exchange between Louisiana Representative Jim McCrery (R) and welfare recipient Cheri Honkala, who is also executive director of the Pennsylvania Welfare Rights Union, suggests just how powerful the belief in hard effort as a solution to misfortune is. Mr. McCrery explained, "I think we need to investigate, based on situations like yours, the possibility of providing incentives for you to work." Ms. Honkala asked, "What if you cannot find a job?" Mr. McCrery responded, "If you have five years to find a job, we are hopeful that you will be able to find a job." Countering with a critique of welfare reform proposals that include a time limit, Ms. Honkala inquired, "But what about people like me that have been on and off of public assistance and would be slated to be cut off, even though I have tried to look everywhere possible for employment? What would I do with my child?" Mr. McCrery replied, "We are counting on you finding a job." More forcefully invoking this notion of the misfortunate welfare recipient who actively seeks employment and cannot acquire living-wage labor, Ms. Honkala retorted, "But I have been on national television saying I need a job, and I would think by now, if there was a job out there, that I would have gotten it by now." In one of the most conspicuous examples of faith in the power of the individual to rise above poverty through self-help, Mr. McCrery ended the discussion by resolutely insisting, "Well, I submit to you that there are jobs out there, and I am hopeful that you will find another job" (House Committee on Ways and Means 1995c, 1115). Such testimony seemingly contradicts the notion that some people may require aid, even on a temporary basis, to succeed.

Cementing the faith in individuals to overcome adversity in the absence of public assistance are narratives of poor individuals who, taking pride in their refusal of public aid, eventually succeed. Former welfare recipient, Cynthia I. Newbille, executive director of the National Black Women's Health Project, proudly affirmed her family's refusal of public aid. As a result, she said, "I know you can pull yourself up" (House Committee on Ways and Means 1994a, 664). Karolin Jappe Loendorf, of Helena, Montana, said she was too proud to take assistance on many occasions, even when public aid would have increased her monthly income. As a divorced mother of four children, she explained that the Transitional Child Care program "automatically entitles you to Medicaid, but not being raised that way, I just chose to purchase the insurance.... I chose to work and go backward.... I do not feel the State of Montana or the Federal Government should carry the burden for the cost of my children, when they...did not conceive my child" (House Committee on Ways and Means 1995c, 1215, 1217).

This theme of pride in self-help as the key to personal success recurs later in the hearings and debates among the legislators. For instance, Representative Joseph P. Kennedy (D-Mass.) narrated: "Let me tell you something friends, I was born 65 years ago into poverty. My dad walked out on my mother and me the day I was born. We never saw him again. Ladies and gentlemen, we went through hell for 10 years. There were no jobs, and my mother would not take a nickel of welfare, and we fought our way out of it" (*Cong. Rec.* 1995, H15509). Later in the debates, Florida Representative Dave Weldon (R) reported:

I was born the youngest of nine children in one of the most distressed communities in Pennsylvania. Neither parent was able to complete high school because of their having to quit school when they were in sixth and eighth grades to help raise their families. Even though we were poor and even though we were a blue collar family, my father worked in a factory 38 years, we were proud. My father was proudest of the fact up until the day he died that...never once did he accept public assistance. There were many times when he was out of work because of strikes...but never once did he have to resort to taking money from the taxpayers. He was proud of that.... And all of us are better for that spirit. (*Cong. Rec.* 1995, H3549)

Still later in the debates, Representative Ensign (R-Nev.) continued: "My mom...would have made more money going on welfare because she had no child support. She had three kids to raise. But I saw my mom each and every single day get up and go to work, and that taught me a work ethic that we are robbing from welfare families today" (*Cong. Rec.* 1996, H7751; 1995, H3363; 1996, H9406). These accounts all suggest that individuals who work hard will eventually succeed. The stories go further, however; they suggest that individuals who refuse public assistance perhaps demonstrate superior character, values, and integrity than those who accept welfare.

In the end, legislators and witnesses crafted an image of the misfortunate poor as an individual who is committed to the family and work ethic and suffers a short-lived calamity. Despite the recognition that some people are temporarily poor, faith in the power of individuals to overcome adversity through hard work and without public assistance led most legislators and witnesses to express strong reservations about the misfortunate poor. No one captured this enduring faith in the American dream better than Lawrence E. Townsend, Jr., director of the Riverside County Department of Public Social Services in California, who testified: "The old-fashioned work ethic that made America great was if you work hard, show your stuff, be reliable, eventually you will prosper. In our country we have found this still to be true" (House Committee on Ways and Means 1995b, 303). Because of this history of "old-fashioned work ethic[s]" and strong faith in the American Dream, legislators have become increasingly skeptical of the misfortunate welfare recipient paradigm and turn to other depictions of welfare recipients as feckless and young to account for poverty and chronic dependence.

The Feckless

The characterization of welfare recipients as feckless acquired a dominant voice throughout the hearings and debates. Whereas structural and systemic challenges prevent the misfortunate welfare recipient from achieving success, poor values and choices prevent the feckless welfare recipient from rising out of poverty. In direct contrast to the misfortunate paradigm, wherein some legislators perceived the system as broken and in need of repair, in the feckless welfare recipient framework, the recipients themselves are broken and need to be made whole. Typically then, legislators and witnesses characterized the feckless welfare recipient as an able-bodied female who is undeserving of public assistance because she refuses to work, engages in criminal activities (e.g., drug abuse, illegal food stamp trade), and makes poor choices with regard to her personal life (e.g., relationships and parenting). As a result, the feckless welfare recipient relies on public assistance for years and bears children who follow suit, thereby perpetuating multigenerational welfare dependency. Two central features mark the depiction of the feckless welfare recipient: (1) failure to adopt key values and observe religious mandates and (2) inability to make sound choices.

According to legislators and witnesses, welfare recipients' lack of values accounts for their welfare dependence. Sister Mary Rose McGeady, president of Covenant House in New York, explained:

I think we are in the midst, in this country, of an enormous values shift, and that the toleration of things that we have traditionally considered immoral, wrong, or just bad for the country and bad for kids, I think a lot of it has gone down the tubes, and this country really needs to put the skids on and ask ourselves, where are we going in terms of values? (House Committee on Ways and Means 1996b, 126)

Perhaps the most damaging evidence comes from Robert Rector, senior policy analyst at the Heritage Foundation, who categorized welfare recipients as behaviorally poor, charging that their poverty "essentially stem[s] from moral character": "The plight of the underclass is rooted in behavior.... It is a chasm of values and behavior which today separates the underclass and the chronically poor from the American middle class" (House Committee on Economic and Educational Opportunities 1995a, 17, 27; Senate Committee on Finance 1995b, 15). Relying on witness testimony in the debates, Senator Dan Coats (R-Ind.) elaborated: "[T]he basic problem lies in the realm of values and character, and those values are shaped, particularly in early childhood, by increasing cultural standards.... People are not pure economic beings analyzing costs and benefits. We are moral beings. We make choices that reflect our values. Incentives are not irrelevant, but it is ultimately our beliefs and habits, I think, that determine our future" (*Cong. Rec.* 1995, S13498). According to this testimony, any decision a welfare recipient makes (to remain a single parent, to decline a job offer, to buy nonnutritious foods) is merely a reflection of her lack of values and is, therefore, at base, a poor choice.

Many witnesses and legislators argued that welfare recipients are morally impoverished because they do not live in accordance with religious beliefs. Former welfare recipient Pam Harris White explained that "a lack of values and the decline in the morals and religious beliefs" are linked to welfare receipt at "high cost to both the person and to society" (House Committee on Ways and Means 1995b, 179). Interestingly, witnesses and legislators invoked religious anecdotes, endeavoring to show the correlation among religion, work, values, and economic well-being. Tracing discussions of Paul the Apostle in the hearings and debates illustrates how religious allusions permeate welfare discussion of faith, work, and a life free from poverty. Reverend Larry Jones, president and founder of Feed the Children, referred to his welfare expert of choice—the Apostle Paul: "I take my notion of what compassion is from my favorite welfare reform expert, who happens to be the Apostle Paul.... [H]e who shall not work shall not eat" (House Committee on Economic and Educational Opportunities 1995a, 73, 74). Invoking a strikingly similar statement, Robert Rector remarked: "My favorite welfare reform expert happens to be the Apostle Paul.... [The] Apostle Paul, in writing down the requirements for basically the Food Stamp Program in the early Christian church, said he who shall not work shall not eat" (House Committee on Agriculture 1995, 517, 525). Paul the Apostle also just happens to be the favorite welfare expert of Senator Jesse Helms (R-N.C.):

But there is another authority who is a favorite of mine. His name is Paul, the Apostle Paul, who...had a thought or two about this issue which we call today welfare. Paul wrote to the Thessalonians and said this: We were not idle when we were with you, nor did we eat anyone's food without paying for it. On the contrary, we worked night and day, laboring and toiling so that we would not be a burden to any of you.... If man will not work, he shall not eat. (*Cong. Rec.* 1995, S11830)

By taking a biblical context and applying it to contemporary welfare reform debates, legislators and witnesses used scripture to distinguish between the deserving and the undeserving poor. As with the Puritans and Calvinists discussed in chapters 2 and 3, these biblical mandates validate the notion that if welfare recipients were morally and spiritually grounded, they would work and, therefore, not be needy.

Another attribute of feckless welfare recipients as portrayed in the hearings and debates is that they make poor life choices. Representative Bill Emerson (R-Mo.) asserted: "I'm not sure that a lot of these folks...know what the right choices for them are. I think they need some counseling and advice to go after the right choices" (House Select Committee on Hunger Domestic Task Force 1992a, 31). These poor choices, legislators explained, lead welfare recipients to indulge in a whole host of intergenerational social ills, including crime, illiteracy, disease, substance abuse, and sexual promiscuity.[1] Ultimately, by linking welfare receipt to social pathologies, welfare recipients, like pathological diseases, are subject to annihilation (House Committee on Ways and Means 1995b, 84). Senator Byron L. Dorgan (D-N.Dak.) remarked in a telling, perhaps Freudian, slip: "We must eliminate those people for whom welfare has become an institutionalized way of life" (*Cong. Rec.* 1995, S12759). Specifically, legislators argued that as a result of making poor choices, welfare recipients possess poor education and skill levels, abuse illegal substances, neglect and abuse their children, and participate in criminal activities.

Unskilled and Uneducated

For a variety of reasons, many welfare recipients were described as unable to obtain the educational competence and skills necessary to find and keep a job. Lawrence Townsend, Jr., explained that welfare recipients have trouble with such basic skills as "setting the alarm clock; getting to work on time; accepting supervision; learning to complete tasks reliably; getting along with coworkers; and, dressing appropriately for work" (Senate Committee on Finance 1995e, 83). Representative Michael Castle (R-Del.) remarked that many recipients "don't have transportation, they don't know how to go about it, they don't show up on time, you have to work with them" (House Committee on Agriculture 1995, 129).

According to depictions, most welfare recipients have less than an eighth-grade education, so they are often functionally illiterate. For example, Sheri Hernandez, case manager with Promise Jobs in Davenport, Iowa, described a typical welfare recipient as a woman with "five children, all under the age of 5,...no driver's license," and an eighth-grade education (Senate Committee on Appropriations 1994b, 30–32). Similarly, Nancy Ebb, senior staff attorney for the Children's Defense Fund, stated, "[T]he average young AFDC mother has reading skills at or below the sixth grade level" (House Committee on Ways and Means 1993a, 88). Testimony by former welfare recipients occasionally reinforced these depictions of the illiterate, uneducated, unskilled welfare mother. For example, in one hearing, Irma Alvarado, an El Salvadoran participant in California's GAIN program, related: "I have three children, my husband left me and I had to apply for welfare.... When I left El Salvador, I...spoke very little English." Alvarado added that in the United States, she "finished the sixth level of study" but was unable to complete high school courses because her welfare benefits expired (House Committee on Education and Labor 1994c, 9–11). These and other statements create an image of welfare recipients as uneducated, unskilled and frequently unemployable.

Welfare Recipients as Substance Abusers

According to witnesses and legislators, a second example of how welfare recipients demonstrate poor choices is by abusing alcohol and drugs. Catherine A. Young, vice president of the Women's Freedom Network in Washington, D.C., related several stories that appeared in newspaper articles to suggest that welfare mothers typically use illegal drugs while they are pregnant (House Committee on Ways and Means 1995c, 1239). Senator Dorgan (D-N.Dak.) supplied a personal narrative: "I toured a hospital...I held in my hand a preemie baby who was born, the third child born to an unwed mother who did not want the third child, who some days before that had presented herself at the hospital with a .25 blood alcohol content and delivered a baby that had a blood alcohol content of .21 upon birth" (Senate Committee on Governmental Affairs 1995, 13). William J. Bennett, codirector of Empower America, surmised, "You will not get ahold of the welfare problem unless you get ahold of the open air drug markets and crack houses" (House Committee on Ways and Means 1995b, 156). Douglas Besharov, resident scholar at the American Enterprise Institute for Public Policy Research, explained that the increase in the African American out-of-wedlock birthrate from 1985 to 1990 may be associated with drug use: "There are many explanations for that increase. My own, by the way, is that this is the effect of crack cocaine on our inner cities. If you look at where those babies are being born, you see a real connection there" (Senate Committee on Finance 1995d, 3). Representative Barbara B. Kennelly (D-Conn.) made a strikingly similar statement when she asserted: "Out to the street when those drug dealers are there. That is when impregnation often happens, when those people are around" (House Committee on Ways and Means 1995b, 170). Drawing on this testimony in the debates, Representative Rangel (D-N.Y.) averred, "Take a look at these communities, take a look and see whether there is a relationship between drugs and out-of-wedlock births, as I know exists" (House Committee on Ways and Means 1996b, 9–10). These statements create an image of welfare recipients as drug dealers and users. Moreover, the passages cast doubt on the ability of welfare recipients to make sound judgments and act responsibly.

Welfare Recipients as Neglectful and Abusive Parents

According to witnesses, a third way in which welfare mothers demonstrate poor choices is by neglecting and even abusing their children. David B. Roth, executive director of Cleveland Works, concluded that until the underemployed and the unemployed "possess the means to earn a decent standard of living," single-parenthood, poverty, and abuse will remain linked: "We prefer to attack problems one by one. Right now it is single-headed households and out-of-wedlock children.... The reason is plain: they are unemployed, poor, uneducated, and lacking access to quality health care. Without fail, it is when the basic necessities are denied—food, clothing, housing, education, health care—that poverty arrives with its dangerous tentacles, such as crime, violence, abuse, and illness" (House Committee on Ways and Means 1995c, 1079). To that end, the hearings and debates sustain an image of welfare recipients as abusive mothers because they do not immunize their children, they feed their children unhealthy foods, they provide hazardous living conditions, and they expose their children to physical and sexual abuse.

The inability of parents to ensure that their children receive required immunizations is one indicator, according to legislators, of the abusive nature of welfare mothers. Representative Marge Roukema (R-N.J.) lamented: "Regrettably, either through ignorance or apathy, many parents in the welfare program today are failing to get their children immunized and vaccinated, making these children the real victims.... In 1992, six children died in New Jersey from an outbreak of the measles" (House Committee on Ways and Means 1995b, 679; 1995a, 210). Representative Grandy (R-Iowa) perceived a correlation between "a lack of parenting skills" and "lack of immunizations" (House Committee on Ways and Means 1993a, 52). Grandy supported this statement with a reference to a study of four inner cities in which 86 percent of all children who were unvaccinated for measles were on AFDC (53). These statements construct welfare mothers as unfit parents because they do not provide for their children's health.

Legislators also charge welfare mothers with neglect on the basis of the food they feed their children. Some, like Representative Grandy faulted mothers with not feeding their children regularly: "In my hometown now, I have put together a cultural camp in two housing projects.... Children are telling us in the camps since school has been out they have been going without food for 1 day, 1 1/2 days, 1 week" (House Committee on Ways and Means 1994a, 600). Even when welfare mothers can afford to feed their children, witnesses testified that the women are ignorant about healthful eating, preferring instead to buy nonnutritious foods. Representative Mark Foley (R-Fla.) recounted in both the hearings and the debates: "I have had a lot of thoughts about food stamps. I was behind a woman the other day, ice cream cones, drum sticks and all these products she was buying that many of us forgo because we don't have the money. Microwave popcorn. It wasn't basic nutrition" (House Committee on Agriculture 1995, 41; *Cong. Rec.* 1995, H3394–95).[2] These passages depict welfare mothers as ignorant, at best, about general nutrition.

Throughout the hearings, the legislators and witnesses also related stories that castigated welfare mothers for failure to provide their children with appropriate housing and supervision. Often these examples are quite graphic in their portrayal of welfare housing as unsanitary, filthy, and associated with drugs, crime, and violence. Representative Ford (D-Tenn.), chair of the Subcommittee on Human Resources, charged that the welfare problem concerns "[c]hildren that are living in poverty and living in these rat-infested shacks that are unfit for human habitation in this country, totally different from the way other Americans are living and they have not been exposed to another way of living" (House Committee on Ways and Means 1994a, 439). Representative James Talent (R-Mo.) supplied a number of vignettes to discuss the horrors associated with this unfit housing. For example, he recounted the story of a 12-year-old boy who was "fatally stabbed in the chest" near a Bronx housing project. Talent also told of Eric Morris, a five-year-old who was dangled out the window of a room on the fourteenth floor of a public housing project by some older kids. These older boys, Talent continued, "dropped him [Morris] deliberately and killed him" (*Cong. Rec.* 1996, H7758). Such examples evoke a visceral response to children residing in filthy, hazardous living quarters.

The depiction of welfare mothers as abusive attains its apex with discussions of welfare mothers as child molesters and abusers. William J. Bennett asserted: "This ridiculous debate that has gone on the last few weeks about snatching babies from the arms of mothers to throw them into orphanages, there is no snatching of babies.... [B]abies are being thrown by their own mothers into dumpsters, out on the street, put on radiators" (House Committee on Ways and Means 1995b, 177).

Tracing one oft-cited story of the Chicago Keystone case throughout the hearings and debates process provides evidence of how witnesses and legislators relied on anecdotal evidence to support their claim that mothers abuse their children. In July 1994, Representative Louise Slaughter (D-N.Y.) described a compelling instance of abuse in Chicago: "[B]ut one of the things that struck me, and I don't think I will ever get over, is the finding of 19 babies in 2 rooms in Chicago who were the children of 4 mothers in their twenties and that they received something like $5,000 a month in welfare payments and what kind of chance do those children have" (House Committee on Ways and Means 1994a, 521). Relying on the same story in his prepared statement of January 30, 1995, Congressman Talent (R-Mo.) reported, "Last year, in a drug raid of an apartment in

Chicago, police found 19 children—the oldest 14 years old, the youngest one-year-old—living in squalor among filth, cockroaches, and broken windows covered with old blankets. When police entered the apartment, they found five children asleep on the floor in their underwear and others gnawing a bone with a dog" (House Committee on Ways and Means 1995b, 534). A few days later, Patrick T. Murphy, public guardian in Cook County, Illinois, recounted: "Perhaps the ultimate example of this was the Keystone case, which happened in Chicago just a year ago. In that case, Chicago coppers investigating drug allegations stumbled across nineteen kids living in a hovel with their five moms who were taking in approximately $6,500 a month in welfare and other benefits for the children. Most of the money was going out the door into the hands of drug pushers" (House Committee on Ways and Means 1995g, 119). One month later, in a March 1995 debate, California Representative Randy "Duke" Cunningham (R) reported: "I look in Chicago, and police found 19 children living in squalor in a cold, dark apartment. Two children in diapers were sharing a bone with the family dog. Why? Because the parents were living on cocaine and drugs. Child abuse services need to be brought in" (*Cong. Rec.* 1995, H3382). The next day, Representative J.D. Hayworth (R-Ariz.) inquired:

How can we, in the name of freedom and decency, stand by silently when we see examples just as we saw a couple of years ago in Chicago during the drug raid when police found 19 children living in squalor in a cold, dark apartment, 2 children in diapers sharing a bone with a family dog, the children belonging to 3 mothers and 6 different fathers who were getting $4,000 in cash benefits per month from the Federal Government? (*Cong. Rec.* 1995, H3506)

These anecdotal passages are typical of countless other stories about abusive welfare mothers. A culture of irresponsibility, substance abuse, and blatant neglect of children characterize the construction of the welfare female-headed family. More important, these passages illustrate how stories told in the hearings infiltrated the debates and eventually warranted welfare reform policies.

Welfare Recipients as Criminals

A final way in which the hearings and debates participants constructed welfare recipients as making poor personal choices was to portray these recipients as fraudulent criminals. This perception of welfare recipients as taking advantage of the welfare system resulted in multiple references to welfare recipients as "training junkies" and "welfare cheats" who "are just playing the system" and are "scamming us" through "padded" claims and "double dip[ping]" (House Committee on Ways and Means 1994b, 970; House Committee on Agriculture 1995, 525; House Committee on

Ways and Means 1995c, 1294; Senate Committee on Agriculture, Nutrition, and Forestry 1994, 11).

The congressional hearings and debate transcripts carefully recorded the various types of fraud in which welfare recipients engage, including lying about their circumstances, trafficking food stamps, bearing children to gain additional welfare benefits, and claiming benefits in two states simultaneously. In all cases, the individuals were depicted as deceiving the system, either intentionally or unintentionally, to receive higher payments. Representative E. de la Garza (D-Tex.) expressed this viewpoint when he noted that in 1993 , AFDC overpayments that were the result of caseworker errors were $763 million, recipient unintentional errors were $637 million, and recipient intentional errors were $424 million (House Committee on Agriculture 1995, 149).

Many legislators also charged welfare recipients with food stamp fraud. Representative Ron Wyden (D-Oreg.) spoke about how welfare recipients frequently trade food stamps for illegal items: "Food stamps are used as an underground currency. They are traded for drugs. They are traded for weapons. All kinds of illegal activity [are] essentially fueled with food stamps" (House Committee on Agriculture 1995, 477). Senator Helms (R-N.C.) added:

[T]he *Los Angeles Times* reported [that] welfare recipients falsified and inflated claims for emergency assistance, once again taking advantage of an already much abused and mismanaged Food Stamp Program.... In fact, the February, 1994, edition of *Reader's Digest* contains an article entitled "The Food Stamp Racket" which reports that of the $24 billion taxpayers fork over for food stamps, nearly $2 billion is lost to fraud, waste and abuse. (Senate Committee on Agriculture, Nutrition, and Forestry 1994, 5)[3]

Later in the debates, Representative Bob Goodlatte (R-Va.) insisted that the welfare program "has historically been beset by all manner of fraud. Food stamps are trafficked on the street, traded for drugs, used in a multitude of methods" (*Cong. Rec.* 1995, H3391). Providing one illustrative anecdote, Representative Philip Crane (R-Ill.) narrated:

Well, I remember one other incident... [of] a well-dressed mother in front of me in the checkout line in the supermarket and she had a quart of ice cream or something and she gave him $20 in food stamps and they gave her change. Now, that is illegal, but what are you going to do, put a cop at the end of every checkout counter? And she could take the money that she got returned to her and buy booze or buy cigarettes or whatever. (House Committee on Ways and Means 1995a, 589)

These statements all charge welfare recipients with misusing food stamps for the purchase of illicit items.[4]

Others who testified accused welfare mothers of having many children to increase their monthly welfare payments. Representative Shaw (R-Fla.) explained: "[T]hese people that are on welfare aren't stupid. They certainly can understand that there is going to be a certain amount paid for them, paid to them once they have children out of wedlock" (House Committee on Ways and Means 1994a, 397). Senator Philip Gramm (R-Tex.) added: "One-third of all the babies born in America today are born out of wedlock. The largest single explanation for why that is the case is that we give larger and larger cash payments to people who have more and more babies on welfare" (*Cong. Rec.* 1995, S13563). Representative Talent (R-Mo.) concluded that "the out-of-wedlock birth rate is so much greater among lower-income Americans" because "it [welfare] is a financial incentive" and it "means more to somebody coming from a lower-income background" (House Committee on Ways and Means 1994a, 553).[5] In these examples, those who testified highlighted how women on welfare bear additional children to obtain higher monthly checks.[6]

Many of the depictions also accuse welfare recipients of claiming benefits in multiple states at the same time or of shopping around to locate a home in a high-paying welfare state. Representative Dick Zimmer (R-N.J.) reported that claiming benefits in more than one state is a serious national problem. He noted that some welfare recipients "were collecting welfare in New Jersey, going to New York, establishing themselves as homeless in New York, and collecting benefits from both States" (*Cong. Rec.* 1995, H3502). In a closely related version of the multiple-state claiming scheme, some representatives suggested that welfare recipients desire to avoid work so desperately that they identify states with the highest benefit ratios and then relocate to those regions. Representative Castle (R-Del.) expressed such a fear when he noted that a problem with raising benefit levels in some states and not others would result in a "migration of welfare recipients from one State to another" (House Committee on Agriculture 1995, 128). Such depictions create an image of undeserving welfare recipients unjustifiably receiving welfare benefits, sometimes not just once but twice, at the expense of hardworking, taxpaying citizens.

The Role of Race and Class

Throughout the hearings and debates, witnesses and legislators explicitly and implicitly linked the feckless welfare recipient paradigm to poor women and minority groups, chiefly African Americans and Hispanics. Notably, this link of minorities to undeserving welfare status is historically consistent and powerful. In contrast to the misfortunate welfare recipient paradigm, in which legislators and witnesses deemphasized differences associated with race, ethnicity, gender, and class in order to highlight the similarities between welfare recipients and non-welfare, hardworking American families, the feckless welfare recipient paradigm fuels stereotypes of poor minority women who cannot achieve the American dream without assistance, frequently take advantage of the welfare system, and violate mainstream middle-class American values. For example, Representative Floyd Flake (D-N.Y.) clarified: "I am saying that at some point, we as African-American people are going to have to deal with the reality that there are some problems endemic to our communities and to our people. . . . Our minorities, and principally African-Americans often need extra help" (House Committee on Ways and Means 1994a, 569). Missouri Senator John C. Danforth (R) explained why African American welfare recipients may need this assistance: "I have worried about the problem of welfare, . . . most particularly, the problem of black Americans who are disproportionately among the poor, among the unemployed who disproportionately go to schools that are not very good, that are from families that are dysfunctional, that have very few activities, other than just to pour into the street at the end of the school day" (Senate Committee on Finance 1994b, 72). Frustrated by the persistent and, what he termed, "false" link between welfare and race, Dr. Ronald Walters, chair of the Department of Political Science at Howard University, commented, "[W]ith the juxtaposition of RACE and welfare dependency in the public imagination, there has been a return to the value system of the 'undeserving poor' and images of the laggard, lazy dull welfare recipient on the 'dole' who deserves the punitive attitude of the elite visited upon them because they constitute a drag upon the economy and a blot upon the moral image of the nation" (House Committee on Government Operations 1994, 83). Unfortunately, few other legislators openly shared Dr. Walters's objections.[7] As a result, race has become intimately associated with characterizations of welfare recipients, especially feckless welfare recipients. By linking welfare to lower-income minority women as well as to major social pathologies, including crime, drug abuse, and violence, legislators encourage people to view these groups with suspicion.

The Young

The third major depiction of welfare recipients centers on welfare mothers as immature youth. Expressing ambivalence about the category of young welfare recipients, representatives are unsure whether these teenagers are deserving or undeserving of aid. Neither completely deserving nor undeserving, the juvenile welfare recipient is constructed as somewhere in between the misfortunate and feckless welfare recipient categories. Clearly, legislators and witnesses expressed sympathy for young welfare recipients and have affirmed their status of welfare mothers as legal minors who are unable to make adult decisions. Calling attention to the immaturity and youth of young welfare recipients, Wisconsin Representative Peter W. Barca (D) noted, "[M]any of these kids still need parenting themselves" (House Committee on Ways and Means 1994a, 615). Eloise Anderson, director of California's Department of Social Services, explained: "But we don't consider them [welfare mothers] women. We consider them girls" (House Committee on Ways and Means 1995a, 674). Representative Jim Ramstad (R-Minn.) wondered how legislators could "reverse this alarming trend in teenage girls having babies" (House Committee on Ways and Means 1995a, 103). One indication of the power of constructing welfare recipients as youth is that Congress held several special welfare hearings solely dedicated to the issue of teenage pregnancy.

In addition to being described as young, these welfare recipients were also depicted as victims of their upbringing. As Representative Eva M. Clayton (D-N.C.) explained, "Teenage pregnancy is just one marker of growing up poor and poorly nurtured, both physically and emotionally, I would say" (House Committee on Ways and Means 1996b, 17). In the debates, Senator David Pryor (D-Ark.) reinforced the idea that "teens from poor and educationally disadvantaged families are more likely to become pregnant than those from more affluent and highly educated parents" (*Cong. Rec.* 1995, S13601). Thus, according to those who testified, welfare receipt is an intergenerational problem marked by teenagers, themselves children of welfare mothers, bearing out-of-wedlock children and relying on welfare.

Teenagers were also depicted in the congressional proceedings as victims of rape and incest. For example, Christopher Shays (R-Conn.), chair of the Subcommittee on Human Resources and Intergovernmental Relations, explained: "[A]dolescent girls need our protection and our guidance. Their cry for help is made even more poignant by recent studies concluding that adult men father more than half the children born to 15- to 17-year-old mothers" (House Committee on Government Reform and Oversight 1996, 1). Senator Joseph Lieberman (D-Conn.) added, "A 1992 sampling of 500 teen mothers revealed that two-thirds had histories of sexual abuse with adult men averaging age 27" (*Cong. Rec.* 1996, S8368). These statements capture legislator sympathy for young recipients who bear children as a result of circumstances beyond their control.

Despite acknowledgment of the immaturity of young welfare recipients growing up in undesirable and abusive circumstances—qualities that seem to warrant public assistance—witnesses and legislators noted that young welfare recipients frequently share some characteristics with the feckless welfare recipient. More specifically, those who testified believed that young welfare recipients are partially to blame for their poor choices. For example, Rebecca A. Maynard, professor of education and social policy at the University of Pennsylvania, explained that teens are susceptible to out-of-wedlock pregnancies and subsequent welfare dependence because of the "disorganization and impulsiveness that characterizes the lives of many of these young, largely poor, teenagers" and the "unwilling-ness on the part of many of the males to cooperate with contraceptive use, at least to do so consistently" (Senate Committee on Finance 1995d, 7). Calling attention to some of these poor choices, Representative Weldon (R-Fla.) argued that some teenagers choose to have children for reasons associated with increased independence: "[A]s a physician...in inner-city obstetrics clinics...I saw 15-year-olds.... I would ask them why they are doing this? And they would tell me they want to get out of their unit, they want to get out from under their mother, they want to get their own place in the project, and they want to get their own welfare check" (*Cong. Rec.* 1995, H3362, H3714). Michael D. Tanner, director of health and welfare studies at the Cato Institute in Washington, D.C., added that teenagers' beliefs about the acceptability of out of wedlock births indicate their poor values, "[T]here was a study in Philadelphia where they asked inner city teenagers, would having a baby be a major crisis in your life[?], and found 60 percent saying, no....As long as that is the predominant attitude among poor inner city teenagers, you are going to have an explosion in illegitimacy" (Senate Committee on Finance 1995b, 17).

Furthermore, as with feckless welfare recipients, young welfare recipi-ents also become associated with a variety of social ills, including gangs, drugs, crime, and violence. Representative Talent (R-Mo.) explained, "These teen moms are children themselves, often living in drug- and gang-infested neighborhoods with no family to speak of" (House Com-mittee on Ways and Means 1995b, 532). Later in the debates, Senator Slade Gorton (R-Wash.) relied on anecdotal evidence to support a claim that juvenile welfare recipients lead lives of crime and violence:

On my way back here from Seattle today, I read a long and fascinating article in the *New York Times* about the cultural difference among various kinds of gangs in the city of Los Angeles. The reporter reports on the particular ethos of black gangs, of Asian gangs, and of Hispanic gangs.... And the principal part of the story is about a 15-year-old gang member with a 17-year-old girlfriend who has a 1-year-old child by this gang member.... So here we are subsidizing gangs and gang warfare in Los Angeles. (*Cong. Rec.* 1995, S13195)

Many of these depictions liken the young and feckless welfare recipient as individuals who make poor choices that have profound consequences for themselves and for society.

The Irresponsible and Absent Father

Notably, all of the foregoing depictions are characterizations largely of female welfare recipients. Because the majority of welfare recipients are women and children, such labeling may not be surprising to some read-ers. Nevertheless, the almost exclusive focus on welfare mothers is alarm-ing to some witnesses and legislators. Penny Young inquired, "[W]hy isn't anyone talking about the father that was involved in this, and the fathers that are involved in all these children's lives?" (Senate Committee on Finance 1995g, 29). Later in the hearing process, Senator John Chafee (R-R.I.) reminded legislators, "By the way, we are always talking about the woman;...there is a man involved in these things, too" (Senate Commit-tee on Finance 1995i, 44). Senator Barbara Mikulski (D-Md.) observed, "Often neglected in the debate has been the role of men, except in a rather tart criticism around something called 'deadbeat dads'" (Senate Commit-tee on Labor and Human Resources 1995a, 11).[8] Although largely sporadic and ineffectual in stimulating prolonged discussion on the role of fathers in welfare, these comments do provoke some discussions about the char-acteristics of fathers.

Two predominant stories[9] address the role of men in welfare. The first account has a sympathetic tone and bears a striking resemblance to the misfortunate welfare recipient paradigm. This narrative relates the tale of poor, unemployed, or disabled men who are unable to fulfill their mascu-line responsibilities as fathers and providers for reasons largely out of their control (e.g., the lack of living-wage jobs). Expanding on the father's limitations, Representative Maxine Waters (D-Calif.) added: "Many low-income fathers are simply unable to meet their responsibilities to their children. They may be disabled, in jail, unemployed, underemployed and working low-wage jobs.... Pursuing child support from these fathers only pushes them deeper into poverty and further alienates them from their children" (House Committee on Ways and Means 1994a, 585). According to Pat Gowens, member of Milwaukee's Welfare Warriors, many men are forced to abandon their families because of unemployment: "[M]ost fathers do not want to marry or stay in home if they cannot provide for their kids.... The fact that they do not have a job pushes them out of the home" (House Committee on Government Operations 1994, 60).

Offering another reason for fathers being unable to fulfill their role as providers, many witnesses and legislators blamed the mothers. For exam-ple, David Ellwood, assistant secretary for planning and evaluation for the Department of Health and Human Services, explained that some welfare mothers refuse to cooperate in establishing the identity of their children's father: "A number of studies suggest that the mother almost always knows the identity of the father as well as his location at the time of the child's birth, and that a high percentage of mothers do provide full information on the father and his whereabouts. Nevertheless, research and anecdotal evi-dence indicate that a lack of cooperation is a problem in a significant num-ber of cases" (House Committee on Ways and Means 1995d, 40). Robert M.

Melia, first deputy commissioner for the Massachusetts Department of Revenue, accused welfare mothers with stalling paternity identification: "If 20 employees are collecting almost all of the money, what do the other 810 staff do all day? The answer is simple:... They're not collecting child support because they're busy trying to pry information out of the 35–40 percent of AFDC recipients who do not want to establish paternity of their children" (House Committee on Ways and Means 1994a, 697). Charles Augustus Ballard, founder and president of the National Institute for Responsible Fatherhood and Family Development, argued, "[M]ost of the problems encountered by fathers are the mothers who reluctantly let their children stay involved with their father's life" (650). David Burgess of the Texas Fathers Alliance and American Fathers Coalition in Austin stated that mothers drive interested fathers away from the moment the father first visits his child in the hospital, preventing him from forming a critical bond with his child (House Committee on Ways and Means 1995c, 1260). These statements all highlight the persistent efforts of mothers to keep their children away from the fathers, even as the fathers indicate a strong desire to participate in family life.

According to those who testified, when fathers are unable to provide for their families and interact with their children, they find destructive ways to act out their masculinity. For instance, Robert C. Granger, senior vice president of the Manpower Demonstration Research Corporation, concluded that "until you start to change the economics for these men, what you are going to end up with is men acting out their manhood in ways that are entirely inappropriate" (Senate Committee on Finance 1995d, 31). Similarly, Professor Rebecca Maynard argued, "If the young man cannot keep house, as he calls it, he cannot provide for the woman and her child, he finds other ways to act out his manliness" (Senate Committee on Finance 1995d, 17). Elaborating on some of these harmful actions, Chair of the Subcommittee on Human Resources Matthew G. Martinez (D-Calif.) stated, "I have seen men who were proud to be the essential head of household, men who have had jobs for a long time who have lost them, who have never been drinkers, never been alcoholics, but then took to drink because of the despair of not being able to provide for the family, and end up as wife-beaters and children-beaters and really cause dramatic upheaval to their family lives" (House Committee on Education and Labor 1994c, 3). These characterizations sympathetically depict fathers as compromised due to a system that prevents them from becoming the fathers and providers they would like to be.

A second, and perhaps the most dominant, narrative regarding men involves the tale of the deadbeat dad. The story begins by discussing men who intentionally father children and then refuse to support them. Senator Mike DeWine (R-Ohio) stated "We are all angry, as the public is, about the men who father children and then run off without paying child support" (*Cong. Rec.* 1995, S11768). Senator Lieberman (D-Conn.) explained, "I was startled as I went through the files—thousands of them—to see the degree to which men who had fathered children refused to accept fiscal responsibility, financial responsibility for those children, and found 100 different ways to try to avoid or make excuses for not doing so" (*Cong. Rec.* 1995, S12699).

What makes the actions of these fathers especially heinous, however, is that they are typically depicted as financially successful and simply unwilling to support their children. Expressing this view, Representative Robert Matsui (D-Calif.) stated:

[I]n the early 1980s, we were talking about the welfare queen as the custodial mother, thinking that she lives in this great palace.... [W]ell, we are going to be talking about the welfare king in the 1990s, because there are about 12 or 13 or 14 billion dollars' worth of moneys that the governments...are paying on behalf of the parent who has the capability, but is not making the payment to that child. (House Committee on Ways and Means 1993c, 155; House Committee on Ways and Means 1993a, 51)

In an even more explicit example, First Deputy Melia wrote: "Without further administrative or judicial action to locate and seize property, however, the child support judgment is often not collected. As a result, obligors acquire real estate, boats, fancy cars, bank accounts, and stocks and bonds, rather than support their children" (House Committee on Ways and Means 1994a, 703). These statements evoke images of professional fathers who are living the American dream in material luxury and deliberately withholding financial payments from their poverty-stricken family living off public assistance.

THE INFLUENCE OF DEPICTIONS ON WELFARE POLICY

Depictions of welfare recipients clearly influence policy proposals and the PRWORA. As mentioned earlier, factors such as partisan politics and negotiations among legislators and special interest groups also influence legislative outcomes. Nevertheless, as is evident in this section, the link between the depictions and corresponding legislation also underscores the significance of language in shaping policy change.

Policy Initiatives Based on the Misfortunate Welfare Recipient Depiction

Reflecting the construction of the misfortunate welfare recipient as a capable, talented, able-bodied individual who is committed to hard work and family and prevented from achieving her full potential due to temporary misfortune beyond her control, the majority of proposals entertain two main solutions: asset-building through microenterprises[10] and through Individual Development Accounts (IDAs), the latter of which is incorporated in PRWORA.

Throughout the hearings and debates, several witnesses attested to the merits of IDA programs. For example, clearly invoking the misfortunate welfare recipient paradigm of a recipient as "rational" and "capable" and eager to live the American dream, Eloise Anderson described a California program that encourages savings accounts:

So we allow people to have a savings account, keep up to $2,000 in one savings account which we call a rainy day account. And we have what we call the American dream account and with that savings account you can save for a home, you can save for your own business, and you can save for your college education for your kids. It is important that we believe that we give a new message in AFDC and that message is that we think that you are a rational, capable human being, capable of getting out here and doing everything else everybody else is doing, that we are not going to treat you differently. (House Committee on Ways and Means 1995a, 681–82)

Incorporating the misfortunate welfare recipient paradigm into his proposal, President Clinton's Work and Responsibility Act of 1994 endorsed "the idea of helping welfare recipients help themselves by proposing to...establish Individual Development Accounts.... An IDA is an optional earning-bearing, tax-benefited trust account in the name of one person. An IDA would be held in a licensed, federally-insured financial institution" (House Committee on Ways and Means 1994a, 298). Later in the debates, Senator Coats (R-Ind.) discussed the Assets for Independence amendment, which allows welfare recipients to save money:

In some respects, IDA's are like IRA's for the working poor. Investments using assets from IDA savings accounts are strictly limited to three purposes: purchase of home, post-secondary education, or business capitalization.... The individual or family deposits whatever they can save—typically $5 to $20 a month—in the account. The sponsoring organization matches that deposit with funds provided by local churches and service organizations. (*Cong. Rec.* 1996, S8368–69).

Reflecting ideas similar to those advanced in the proposals, PRWORA contains a provision for IDA's. Under the TANF block grant, states may use a portion of their grant to establish IDAs for individuals to accumulate funds for any qualified purpose, such as post-secondary educational expenses, first home purchase, or business capitalization (*PRWORA of 1996*, 2125–27; *Cong. Rec.* 1995, S126730).

The inclusion of asset-building provisions in the 1996 welfare reform bill attests to the relative power of constructing the misfortunate welfare recipient as a capable and responsible individual. By encouraging owner-ship of property, IDAs reinforce capitalist and work ethic ideologies and affirm the historical importance of property in America as a precursor to participation in American sociopolitical life. IDAs are the only major solutions apparent in the PRWORA that are driven by the misfortunate welfare recipients paradigm. This fact may reflect legislator skepticism of the paradigm. Legislators instead endorsed numerous policy initiatives consistent with conceptions of welfare recipients as feckless and young, perhaps indicating that legislators viewed these accounts as more accurate descriptions of the welfare population.

Policy Initiatives Arising from the Feckless Welfare Recipient Paradigm

Many proposals and provisions in the 1996 act respond to the construction of welfare recipients as immoral, unskilled, substance-abusing, neglectful parents.

Responding to Constructions of Welfare Recipients as Immoral

Constructions of welfare recipients as lacking in values and morals, combined with proposals designed to reinforce those values, encourage legislators to view religious organizations as a main solution to the welfare problem. Basically, the act authorizes states to contract with religious, charitable, and private organizations to supply social services to welfare recipients (*PRWORA of 1996,* 2161–62). The emphasis on religious and charitable organizations also reflects a growing perception of poverty as rooted in poor morals and values.

Responding to Constructions of Welfare Recipients as Unskilled and Uneducated

PRWORA also continues to reflect the construction of an unskilled, feckless welfare recipient, providing for work activities that include "job search and job readiness assistance," "vocational educational training (not to exceed 12 months)," and "job skills training directly related to employment" (*PRWORA of 1996,* 2133). Although the thrust of the act is to encourage work activities, the legislation nevertheless responds to constructions of the feckless and young welfare recipients who may not be equipped to work due to lack of skills and training.

Responding to Constructions of Welfare Recipients as Substance Abusers

PRWORA validates the construction of welfare recipients as substance users by containing provisions that allow states to require that individuals undergo substance abuse treatment. A statement by Representative Gary

A. Franks (R-Conn.) powerfully illustrates the influence of depictions emergent in the hearings and debates on the resulting legislation:

Today I would like to talk about one bill that would deal with a debit card, H.R. 4764. Mr. Chairman, I strongly believe that we should take cash out of our welfare system and replace welfare checks with a debit card. This would give us as taxpayers an accounting of all dollars spent by a welfare recipient. However, I do recognize that there may be a need to allow a small amount of cash for incidental items but I would hope that the vast majority of welfare funds would be dispensed via a debit card.... I believe that billions of taxpayers' dollars intended for families with dependent children are ending up in the hands of drug dealers via the purchase of drugs by some welfare recipients.... In Chicago, we all read how 20 people were living in a 2-bedroom apartment with the 4 adults receiving approximately $4,500 in welfare cash. It was alleged that all four adults were drug users. Part of their $4,500 was going to support their alleged drug habits, not going to supporting their children.... [B]ut we cannot have a card system that would allow welfare recipients to draw out their funds in the form of cash. That defeats the purpose of having an accounting of the taxpayers' funds and, thus, under the administration's plan, recipients would still be able to buy illegal drugs with their welfare money. (House Committee on Ways and Means 1994a, 596; 1995c, 795)

The reference to the Chicago incident, discussed earlier, provides a clear image of welfare recipients; a construction that obviously warrants Franks's support of an amendment directed toward drug-addicted welfare recipients (House Committee on Ways and Means 1995b, 534). Following this lead, a section in PRWORA, entitled "Sanctioning for Testing Positive for Controlled Substances," allows states to condition welfare receipt on testing negative for controlled substances (*PRWORA of 1996*, 2141, 2278). Other PRWORA provisions deny assistance to individuals convicted of "any offense which is classified as a felony by the law of the jurisdictions involved and which has as an element the possession, use, or distribution of a controlled substance" (2180).

Responding to Constructions of Welfare Recipients as Abusive and Neglectful Parents

In a manner reminiscent of nineteenth-century Poor Law reforms, constructions of young, never-married mothers on welfare who are abusive and neglectful result in many proposals[11] and eventually legislation designed to improve welfare mothers' parenting skills, enforce welfare mothers' proper care of their children, and remove children from harmful environments. For example, upon penalty of grant reduction, individuals are required to set up and adhere to an individual responsibility plan that "sets forth the obligations of the individual, which may include a requirement that the individual attend school, maintain certain grades and attendance, keep school age children of the individual in school, immunize children, attend parenting and money management classes, or do other things that will help the individual become and remain employed in the private sector" (*PRWORA of 1996*, 2140–41). In addition, PRWORA permits states to sanction welfare recipients for failing to ensure that their minor children attend school (2127, 2128). Finally, codifying the perception that some welfare families are ill equipped to raise children, Title IV-E requires that states certify that they "will operate a foster care and adoption assistance program" (2114). These provisions all reflect varying levels of suspicion about the quality of welfare mothers' parenting.

Responding to Constructions of Welfare Recipients as Criminals

Reflecting the construction of welfare recipients as criminals, PRWORA contains many provisions that deny assistance to felons, parole violators, and others engaged in criminal behaviors, such as food stamp trafficking, bearing children to gain additional welfare funds, and claiming benefits in multiple states simultaneously. For instance, the Act doubles penalties for violating food stamp requirements (*PRWORA of 1996*, 2314). It also requires that states must demonstrate "[c]ertification of standards and procedures to ensure against program fraud and abuse" and that states must deny "assistance for fugitive felons and probation and parole violators" (2115, 2138, 2185). Indeed, entire sections of PRWORA deal with the "Treatment of Prisoners," "Expanded Criminal Forfeiture for Violations," and "Elimination of Housing Assistance with Respect to Fugitive Felons and Probation and Parole Violators" (2186, 2187, 2334, 2348, 2349).

The construction of welfare mothers as bearing additional children to increase their welfare benefits also influences the Act in a subtle, but important, way. Previous bill proposals included family-planning alternatives[12] and a highly contentious and publicized family cap designed to limit payments to women who bear children while on welfare. Although the family cap does not appear in the 1996 Personal Responsibility and Work Opportunity Reconciliation Act by specific reference, the TANF block grant contains two significant sections that implicitly encourage states to implement a family cap or child exclusion provision in their welfare bills. First, under TANF, states do not need to apply for a waiver to implement a family cap. As a result, the 14 states that enforced a family cap at the time of TANF's passage can continue to implement this cap and receive federal funding (*PRWORA of 1996*, 2157).[13] Moreover, TANF may actually encourage states to continue such waivers with a provision for "Secretarial Encouragement of Current Waivers," which states: "The Secretary shall encourage any State operating a waiver described in subsection (a) to continue the waiver and to evaluate, using random sampling and other characteristics of accepted scientific evaluations, the result or effect of the waiver" (2158).

Second, TANF makes the family cap attractive by promising five eligible states a share of $20 million ($25 million if fewer than five are eligible) for reducing out-of-wedlock births without a corresponding increase in abortion for fiscal years 1999, 2000, 2001, and 2002 (2121, 2122). Although the exclusion waivers are stricter than those in prior policies, they respond to a growing social perception that promiscuous welfare mothers are having many illegitimate children, resulting in a significant and costly problem. The waivers also signal prevailing beliefs best expressed in the hearings and debates by Subcommittee on Human Resources Chair E. Clay Shaw (R-Fla.): "The correct birth rate for mothers already on welfare is zero" (House Committee on Ways and Means 1996b, 5).

Finally, perhaps in response to stories that welfare recipients migrate to states with higher benefits, PRWORA contains a provision expressly designed to discourage welfare recipients from migrating to states to claim higher benefits. For example, the act asserts that states can deny "assistance for 10 years to a person found to have fraudulently misrepresented residence in order to obtain assistance in 2 or more states" (*PRWORA of 1996*, 2139, 2321; *Cong. Rec.* 1995, H3453, H3497). In addition, PRWORA requires states to indicate whether and how the state intends to treat families that move from one state to another differently from families that currently reside in the state (*PRWORA of 1996*, 2114, 2124).

Policy Initiatives Arising from the Young Welfare Recipient Paradigm

The depictions of the young welfare recipient and corresponding proposals also clearly influence PRWORA. Specifically, many provisions respond to the construction of welfare recipients as young, poorly nurtured, and victims of sexual abuse. One dramatic example of the influence of testimony and depictions on policy aimed at teenage welfare recipients comes from Senator Kent Conrad (D-N.Dak.). After speaking in support of Conrad-Lieberman Amendment 2528, which allocates money for states to develop second-chance homes or adult-supervised living arrangements in which "young, unmarried mothers can get the structure and supervision that they need to turn their lives around," Senator Conrad cited the evidence he used to justify his support of the amendment (*Cong. Rec.* 1995, S13529, S13532):

I wish to share a couple of vignettes.... They are real life experiences.... Elena is an 18-year-old single mother with a 2-year-old son, Andrew. She has never been married, has never lived independently, and she receives public assistance.... Elena has a fractured and unstable past. She shuffled between her mother and father until age 5, when she was placed in the first of three foster homes due to physical abuse from her mother.... Her relationship with her baby's father deteriorated as he continued . . . his drug use. . . . Elena had no other choices but to enter the shelter system. . . . The day after, she enrolled in the one-step programs, including the alternative high school where she is working toward completing her GED, the licensed day care center where her child is being socialized to the norms of education and the independent living skills workshops where she is learning topics such as parenting, budgeting, nutrition, and family violence prevention. (*Cong. Rec.* 1995, S13533, S13599)

Based on this anecdotal evidence and what he referred to as the "most compelling" anecdotal testimony of Sister Mary Rose McGeady and her experiences with teenage mothers in a second-chance home, Conrad supported proposals for second-chance homes (*Cong. Rec.* 1995, S13529–30).[14]

Variations of these proposals are included in the enacted legislation. In the case of unmarried mothers under the age of 18, PRWORA includes a provision for second-chance homes defined as programs that provide individuals "with a supportive and supervised living arrangement in which such individuals are required to learn parenting skills, including child development, family budgeting, health and nutrition, and other skills to promote their long-term economic independence and the well-being of their children" (*PRWORA of 1996,* 2137). PRWORA also denies assistance to all teenage parents who are not living in an adult-supervised setting, with the exception of those who have been "subjected to serious physical or emotional harm, sexual abuse, or exploitation" (2136). In the case of those exceptions, the states must "provide or assist the individual in locating a second chance home, maternity home, or other appropriate adult-supervised supportive living arrangement" (2136). Finally, PRWORA allows states to use funds to support a voucher system[15] rather than to give cash aid to recipients (2351). This provision responds to legislator uncertainty about whether youth are deserving or undeserving of aid. Such measures as second-chance homes are sympathetic to the needs of young teens for adult guidance, whereas others, such as denial of cash assistance, reflect legislator skepticism of the young welfare recipients' tendency to act like feckless welfare recipients and misuse public assistance. In the same manner that outdoor relief typically provided the needy with basic necessities rather than cash aid, PRWORA vouchers give recipients essential items (e.g., diapers, clothing, school supplies, cribs) instead of monetary assistance.

Further, PRWORA reads that states must provide evidence of how they are going to "prevent and reduce the incidence of out-of-wedlock pregnancies, with special emphasis on teenage pregnancies" (*PRWORA of 1996,* 2113–14).[16] To that end, PRWORA provides for the allocation of money to states for abstinence education.[17] The law specifies that the purpose of such education is to teach people "that a mutually faithful monogamous relationship in context of marriage is the expected standard of human sexual activity," and that "sexual activity outside of the context of marriage is likely to have harmful psychological and physical effects" and "harmful consequences for the child, the child's parents, and society" (2354). The underlying rationale that informs these changes is that welfare parents are unable to provide their children with moral instruction. Because feckless welfare recipients are depicted as incompetent parents, ensuring that welfare recipient children learn when sexual activity, child-bearing, and marriage are appropriate requires nationally supervised school programs.

Finally, depictions of young welfare recipients as victims of rape and abuse by older men rationalize legislation designed to reduce statutory rape and prosecute offenders more harshly. Specifically, in PRWORA, Congress noted, "An effective strategy to combat teenage pregnancy must address the issues of male responsibility, including statutory rape culpability and prevention" (*PRWORA of 1996*, 2111, 2349–50). Consequently, Section 402 dictates that states must include education and training on the problem of statutory rape as part of their family assistance plan (2114).

Policy Initiatives Arising from Constructions of Fathers

Constructions of fathers also influence policy proposals[18] designed to improve paternity identification and child-support enforcement measures.[19] Responding to constructions of mothers as willfully obstructing paternity identification, PRWORA requires women to cooperate in establishing paternity and obtaining child support upon penalty of reduction or elimination of assistance (*PRWORA of 1996*, 2135, 2321). Until the child reaches adulthood at 18 years of age, the child is eligible to use the paternity-establishment process, including genetic testing and voluntary paternity acknowledgment procedures (e.g., hospital-based programs, state-offered services) (2227–78).

The act includes some of the toughest child-support enforcement measures in history. Under Title IV-D, states are required to operate a child-support enforcement program (*PRWORA of 1996*, 2114).[20] According to the act:

It is the sense of the Senate that (a) States should diligently continue their efforts to enforce child support payments by the non-custodial parent to the custodial parent, regardless of the employment status or location of the non-custodial parent; and (b) States are encouraged to pursue pilot programs in which the parents of a non-adult, non-custodial parent who refuses to or is unable to pay child support must—(1) pay or contribute to the child support owed by the non-custodial parent; or (2) otherwise fulfill all financial obligations and meet all conditions imposed on the non-custodial parent, such as participation in a work program or other related activity. (2349)

To ensure compliance with child support, state agencies are authorized under PRWORA to order genetic testing, "subpoena financial or other information needed to establish, modify, or enforce a support order," and request information, such as vital statistics, state and local tax and revenue records, "records concerning real and titled personal property," "records of occupational and professional licenses,... records concerning the ownership and control of corporations, partnerships, and other business entities," "records of the motor vehicle department," and "correction records" (2224). There are also provisions that allow states to intercept and seize lump-sum payments, such as judgments or lotteries, and to impose liens on property (2225, 2251). Furthermore, PRWORA includes provisions to improve links among automated local, state, and federal registries of child support orders; to compel states to create a "State Directory of New Hires"; to enforce stringent income-withholding procedures of "wages, salaries, commissions, bonuses, worker's compensation, disability, payments pursuant to a pension or retirement program, and interest"; and to expand the federal parent locator service (2205–6, 2209–14). Such provisions rely on constructions in the hearings and debates of welfare fathers as deadbeat dads who are employed and who choose not to spend their bonuses, commissions, and lump-sum payments on their children. Perhaps influenced by narratives of fathers who prefer to pay off their car loans rather than their child support, the act specifically allows states to suspend a father's driver's license, request his motor vehicle records, and put a lien against his property.

"THE MORAL SIGNIFICANCE OF BEING NEGATED": RHETORICAL IMPLICATIONS

As demonstrated throughout this chapter, legislators and witnesses rhetorically construct four distinct depictions of welfare recipients—the misfortunate, the feckless, the young, and the fathers—to account for the existence of poverty and welfare dependence in America. These depictions and the narratives they evoke frequently warrant legislator actions in terms of specific proposals and the resulting 1996 act. The rhetorical force of some depictions is so powerful that legislators often rely on these depictions to the exclusion of other forms of evidence, an issue discussed in more detail in subsequent chapters. Thus, this chapter advances our understanding of a process frequently overlooked in policy-making studies—the role of depictions and language in guiding policy decisions. In so doing, this chapter also makes at least three important contributions.

First, this chapter challenges the democratic and participatory functions of the narrative paradigm as conceived by Walter Fisher. Implying that audiences have the power to interpret and assess narratives, Fisher's narrative paradigm endows audiences with significant control in the creation of meaning. Fisher's insistence upon audiences' ability to judge a text critically based on its narrative rationality, however, discounts the power of discourse to shape and position audiences' understanding of their world in particular ways. Thus, whereas Fisher claimed that "[t]he sort of hierarchy condemned by the narrative praxis is the sort that is marked by the will to power, the kind of system in which elites struggle to dominate and to use the people for their own ends" (1984, 9), this chapter suggests otherwise. An analysis of the congressional hearings and debates that led to the passage of PRWORA points to the power of some depictions to facilitate elite discourse and to exclude and delegitimate particular public voices.

Interestingly, the hearings appeared to solicit a variety of opinions from concerned citizens, including clerics, social scientists, policy experts, and, occasionally, former welfare recipients. Some hearings announcements also invited interested citizens to submit statements for inclusion in the public record. In addition, some hearings included the testimony of unsolicited witnesses. This evidence seems to confirm Lloyd F. Bitzer's conclusion that "legislative bodies provide explicitly for the active participation of interested parties" (1987, 426).

Despite an apparent openness to the hearings, however, the legislative process possessed an elitist tenor. Because legislators exercised considerable control in selecting witnesses, most panels comprised invited witnesses. The written statements of other unsolicited individuals were appended to the printed public record and were rarely invoked in the actual proceedings. Although witnesses who testified in the hearings represented a diverse demographic and professional group, almost all shared similar views on welfare reform. Indeed, according to Ron Haskins, Republican staff invited people to testify because they knew these witnesses held similar beliefs. In so doing, they could promote Republican welfare strategies, educate their constituency, and lessen the force of oppositional testimony. Rather than bypassing elite audiences as Fisher would hope, this form of public moral argument privileges the interpretations of the elite audience of legislators who are able to invite witnesses, structure the hearings, evaluate the narrative rationality of testimony, and develop policies in line with their agendas. As highly controlled, disciplined public conversations, the hearings and debates assumed a Foucaultian quality. The Republican party largely determined who would speak and on what topic, and a select audience of legislators applied the tests of fidelity and coherence to the testimony.

Further, the hearings and debates can be considered elitist because depictions of welfare, from the perspective of welfare recipients, were almost absent. In this sense, the congressional proceedings relegated welfare recipients to what Philip Wander termed the "Third Persona," or the audience negated by the discourse:

"[B]eing negated" includes not only being alienated through language—the "it" that is the summation of all that you and I are told to avoid becoming, but also being negated in history, a being whose presence, though relevant to what is said, is negated through silence. The moral significance of being negated through what is and is not said reveals itself in all its anguish and confusion in context, in the world of affairs wherein certain individuals and groups are, through law, tradition, or prejudice, denied rights accorded to being commended or, measured against an ideal, to human beings. The objectification of certain individuals and groups discloses itself through what is and is not said about them and through actual conditions affecting their ability to speak for themselves. Operating through existing social, political, and economic arrangements, negation extends beyond the "text" to include the ability to produce texts, to engage in discourse, to be heard in the public space. (1984, 210)

Similarly, constructions of the feckless welfare recipient as immoral and incompetent and the young welfare recipient as immature and inexperienced largely warranted the exclusion of welfare recipient testimony. In other words, legislators and witnesses constructed welfare recipients as forfeiting their right to speak authoritatively on welfare precisely because they were on welfare. The relative absence of any welfare recipient testimony until March 10, 1994, a full two years after the incipience of welfare reform hearings on March 25, 1992, provides some indication of the pertinence of welfare recipient testimony in the eyes of legislators. The few welfare recipient stories included in the hearings were largely those of the misfortunate welfare recipient, the individual who conforms to the family and work ethics and eventually succeeds. More important, the recipients who testified were typically *former* welfare recipients. By using former welfare recipient testimony and stories about welfare recipients whom legislators knew, Republicans could give the illusion that welfare recipient voices were being heard in the hearings, when in fact others were speaking on behalf of recipient interests. Far from being inclusive, the depictions invoked in the hearings justified the exclusion of testimony from welfare recipients, who are arguably among the most experienced groups of individuals on the topic. As a result, welfare recipients lost the right to speak about legislation that has profound implications for their lives.

Second, the depictions in this chapter signal an important historic return to explanations of poverty. Characterizing welfare recipients as behaviorally and spiritually impoverished, many witnesses and legislators argued that poverty is the result of poor values and morals. This spiritual explanation of poverty is made even more explicit with religious allusions. Given these concerns, it is not surprising that religious leaders

rendered a considerable portion of congressional testimony. So pronounced was the influence of religious testimony that Reverend William
Cunningham, director of Focus Hope, stated: "I don't know if you realize
you got three clerics up here today.... I brought a Presbyterian with me,
but you got all Catholics here, and if you are not suspicious of what happened, you ought to check with Lynn Gallagher, because she is a very fine
aide, but I think she may have had a little bit of bias here in the way this
thing is turning out" (House Committee on Agriculture 1995, 199). One
hearing panel was devoted exclusively to testimony from religious figures, such as Robert Sirico, president of the Acton Institute for the Study
of Religion and Liberty in Grand Rapids, Michigan; Fred Kammer of
Catholic Charities USA in Alexandria, Virginia; Mary Nelson, Bethel New
Life, Inc., Evangelical Lutheran Church in America; and John L. Carr, secretary of the Department of Social Development and World Peace, United
States Catholic Conference, Washington, D.C.[21] Robert Rector, however,
insisted that "we are not talking about promoting a Christian agenda, or a
Jewish agenda, or a Muslim agenda, or anything; we are just saying...we
have to have a spiritual basis for our compassion" (Senate Committee on
Finance 1995b, 15). By quoting passages from the Bible and including testimony almost entirely from persons of a Judeo-Christian faith, however,
legislators marked the policy proposals with a Judeo-Christian tone.

This spiritual tone has several consequences. The religious testimony
established a spiritual frame for evaluating welfare recipients, the welfare
system, and welfare reforms. As a result, the religious imagery lent an air
of righteousness to the welfare reform deliberations and resulting policy.
By invoking scripture and religious imagery, legislators could argue that
their political preferences and policies were part of a higher, perhaps
divine, plan. In this frame, legislators were above partisan politics and
were acting morally and ethically. The religious imagery also cast doubt
on the morality of welfare recipients. Within the frame of the religious narrative, those who are spiritually sound will work and will live pure lives.
Already, the spiritual and moral character of welfare recipients is implicitly in question because of depictions of single mothers as sexually
promiscuous, abusive (of alcohol, drugs, and children), and criminally
intentioned. In the end, the religious symbols shifted the discussion of
welfare from one of poverty to one of values, foreshadowing policies
designed to enforce work and family ethics. From this vantage, poverty is
not the problem, but rather it is the moral integrity of the welfare recipients. The sheer weight of religious testimony, then, underscores the heart
of the welfare reform debate as a struggle over values and morals. Indeed,
as the next chapter evinces, the purpose of the 1996 Act and reauthorization proposals is not to alleviate poverty but rather to inculcate recipients
with normative family values, attitudes, and beliefs.

Third and finally, this essay implies the need to examine mediated portrayals of welfare in greater detail. Legislator and witness perceptions of welfare families are often supported in the media. Those who testified frequently mentioned stories they read in newspapers or popular magazines such as the *Reader's Digest* to support their claims. The Chicago Keystone Case described in this chapter, for example, is invoked numerous times to support depictions of welfare recipients as child and drug abusers and to warrant specific policy proposals. Providing another example of how the media permeate welfare deliberations, Representative Roukema (R-N.J.) argued in one debate that some welfare recipients were "skillfully gaming the system" so they could "live off welfare." As support she said, "we all saw the article last month in the *Boston Globe* about four generations of one family—1 mother, 17 children, 74 grandchildren, and an unknown number of great-grandchildren—living in Massachusetts on welfare of some kind or another." Representative Roukema used this instance to justify her endorsement of time limits included in the Personal Responsibility Act of 1995 (*Cong. Rec.* 1995, H3374). "Policymakers read stories in the newspapers about welfare recipients who have six or seven children by different fathers, abuse drugs, and raise children who themselves go on to become welfare dependent for long periods" (Weaver 2000, 135). This "ordinary knowledge" that is not based on systematic social science methods, says Weaver, "paints a vivid portrait of real people with names and faces attached; it can seem far more real than piles of statistics, especially if it fits with and reinforces images or stereotypes that people already hold about how the world works" (136). The force of such ordinary knowledge in policy deliberations may be magnified because, as Weaver observed, much of the information legislators receive can be categorized, not as social science, but rather as "ordinary knowledge" (135). Given the influence of this ordinary knowledge, further study of mediated representations of welfare recipients and families in general, as well as the impact of such representations on public perception and legislative outcomes, is warranted.

NOTES

The question "Are we going to now govern by anecdote?" in the chapter title was asked by the late Senator Paul Wellstone (D-Minn.) in an August 7, 1995, debate (*Cong. Rec.* 1995, S11749).

1. Legislators and witnesses offered an abundance of examples of welfare mothers who violate marriage as normative behavior, sleep with numerous men whom they do not know, and engage in other illicit activities. For example, welfare recipient Pamela Cave related the story of a single mother on welfare who has four children by "several ex-husbands" (House Committee on Ways and Means 1995c, 1211–12). Robert A. Sirico, president of the Acton Institute for the Study of Religion and Liberty and member of the Michigan Civil Rights Commission, argued that

welfare mothers need to be discouraged from their "promiscuity" (House Committee on Ways and Means 1995b, 210). In another hearing, Bryce Suderow, editor of *Street Stories*, related anecdotes about mothers with four and five children by multiple sexual partners (House Committee on Ways and Means 1995c, 1680–88). In addition, Patrick T. Murphy, public guardian in Cook County, Illinois, narrated a frequently cited instance about a family in Chicago with five mothers who had "twenty-three children by seventeen fathers" (House Committee on Ways and Means 1995g, 119). This focus on promiscuity and the resulting out-of-wedlock births prompted many legislators to conclude, along with Representative Rick Santorum (R-Pa.), that out-of-wedlock births may be "the most serious social problem facing this country in America today and in the future" (House Committee on Ways and Means 1994a, 424).

2. Related comments include the following. In one hearing, Representative Emerson (R-Mo.) asked Joyce Walsh, local administrator for the LaRue County Health Center in Hodgenville, Kentucky, "So you really don't believe the Food Stamp Program promotes healthy eating?" Ms. Walsh replied: "No, I do not. How could it? We give them the coupon. They buy what they want to" (House Committee on Agriculture 1995, 402). Representative Gerald B.H. Solomon (R-N.Y.) related: "Twice this week... I went into a chain grocery store... [and] I watched the people going through those checkout lines. They were very, very young people.... One fellow was drunk as a skunk and he had a whole handful of food stamps, and he could not even count them. The things they were buying were not nutritious food" (*Cong. Rec.* 1996, H7788).

3. These articles are appended to the Senate Committee on Agriculture, Nutrition, and Forestry, 2 February 1994, hearing.

4. See the related comments of Representative David Dreier (R-Calif.), who is vice chair of the Rules Committee. He reported:

[J]ust a couple of hours ago I was running here on Capitol Hill [and]...had seen a number of people who obviously rely on food stamps for their survival, and what was on the ground but cracked crab legs. It seems to me that when we have people who are abusing the Food Stamp Program and living extraordinarily well off the Food Stamp Program, it obviously is a system that has failed. (*Cong. Rec.* 1996, H7789)

5. See also the related comments of Charles A. Murray from the American Enterprise Institute for Public Policy Research in Washington, D.C., who stated: "For a poor young woman, the welfare system is highly relevant to her future if she has a child, easing the short-term economic penalties that might ordinarily restrain her childbearing. The poorer she is, the more attractive the welfare package, and the more likely that she will think herself enabled by it to have a baby" (Senate Committee on Finance 1995i, 100).

6. A few scholars and legislators provided evidence contradicting the perception that women have children to receive higher benefits. Consult, for example, Representative Ford (D-Tenn.): "But there were about 70 scholars and researchers in this country that suggested very strongly to us that there was no evidence that would suggest in any way that these teen mothers were having these babies for the purpose of welfare benefits" (*Cong. Rec.* 1995, H3517); and Sociology Professor

Frank Furstenberg: "[T]here are very few people who say that they got pregnant to get on welfare, to stay on welfare. The vast majority are like the women in my study. They go on welfare out of necessity, not out of desire" (House Committee on Ways and Means 1996b, 73).

7. Exceptions include Representative Major R. Owens (D-N.Y.), who argued:

Clearly the shotgun is aimed at the places where poor people live. Clearly there is a demonization and there is a targeting of poor people to begin with. Then there is a more specific targeting of poor people who live in urban areas.... The more specifically large numbers of the people who are the ben-eficiaries are minorities. Large numbers more specific than that are people of African descent, black people.... Welfare is...a vehicle for the demonization of African-Americans. (*Cong. Rec.* 1995, H3400, H3404)

Illinois Senator Carol Moseley-Braun (D) charged that the welfare debate was replete with "racially inflammatory" arguments (Senate Committee on Finance 1995i, 90). Sonia M. Pérez, director of the Poverty Project at the National Council of La Raza, and Katherine McFate, associate director of research for Social Policy at the Joint Center for Political and Economic Studies, both argued that the welfare reform discussions and proposals were replete with racist tendencies (House Committee on Ways and Means 1995c, 1091, 1103,). Chapter 7 offers an explana-tion for why these objections do not have persuasive force in the congressional proceedings.

8. For similar comments, consult Dr. Nicholas Zill, vice president and director of Child and Family Studies for Westat, Incorporated, in Rockville, Maryland, who encouraged representatives not to forget the importance of fathers in welfare reform discussions: "[A]nother thing that many of us would plead is not to forget to focus on the father. I mean, one of the ways to get people above poverty is to have more than one wage earner contributing to the support of the family" (House Committee on Ways and Means 1996b, 94); and California Representative George E. Brown (D), who argued: "We must also stop pretending that the problem of ille-gitimate births is strictly a women's problem" (*Cong. Rec.* 1995, H3369).

9. Arguably, a second narrative about fathers in the welfare debate centers on men who rape young women. Throughout the hearings and debates, numerous witnesses and legislators testified that older men are sexually exploiting younger women and frequently committing statutory rape. Underscoring the youth of female victims, Governor Howard Dean explained, "Often, pregnancy is a result of predatory sexual behavior by older males on younger children, particularly those children who are under the age of 16" (Senate Committee on Finance 1995a, 39). Elayne Bennett, founder and president of the Best Friends Program, pleaded, "Please understand...that we are talking about girls who are 11, 12, and 13, and men who are 25, 26, 27, 30, and 35." (House Committee on Government Reform and Oversight 1996, 77–78). Representative Edolphus Towns (D-N.Y.) added: "[O]ften the partners of these girls are not boys their own age, but grown men who are victimizing the immaturity of these girls. It is 71 percent of adolescent girls who give birth report that the father of their child is a man of 20 or older. Clearly, we can no longer afford to focus attention on just adolescent girls" (House Committee on Government Reform and Oversight 1996, 3). Senator

Joseph Lieberman (D-Conn.) commented: "As I understand it, it is men who are typically older than these teenaged girls who, in a setting that is often abusive, exploitive, or overpowering, are fathering these children in acts that from a legal point of view are pure and simple statutory rape" (*Cong. Rec.* 1995, S8367, S12699–700). These passages all reinforce the idea that fathers of children on welfare prey on the immaturity of young girls, frequently engaging in coercion and rape. Although important, this perception of men is developed in the context of depictions of teenage welfare recipients. Consequently, provisions to address rape are discussed in response to the young welfare recipient paradigm and not as part of a description of fathers.

10. One outspoken advocate for microenterprises, Executive Director of the Community Nutrition Institute Rod Leonard, argued early in the hearing process: "We should invest in these Americans. I think we could create a small enterprise loan fund, SELF. It's an acronym. It's self-employment, to help people create their own jobs or one job for themselves and one job for someone else" (House Select Committee on Hunger 1992a, 7). Echoing Leonard's views, Robert Friedman argued: "[W]e should support enterprise—the ability of low-income folks to create jobs for themselves, as well as other innovative job creation strategies.... [A]ny welfare reform should make self-employment an option, and a supported option.... The only way, it seems to me, to engender enduring escapes from poverty is to enable low-income Americans to make a down payment on the American dream" (Senate Committee on Finance 1995e, 24–25, 41; House Committee on Ways and Means 1995c, 1192, 1184, 1190). Representative Cardiss Collins (D-Ill.) explained: "[T]here are many people receiving public assistance who have skills, ideas, and the desire needed to make a living on their own. In some cases, microenterprises are the perfect vehicle for their ambition. Such programs and microloans help ensure that these potential business owners have the support and technical assistance that they need to succeed" (House Committee on Ways and Means 1994a, 531). Relying on such testimony, some representatives included provisions for microenterprise development in early welfare reform proposals. For example, President Clinton's Work and Responsibility Act of 1994 proposed "to increase the number of microenterprises" (House Committee on Ways and Means 1994a, 298). Representative Jill Long (D-Ind.) and Representative Dave McCurdy (D-Okla.) supported H.R. 4414, the Independence for Families Act, which provided assistance for microenterprises (House Committee on Education and Labor 1994a, 115–21). In addition, Senator Spencer Abraham (R-Mich.) sponsored Amendment 2511 for "passing enterprise zone legislation," because he believed: "Enterprise zones are a crucial part of our effort to help poor people in this country.... [I]t is clear that enterprise zones will spur investment, entrepreneurship, public spirit and the development of skills necessary for participation in our market economy" (*Cong. Rec.* 1995, S13377).

Despite some support, the microenterprise strategy did not receive a hearty endorsement from most witnesses and legislators. Skepticism of microenterprises likely stemmed from testimony that they would only work for between 1 and 3 percent of the welfare population (Senate Committee on Appropriations, 1994b, 38). Although Friedman noted that "each 1% of welfare recipients choosing self-employment means nearly 50,000 businesses and 90,000 jobs," he also acknowledged that "self-employment is not an option for most welfare recipients" (House Committee on Ways and Means 1995c, 1191; Senate Committee on Finance 1995e, 8).

11. Addressing the perceived need for welfare mothers to learn parenting skills and to role model family values, Erica E. Tollett, senior public policy analyst for the National Black Child Development Institute, argued that "[s]tates must require parents to participate in long-term parenting programs" (House Committee on Ways and Means 1995c, 937). House Democratic Leader Richard A. Gephardt (Mo.) proposed a national program based on his state's success: "We have a program in Missouri...called Parents as First Teachers.... It is a family-based program. It tries to help parents be not only good parents but teachers. And we all know that our parents are our most important teachers throughout our life. Should we not encourage, as a goal, States to have programs like that?" (House Committee on Ways and Means 1995a, 37). The "Summary of Welfare Reform Legislation Sponsored by House Republicans, Fall, 1993" suggested requiring welfare parents to take parenting and money management classes (House Committee on Education and Labor 1994a, 126). Clearly, these provisions were consistent with constructions of young and feckless welfare mothers as lacking in basic parenting knowledge.

To ensure that welfare parents do not neglect their children, many proposals condition aid on parental adherence to health guidelines. For example, some proposals enforce the nutrition of pregnant at-risk mothers. Explaining one option, South Carolina Governor Campbell proposed a voucher system used in his state:

> We created a book, and it was called "Caring for Tomorrow's Children." "Caring for Tomorrow's Children" allows people to give free coupons in that book for an expectant mother that tells her what to do. We give them out to any female. It tells them how not to get pregnant; if they get pregnant, what to do, where to go.... Every fourth or fifth coupon has a transportation by cab that you can validate to get to the doctor. There is a coupon to go to a technical school for training. There is also a coupon for milk, pizza, and a few other things. And if it takes a pizza to get a girl to go get a physical to make sure she gets a healthy baby in the world, it is a cheap price. (Senate Committee on Governmental Affairs 1995, 39)

To ensure proper nutrition for welfare recipients, one of the amendments to H.R. 4, entitled "Model Nutrition Standards for Food Assistance for Pregnant, Postpartum, and Breastfeeding Women, Infants, and Children," reads:

> (a) In General—Not later than April 1, 1996, the Food and Nutrition Board of the Institute of Medicine of the National Academy of Sciences, in cooperation with pediatricians, obstetricians, nutritionists, and directors of programs providing nutritional risk assessment, food assistance, and nutrition education and counseling to economically disadvantaged pregnant women, postpartum women, breastfeeding women, infants, and young children, shall develop model nutrition standards for food assistance provided to such women, infants, and children under this Act. (b) REQUIREMENT.— Such model nutrition standards shall require that food assistance provided to such women, infants, and children contain nutrients that are lacking in

the diets of such women, infants, and children, as determined by nutritional research. (*Cong. Rec.* 1995, H3462, H3460)

Such proposals respond to constructions of welfare mothers as unable to provide their children with basic needs. In addition, the proposals offer a remedy to depictions of welfare mothers who use their food stamps to purchase nonnutritious foods.

In addition to nutrition requirements, some proposals require parents to immunize their children, reflecting witness and legislator fears that welfare parents will not provide their children with adequate health care. The "Summary of Welfare Reform Legislation Sponsored by House Republicans, Fall, 1993" contained a suggestion for "required immunizations for children" (House Committee on Education and Labor 1994a, 141). Representative Roukema (R-N.J.) added: "For decades, States have required that children entering the school system be properly immunized and vaccinated.... [I]t is essential that we put it as a requirement for continuing AFDC benefits, that families have their children immunized, using the medical protocol which is within the first 2 years" (House Committee on Ways and Means 1995a, 207). Representative McCrery (R-La.) suggested that "simply requiring the parents to show proof of immunization for their children in order to get their checks" is "one concrete way I think we could get the parents involved" (House Committee on Ways and Means 1995b, 301). Responding to such concerns, Representative Flake (D-N.Y.) explained his proposal: "Therefore, I have included a child immunization provision which allows a state an option to deny the family portion of AFDC benefits to any family which does not bring its child into compliance with Health and Human Services (HHS) immunization requirements" (House Committee on Ways and Means 1994a, 565). In response to constructions of welfare mothers as neglectful, these provisions attempt to ensure that children's basic health needs are met.

Throughout the hearings and debates, legislators also expressed concern about the commitment of welfare parents to providing their children with a quality education. This consideration prompted several witnesses to redefine the role of public schools and condition public assistance on welfare parents' ability to keep their children in schools. For example, Robert Rector suggested that children of parents on welfare be placed in moral church schools (House Committee on Economic and Educational Opportunities 1995a, 29). Andrea Sheldon, of the Traditional Values Coalition, proposed a voucher system to allow parents to send their children to religious schools (House Committee on Ways and Means 1996b, 106). Discussing one program, Virginia Senator Stephen H. Martin (R) explained, "In Virginia, we will require parents who want to continue receiving benefits for their children to ensure their attendance in school" (House Committee on Ways and Means 1995b, 336). Other proposals sanction welfare recipients for failure to keep their children in school. The "Summary of Welfare Reform Legislation Sponsored by House Republicans, Fall 1993" suggested that "Families with school-age children who attend school less than some state-established minimum without good cause can be subject to a sanction of up to $75.00 per child per month" (House Committee on Education and Labor 1994a, 133). Going further, Senator Danforth (R-Mo.) proposed that schools remain open 24 hours a day every day of the year to provide a safe, supervised environment for at-risk children:

The idea is to keep schools open 24 hours a day, 365 days a year. Why? Because a lot of the problem of poverty is a kid issue and these kids often times are in communities that have no resources for them, no place for them to go.... Why not create some place where they can be supervised, some place where they can have structure, some place where they can have activities, play sports, be tutored, mentored, whatever, to give them a chance to move out of this desperate situation where they have been locked. (Senate Committee on Finance 1994b, 73)

Based on this idea, Senator John F. Kerry (D-Mass.) proposed amendments 2662 and 2664:

In cities beset by crime and violence, and in rural areas with little to inspire or occupy children, the neighborhood public school must become a beacon—a warm, safe haven of learning, of values, or friendship, of intellectual growth.... Mr. President, it is well-established that some children of welfare dependent parents are subjected to inadequate care, supervision, and parental love and attention, to unsafe environments and undesirable influences.... My first amendment would provide funds for demonstration projects [to] keep schools that serve at-risk children open for more hours and initiate new programs so that schools can offer an alternative to the street for our Nation's unsupervised youth.... My second amendment would require parents to sign a parental responsibility contract that would demand, in exchange for benefits, that parent take an active role in the supervision and education of their children. (*Cong. Rec.* 1995, S13570–71)

Along similar lines, Senator John Ashcroft (R-Mo.) argued, "Government should certainly not be paying parents to let their kids play hooky and skip school. If you are on welfare, your kids should be in school" (*Cong. Rec.* 1996, S8407, S8503). As a result, Ashcroft proposed Amendment 4944 to allow states to "sanction welfare recipients...that do not ensure that their children are attending school" (*Cong. Rec.* 1996, S8493). Such provisions clearly draw on constructions of welfare parents as ill equipped at providing their children with education and acting as role models of cherished values.

The most popular proposal for removing children from harmful environments concerns adoption. As Lou Ann Bassan, of Family Law Reform News in San Francisco, summarized, "If mothers don't want to be responsible, or cannot be responsible, then the children need to be removed" (House Committee on Ways and Means 1995c, 1499). Carol Statuto Bevan, vice president for research and public policy at the National Council for Adoption, argued: "Adoption is clearly, when you review the research, in the children's best interest. There is no reason why adoption is the last resort in terms of providing services. It should be for some children clearly the first resort; not the last.... Financial, social, and legal barriers to adoption must be removed to allow more children the benefits of adoption" (House Committee on Ways and Means 1995g, 103, 147). William J. Bennett stated: "I believe that making adoption easier is an essential and compassionate part of welfare reform. Adoption is the best alternative we have to protect a child's interest in a post-welfare world" (House Committee on Ways and Means 1995b, 161). Wade F. Horn, director of the National Fatherhood Initiative, recommended that the Adoption Assistance and Foster Care Maintenance programs remain entitlements where the Adoption program "provides cash assistance to families who adopt children who are AFDC or SSI [Supplemental Security Income] eligible and who have special needs" (House Committee on Ways and Means 1995g, 144, 145). The National Governors Association promotes adoption assistance (Senate Committee on Finance 1996a, 175). In addition, Robert Rector recommended adoption as a strategy to combat welfare dependence (House Committee on Economic and Educational Opportunities 1995a, 26).

Drawing on witness suggestions, Representative Talent (R-Mo.) lauded the benefits of placing children on welfare in adoptive homes: "It [adoption] is a win-win situation if it is done right. I mean, the statistics tell us what everyone knows, which is that the child's life expectancies and hopes go up by thousands of percent if the adoptions occur.... [E]very time that a successful adoption occurs, the State has dealt with the problem" (House Committee on Ways and Means 1995b, 544). Congressman Shays (R-Conn.) argued, "[M]easures such as orphanages and foster homes must be considered as possible solutions in reforming the existing welfare system" (House Committee on Ways and Means 1995a, 734). Recognizing that the link between welfare and adoption is tenuous, Senator Larry E. Craig (R-Ind.) explained: "Some people may ask, 'What does this have to do with welfare?' It has very little to do with our current welfare system, but a great deal to do with a dramatically reformed system.... Adoption is a viable option that results [in] the best of all worlds: Uniting a wanted child and a loving family" (*Cong. Rec.* 1995, S8363, S13585). One of the amendments offered en bloc by Representative Bill Archer (R-Tex.) regards the timely adoption of children: "It is the sense of the Congress that—(1) too many children who wish to be adopted are spending inordinate amounts of time in foster care; (2) there is an urgent need for States to increase the number of waiting children being adopted in a timely and lawful manner" (*Cong. Rec.* 1995, H3497).

To facilitate adoption, many representatives proposed tax credits for families that adopt children on welfare. Drawing on depictions of welfare parents as abusive, Wisconsin Representative Toby Roth (R) stated:

> Some have said this is mean legislation, it does not consider the welfare mother. But let us take a look at what really happens.... Let us take a look at how your particular system, the present system operates. Here [it] is right out of the newspaper: Kids go hungry while parents buy drugs. Three children live in a house of roaches, without food, while the parents spend their monthly welfare benefit in narcotics. In 1988, this woman had six children taken from her, put in foster homes. Now she has three more children after her boyfriend moved in, one 15 months, one 2 1/2 weeks. (*Cong. Rec.* 1995, H3504)

This description clearly warrants Roth's support of "a $5,000 tax credit for parents that adopt children who are in foster care" (*Cong. Rec.* 1995, H3505). Senator Gramm (R-Tex.) also favored an amendment for a refundable credit for adoption expenses: "I want, as we promised in the Contract with America, to have a tax credit for families that adopt children, something we desperately want to promote" (*Cong. Rec.* 1995, S11747, S12899, S13488). Speaking on behalf of adoption tax credits, Senator Richard C. Shelby (R-N.C.) stated:

Society is unambiguously better off as a result of adoption. Statistics show that time and again that children with families intact are more likely to become productive member of the community than children without both parents. Unfortunately more times than not a financial barrier stands in the way of otherwise qualified parents.... Our amendment seeks to address this problem. It would allow a $5,000 refundable tax credit for adoption expenses...to any individual with an income up to $60,000 and phased out up to an income of $100,000.... A fully-refundable adoption tax credit is an essential part of any welfare reform measure...[and] will go a long way in making adoption a reality for many children and helping them find the loving homes they so desperately need in America. (*Cong. Rec.* 1995, S13585)

Senator Barbara Boxer (D-Calif.) added: "If we have to get a child out of an abusive home situation, we want to give a little assistance to the foster family or the adopting parents (*Cong. Rec.* 1995, S13376).

12. For example, an early Senate bill (2895) from the state of Mississippi contained a requirement for women on welfare to use the contraceptive Norplant (House Select Committee on Hunger, Domestic Task Force 1992a, 106). Representative James P. Moran (D-Va.) asked in one hearing if "other jurisdictions throughout the state considered that [Norplant]" (House Select Committee on Hunger Domestic Task Force 1992b, 16).

13. By 2000, 23 states had adopted family caps (Gais and Weaver 2002).

14. Constructions of young welfare recipients as needing a more structured, disciplined upbringing influenced a number of discussions about maternal and second-chance homes. Carol Statuto Bevan explained the need for such homes: "[W]e need a place for young moms to bear their children, to learn parenting skills, to promote adoption, if that is part of what they want to do. But to really have a real choice in this country, and to avoid the choice of only having an abortion, we do need to bring back residential settings, supervised settings" (House Committee on Ways and Means 1995g, 149). Eloise Anderson favored establishing a "group setting with other young girls who have children where they would be supervised, where they could finish their high school education, where they can learn the kind of parenting skills they need, where we can teach them the kind of financing skills they need, where we can teach them cooking and all those other kinds of home maintenance skills they are going to need as they get out on their own" (House Committee on Ways and Means 1995a, 679). Robert Greenstein, executive director for the Center on Budget and Policy Priorities, added, "Teen parents should live in supervised settings either with parents or with other responsible adults" (Senate Committee on Finance 1995b, 50). In one hearing, Representative Y. Tim Hutchinson (R-Ark.) supported "closely supervised group homes in which the moms lived with the children and in a closely supervised environment and learned parenting skills" (House Committee on Ways and Means 1994a, 556). Representative Ford (D-Tenn.) argued: "We think the solution is to put them [teenagers on AFDC] in a residential home with their children, teach them parental skills, provide the children with early education, Head Start, and to make sure the mothers stay in school" (House Committee on Ways and Means 1995b, 135). Later in the debates, Senator Coats (R-Ind.) concluded: "[M]any young pregnant women are still in need not of cash, but of direction, compassion and support.... [P]rivate

and religious maternity homes, also known by some as second chance homes, provide that help. They are a one-stop supportive environment where a young woman can receive counseling, housing, education, educational services, nutrition, and job and parenting training that gives them a real opportunity for growth and decision making" (*Cong. Rec.* 1995, S13601).

Indeed, stories about young unmarried mothers who experience a childhood of neglect and then flourish in alternative supervised living situations have inspired a number of welfare reform proposals and amendments. For example, speaking on behalf of the Personal Responsibility Act (PRA), Representative Talent (R-Mo.) observed: "Under the PRA, the States would be empowered to use Federal money for the kind of care these children really need—residential care in a closely supervised nurturing environment where they can be taught work, parenting and life skills" (House Committee on Ways and Means 1995b, 532). In Section 1202, there is a provision for a "Role Models Academy Demonstration Act" to provide education for at-risk youth with "valuable instruction and insights regarding…(A) the tools to become productive citizens; (B) learning skills; (C) traditional, moral, ethical, and family values; (D) work ethics; (E) motivation; (F) self-confidence; and (G) pride" (*Cong. Rec.* 1995, S12718). Title I of Senate Amendment 1214, entitled "Maternal Health Certificates Program," provides for maternity homes where mothers can receive support services such as the following:

> (i) instruction and counseling regarding future health care… ; (ii) nutrition counseling; (iii) counseling and education concerning all aspects of prenatal care, childbirth, and motherhood; (iv) general family counseling, including child and family development counseling; (v) adoption counseling; (vi) employability training, job assistance, and counseling; and (vii) medical care or referral for…(I) prenatal, delivery, and post-delivery care; (II) screening or referral for…illegal drug use…and sexually transmitted diseases. (*Cong. Rec.* 1995, S12733)

15. Several legislators spoke in favor of denying cash benefits to those under 18 who bear children. Representative Archer (R-Tex.) averred, "The most effective direct attack on illegitimacy is to stop, to stop cash welfare benefits to young mothers" (House Committee on Ways and Means 1994a, 12). Later in the debates, Representative Ford (D-Tenn.) spoke in favor of an amendment that "[cuts] off the cash benefits from those children who are born to unmarried women under the age of 18" (*Cong. Rec.* 1995, H3517). Senator John Breaux (D-La.) added: "I kind of like the idea of vouchers…. I guarantee you, there are some teenage mothers who, when they do get extra cash assistance, may not use that cash assistance for the benefit of the child. They may use it to buy things which are not necessary. They may use it to feed an alcohol abuse problem or a drug problem" (*Cong. Rec.* 1995, S13515). Representative Jim Bunn (R-Oreg.) also favored an amendment that allows states to use funds for "vouchers…to pay for particular goods and services specified by the state as suitable for the care of the child such as diapers, clothing, and school supplies" (*Cong. Rec.* 1995, H3515).

For objections to vouchers, consult Representative W. G. (Bill) Hefner (D-N.C.), who feared that young welfare recipients will not act responsibly even with vouchers: "[T]here are certain things you cannot buy with food stamps. If you have vouchers for diapers or what have you, what is to keep unscrupulous people from taking a voucher for diapers and trading it for a six-pack or what have you? Just because you have restrictions...does not...guarantee that that is what the money is going to go for" (*Cong. Rec.* 1995, H3521). Representative Rangel (D-N.Y.) doubted whether vouchers would be effective (*Cong. Rec.* 1995, H3515). Representative Jim McDermott (D-Wash.) was uncomfortable with proposals that "micromanag[e] down to the level of the number of diapers that a woman needs to buy for a child" (*Cong. Rec.* 1995, H3518, S9384).

16. Similar provisions are included in previous proposals and bills. For instance, Donna E. Shalala, secretary of Health and Human Services, explained President Clinton's welfare reform strategy, noting that "[w]orking to prevent teen pregnancy...is a critical part of our plan" (Senate Committee on Finance 1994a, 10; Senate Committee Finance 1995c, 3; House Committee on Ways and Means 1994a, 361). In addition, the March 1996 "Provisions to Combat Rising Out-of-Wedlock Birth Rates Conference Report on H.R. 4," "Requires state plans to establish goals and take action to prevent and reduce the incidence of out-of-wedlock pregnancies, with special emphasis on teenage pregnancies" (House Committee on Ways and Means 1996b, 6).

17. Many of those who testified suggested abstinence education as a means of preventing teenage out-of-wedlock births. For example, Heidi Stirrup, of the Christian Coalition, suggested, "[F]irst of all, to increase funding in abstinence education.... I would also recommend that the Federal Government require States to devise their own plans to reduce out-of-wedlock births" (Senate Committee on Finance 1996a, 117). Building on witness suggestions, Representative Nancy L. Johnson (R-Conn.) stated: "Abstinence, I think, has to be pressed harder just like the DARE program in fifth grade. Say no to drugs. Young girls don't know how to say no to sex. They want to. They feel pressure" (House Committee on Ways and Means 1994a, 94). Later in the debates, Senator Lieberman (D-Conn.) concluded: "Programs that are effective focus on three behaviors: One is to protect oneself sexually. The second is abstinence. And the third is how to resist the pressure—peer pressure, or pressure from an individual, a man—to have sex" (*Cong. Rec.* 1995, S13531–32). Citing a successful abstinence education program in Atlanta, Georgia, targeted to young girls, Senator Lauch Faircloth (R-N.C.) proposed Amendment 2608 to provide for an abstinence education program.

18. Many witnesses and representatives suggested proposals that improve men's employment options through education and job training. For example, Kristin A. Moore, executive director and director of research for Child Trends in Washington, D.C., argued that men need job training to locate work: "[I]f they are unemployed, fathers as well as mothers should receive education and job training, and be subject to workfare to enable them to provide child support" (Senate Committee on Finance 1995d, 11). Robert C. Granger advocated "employment and other training programs" to improve the "marriageability of men,...increas[e] their ability to support a family" and "improve [their] economic prospects" (14). The vision statement for the Work and Responsibility Act of 1994 notes that successful programs provide noncustodial parents with the "skills they need to hold down a job" while others "give non-custodial parents the opportunity to meet their child support obligations through work" (House Committee on Ways and

Means 1994a, 182). Later in the debates, Senator Mikulski (D-Md.) proposed Amendment 2669, which "sets aside a very small amount of money in the welfare block grant for States to enroll unemployed fathers in job training and placement so they can meet their child support and family obligations. Employing these fathers is the most significant step we can take to promote two-parent families" (*Cong. Rec.* 1995, S13588).

19. Child-support measures were discussed frequently in the hearings and debates. Several measures included strategies for monitoring and sanctioning men who owe child support. Ruth E. (Betty) Murphy, marketing consultant on behalf of Electronic Parent Locator Network (EPLN) and the Consortium of EPLN States (Alabama, Arkansas, Florida, Georgia, Kentucky, Louisiana, North Carolina, South Carolina, Tennessee, and Virginia), advocated a state-run EPLN system to track the movement of deadbeat fathers (House Committee on Ways and Means 1995d, 257). Outlining President Clinton's welfare reform measures, David Ellwood explained that states "would be given the enforcement tools they need...revoking professional, occupational, and drivers' licenses to make delinquent parents pay,...expanded wage withholding, improved use of income and asset information, easier reversal of fraudulent transfers of assets,...[and] expanded use of credit reporting" (House Committee on Ways and Means 1995d, 43). Mary Jo Bane, assistant secretary for children and families of the Department of Health and Human Services and co-chair of the President's Working Group on Welfare Reform, Family Support, and Independence, stated that measures such as "[r]outine license screening, processing on motor vehicles" will enable men to understand that "their child support obligations are more important than their car payments, that indeed they can lose their cars if they don't pay their child support" (House Committee on Ways and Means 1994a, 389). Building on witness testimony, Representative Roukema (R-N.J.) advocated criminal penalties for willful violation of child support, including prison time and the withholding of licenses (House Committee on Ways and Means 1995d, 9). Representative Kennelly (D-Conn.) supported a wage-withholding system, a national registry, and anything that would "increase penalties for noncustodial parents who refuse to pay child support" (House Committee on Ways and Means 1995d, 7). Representative Olympia J. Snowe (R-Maine) suggested policies that revoke professional licenses (House Committee on Ways and Means 1994a, 502, 504). Later in the debates, Delaware Representative Castle (R) reported: "A Columbia University study found almost 40 percent of welfare beneficiaries could be self-sufficient if noncustodial parents paid their support. The proposal to deny licenses, along with other measures in our bill to crack down on deadbeat dads, would increase child support collections by $24 billion over 10 years, and help 800,000 mothers and children off welfare" (*Cong. Rec.* 1995, H3632). Senator DeWine (R-Ohio) proposed financial tracking of deadbeat fathers: "My amendment will allow states to enter into agreements with the financial community in their States to match financial data with child support delinquency lists on a more frequent basis" (*Cong. Rec.* 1995, S13594).

20. For noncustodial parents under the age of 18, the legislation encourages states to count community service and educational classes as a form of child sup-

port. "It is the sense of the Congress that the States should require noncustodial, nonsupporting parents who have not attained 18 years of age to fulfill community work obligations and attend appropriate parenting or money management classes after school" (*PRWORA of 1996*, 2134).

21. See House Committee on Ways and Means 1995b, 209, 714, 723; Senate Committee on Finance 1995g, 41.

Chapter 5

Legislating a "Normal Classic Family": The Rhetorical Construction of Families in American Welfare Policy

The Congress makes the following findings:
(1) Marriage is the foundation of a successful society.
(2) Marriage is an essential institution of a successful society which promotes the interests of children.
(3) Promotion of responsible fatherhood and motherhood is integral to successful child rearing and the well-being of children.

Personal Responsibility and Work Opportunity Reconciliation
Act of 1996, 2110

With a clear and strong emphasis on marriage, these words mark the introduction to the 1996 Personal Responsibility and Work Opportunity Reconciliation Act. As part of PRWORA's scheduled October 1, 2002 reauthorization, congressional representatives debated a variety of welfare proposals, many of which complement the Bush administration's emphasis on marriage. On May 16, 2002, the House of Representatives passed H.R. 4737, the Personal Responsibility, Work, and Family Promotion Act which would have amended the TANF program to encourage states to promote marriage and responsible fatherhood by redirecting "substantial funds—$1.6 billion over five years—focused almost exclusively on grants for the promotion and support of marriage" (Pance 2003, 3). These grants included Healthy Marriage Promotion Grants, Marriage Research and Demonstration Funds, and Promotion and Support of Responsible Fatherhood and Healthy Marriage Grants.

Of importance for the purposes of this chapter is that H.R. 4737 also amended the TANF purpose language to emphasize marriage and family. Specifically, H.R. 4737 replaced a reference to "parents" with a reference to "families." H.R. 4737 also further defined the original TANF reference to two-parent families as "healthy two-parent married families" (Parke 2003, 1–7). On February 13, 2003, the House of Representatives passed H.R. 4, the Personal Responsibility, Work, and Family Promotion Act of 2003. The marriage provisions of H.R. 4 are similar to those of H.R. 4737; one main difference is that most of the funding in H.R. 4 is over 6 years for a total of $1.9 billion dollars (Parke 2003, 5). H.R. 4 also extends a controversial $50 million program for promoting sexual abstinence until marriage. This abstinence education program does not include contraceptive education. Since the 1996 Act, Congress also enacted a similar program called Special Projects of Regional and National Significance (SPRANS) (email correspondence with Ron Haskens of the Brooklyn Institution, 10/3/03).

On September 10, 2003, the Senate Finance Committee approved reauthorization legislation of a bill called Personal Responsibility and Individual Development for Everyone (PRIDE) that earmarks $1.5 billion in federal funds over five years for marriage promotion activities. For a variety of reasons, however, PRWORA has not yet been reauthorized. A series of continuing resolutions have allowed PRWORA to operate while congress debates reauthorization proposals. With marriage promotion, and to a lesser extent sexual abstinence, and responsible fatherhood, as central features, PRWORA and its reauthorization proposals codify a series of American family values.

Despite the increasing importance of family values in this and other social policies, rhetoric scholar Dana L. Cloud noted, in an ideographic analysis of political speeches surrounding the 1992 presidential elections, that few rhetorical scholars attend to family values language. Cloud attributed this "scant writing" to "perceptions that this rhetoric was marginal to mainstream politics or that it was unsuccessful in the long term" (1998, 388). Observing that few rhetorical scholars have explored the relationship between argument and public policy, Linda Miller concluded in a *Quarterly Journal of Speech* article on legislation debates that despite a few empirical studies of public controversies[1] in legislative contexts, "the relationship between public argument and policy change remains unclear." Consequently, she called for "further analysis of the formation of a variety of public policies at the municipal, state, or federal legislative levels" (1999, 375). Exploring the connection between family constructions and public policy is critical, because some family forms often appear in policy discussions as normative and influence policy outcomes (Neisser and Schram 1994).

Based on a rhetorical-critical examination of the hearings and debates from the 102nd, 103rd, and 104th Congresses surrounding welfare reform, as well as of the PRWORA reauthorization deliberations, this chapter discusses the policy construction of families on welfare. The chapter focuses on discussions in the hearings and debates as a process of negotiating or constructing a particular symbolic reality, which provides the basis for future legislative action. In contrast to the legislation's goals, depictions of welfare families in the hearings and debates have led to legislation that reaffirms a family structure predicated on the historic family-wage model. The 1996 act and subsequent proposals reinforce this family ideal (defined as married adults living with their biological children), despite significant research demonstrating that many Americans do not live in traditional nuclear families. Consequently, because much of this legislation responds to and affirms an ideal family, what political communication scholar Darlaine C. Gardetto termed a "social imaginary family," it cannot offer adequate solutions to the material needs of many "real" families (1997, 226). Furthermore, the legislation ultimately promotes ends (e.g., dependence) antithetical to the legislation's stated goals of independence and self-sufficiency, even as it cleaves society along gender, racial, and class lines.

The chapter begins by reviewing the methodological and theoretical assumptions that guide this inquiry. Next, the chapter contextualizes the study by reviewing two significant welfare reforms—mothers' pensions and Aid to Dependent Children (ADC)—with special attention to gender, racial, and class issues. Third, the chapter outlines how those who testified in the hearings and debates characterized welfare families and evaluated those families through the lens of an idealized nuclear family. The chapter concludes with a discussion of implications.

PUBLIC POLICY AS SOCIAL CONSTRUCTION: RHETORICAL, POLITICAL, AND FEMINIST APPROACHES

This chapter's objectives suggest a methodological approach rooted in the intersection of rhetorical, political, and feminist studies. These disciplines provide the methodological framework for identifying significant characterizations of welfare families (that are emergent in contemporary legislative hearings and debates) and for assessing the implications of those characterizations for legislation and society. Moreover, these studies suggest the utility of feminist and rhetorical analyses as methods for deconstructing gender, race, and class in legislation and understanding how such constructions are accomplished and sustained in legislative decisions. Notably, the scholars cited in the text that follows recognize the value of discursive analyses for understanding public policy and, to varying degrees, assume that public policies are social constructions.

The works of political scientist Murray Edelman, law professor Martha Fineman, and rhetorical theorist Michael Osborn deserve special note. Edelman's work challenges traditional political science and communication approaches by focusing on the power of political language to construct meaning and shape responses. In *Constructing the Political Spectacle*, Edelman (1988) reflected on the complex linguistic construction of leaders, institutions, policy stances, and social problems and the ways in which political language reinforces dominant ideologies and existing power relationships, thereby partially shaping the reality to which the language responds. In *Political Language: Words that Succeed and Policies that Fail*, Edelman considered how language and symbols function to justify public acceptance of policies that result in inequality and deprivation as well as a persistent tolerance of chronic social problems (1977, 2). This chapter builds on Edelman's work regarding the constitutive power of public policy by providing a case study of how symbolic representations of welfare families within the hearings and debates reinforce dominant ideologies (e.g., about marriage) and ultimately influence public policy.

Martha Fineman drew on an approach similar to Edelman's to demonstrate how historic ideologies about families continue to regulate family law. According to Fineman, "[L]egal regulation is grounded on societal beliefs and expectations that continue to reflect unexamined gendered politics, policies, and practices" (1995, 6). Fineman argued: "Shared societal presumptions about the naturalness and inevitability of existing gendered role definitions and divisions continue to be pervasive," resulting in the maintenance of patriarchy to the detriment of many women and children (7, 27). As this chapter on welfare evinces, ideologies about the normalcy of two-parent families with the father as breadwinner and mother as caretaker exert a powerful influence on legislative reform.

To assess the constructions of welfare families, this chapter relies on depictive rhetoric as outlined by Michael Osborn (1986). In the case of welfare reform deliberations, depictive forms (e.g. anecdotes, metaphors, and narratives) craft a vivid image of the typical welfare family and normalize a two-parent family framework for evaluating welfare families. Ultimately, these depictions of welfare families serve as evidence to support legislative proposals and policies designed to enforce marriage, paternal economic support, and maternal dependence.

THE MYTHICAL FAMILY IDEAL: A REPRESENTATIVE ANECDOTE?

Understanding the emphasis on marriage in the contemporary welfare reform debate requires contextualizing the American family in light of historical views of the family and significant pieces of welfare legislation. Such a historical perspective reveals the dominance of a nuclear-family form as a legal and social norm.

Many scholars have acknowledged the central role of the nuclear family in U.S. legal and welfare history (Coontz 2000; Dornbusch and Strober 1988; Gutman 1976; Pleck 1998; Stacey 1996; Weiss 2000). Mimi Abramovitz, author of *Regulating the Lives of Women*, traced the dominance of the traditional family model to colonial America. She argued convincingly that the family ethic ideology rationalizes a sexual division of labor, assigning women the tasks of homemaking and child care and men the responsibility for earning an income (1996, 36–40). In *Life without Father*, David Popenoe stated, "Marriage and the nuclear family—mother, father, and children—are the most universal social institutions in existence" (1996, 2–3). In addition, Fineman noted, "In law, marriage traditionally has been designated as the only legitimate sexual relationship" (1995, 146). Fineman further argued that "although the image of the traditional family has undergone some revisions in light of the modern concerns with gender equity and equality, the nuclear-family form, with a sexual affiliation between man and woman as the paradigmatic intimate associational bond, is still dominant" (103). Like Abramovitz, Fineman recognized the role of cultural ideologies in sustaining the dominance of the nuclear-family form: "The shared assumption is that the appropriate family is founded on the heterosexual couple—a reproductive, biological pairing that is designated as divinely ordained in religion, crucial in social policy, and a normative imperative in ideology" (145).

The dominance of a nuclear family as normative imperative has had profound implications for federal welfare legislation. As historian Linda Gordon explained in *Pitied but Not Entitled:* "It is a commonplace that a key function of a welfare state is to replace *wages* lost through illness, disability, unemployment, or death. A more inclusive generalization is that welfare programs were intended to replace and defend the *family wage,* by which is meant the wage that should (theoretically) allow a husband to earn enough to support a nonemployed wife and children" (1994, 12, emphasis in original). In his book *After Welfare,* Sanford Schram added that "although the family-wage system has become harder to sustain in the face of postindustrial economic change, the rise of families with two wage earners, increased single motherhood, and other changes, the welfare system continues to be tied to reinforcing this idealized breadwinner model" (2000, 21).

Mothers' pensions and the ADC provision of the 1935 Social Security Act—two reforms credited with institutionalizing the family-wage model in welfare legislation—illustrate the prominent role of the nuclear family in U.S. welfare legislation. This chapter expands on previous discussions of these legislative forms in Chapter 2 , focusing on specific issues of gender, race, and class.

Mothers' pensions and ADC both reflected reformers' concerns with preserving the family, protecting children, and reinforcing a woman's caretaking roles. Progressive reformers introduced mothers' pensions to allow mothers to remain home to care for their children. As women's historian Julie Matthaei observed: "Certainly, other ways of rescuing such children were imaginable, such as providing their mothers with job training, jobs, and subsidized day-care facilities. The state's decision to provide cash child-support payments to female heads of households reflected the prevailing public views of family life as woman's vocation and proper parenting as mothering within the home" (1982, 139). Joanne L. Goodwin, author of *Gender and the Politics of Welfare Reform*, made a similar point, arguing that despite increased awareness of women's rights, "a majority of organized women continued to see women's greatest potential in traditional terms—as wife and mother. Those who linked mothers' pensions to maternal service shared this view and focused on a woman's ability to rear good citizens" (1997, 5).

By 1921, 48 states had adopted a form of mothers' pensions. Although the program may be viewed as a radical and feminist program in that it rewarded women economically for their caretaking work and theoretically[2] reduced women's economic dependence on men, the program also reinforced the sexual division of labor with important gender, class, and racial consequences (Gordon 1994, 56, 290). For example, the privileged, largely white female reformers who supported mothers' pensions advocated a family-wage, breadwinner-housewife structure as ideal, even though they themselves did not live or aspire to such a lifestyle.

Above all the welfare reformers' feminism was characterized by a class double standard. . . . For women of education and high status, they supported careers, public-sphere activism, and economic independence. For poor women, they recommended domesticity and economic dependence on men. They continued to view a career and motherhood as by and large alternative choices. Their view also rested on the assumption that a whole society could never run without working mothers as the norm; the children would not be properly raised or homes properly maintained. (107)

Reflecting this preference for the family-wage model, and as mentioned previously, mothers' pensions, for the most part, aided women whose husbands were absent due to death, imprisonment, or physical or mental incapacitation, whereas divorcees, unmarried women and mothers, and women of minority groups remained largely ineligible. By 1931, over 80 percent of more than 60,000 families receiving aid nationwide were headed by widows. By comparison, "just three states—Michigan, Nebraska, and Tennessee—officially aided unmarried women. Although the statutes of eight others [states] were broad enough to include them [unmarried women], a 1931 survey found that only fifty-five families headed by unmarried mothers were receiving aid" (Abramovitz 1996, 201). Poor two-parent families remained ineligible for the mothers' pensions, the assumption being that two-parent families already had a wage-earner present.

Issues of race and ethnicity also haunted mothers' pensions. For example, Gordon argued that the emphasis of mothers' pensions on "proper family" with a "male breadwinner and full-time housewife" did not reflect the "attitudes, experiences, and aspirations" of "many black and/or poor women" (1994, 32, 72–80).[3] Evidence of racial bias is also evident in available statistical data. In a 1931 survey, 96 percent of 46,597 families that reported their race on the survey were white[4] (Abramovitz 1996, 201). In 1906, of 100 institutional homes for single mothers in Chicago, only one assisted African American women (Gordon 1994, 131). Other forms of racial and ethnic discrimination were manifest in the existence of two different pensions for white and African American mothers in Washington, D.C. (because of a higher economic standard for white families), a refusal to recognize the family practices of African American and Mexican American families as legitimate, and repeated efforts to reculture immigrant families and transform them into "American" families (46–49, 84–88). Those who qualified for aid received pensions only after enduring an intense and reportedly humiliating investigation process that verified the women's status as deserving and their provision of a suitable home. Ultimately, however, mothers' pensions provided relief for a significant number of women and their families, and paved the way for a program to aid dependent children in the Social Security Act of 1935.[5]

Aid to Dependent Children, or Title IV of the 1935 Social Security Act, was the predecessor to Aid to Families with Dependent Children (AFDC).[6] Unlike social insurance programs, which were entirely administered by the federal government, ADC was a federally aided, state-administered categorical assistance program. Like the mothers' pension program, ADC was fraught with gender, class, and race issues. For example, ADC grants were insufficient to raise a family above the poverty level, a practice designed to promote a family-wage structure. Tracing this practice to colonial poor laws, Abramovitz explains: "Trying to keep benefits below current wages continues the poor law practice (known as 'less eligibility') of lowering the social wage to assure that public aid does not become more attractive than the lowest paying job, and for women, more attractive than marriage and family life" (1996, 317). But unlike mothers' pensions which valued women's caretaking labor with wage compensation, ADC, as its name suggests, supported the child and not the caretaker, thereby not explicitly valuing women's labor at home in economic terms.

Perhaps the greatest indication that ADC was designed to promote the family-wage structure, however, lies in comparing it with other social insurance programs developed as part of the 1935 Social Security Act. Reformers believed that ADC and other welfare programs would cease to be necessary as Old Age Insurance expanded to cover widows and orphans (Abramovitz 1996, 317–18).[7] But this view, which is based on the acceptance of a normative family-wage model, has had significant gender and racial implications.

By conceptualizing ADC as a problem to be solved eventually . . . by the retirement program—white widows of working men who would eventually be covered—the administration reflected both the thinking and the realities of that period: Divorced, deserted, and never-married women of color were simply not considered to be part of organized public welfare; rather, they and their children were lumped with the general mass of undifferentiated undeserving poor. (Handler and Hasenfeld 1991, 104)

ADC also reflected a class and racial bias, perhaps due, in part, to the exclusion of African American, immigrant, and poor women's influence on legislative discussions. White female reformers who had been so active in mothers' pensions played a minor role in developing ADC legislation, preferring to accede such family provision matters to the largely white, male policy makers (Gordon 1994, 145). Furthermore, "blacks were systematically deprived of access to ADC benefits. In 1937–1940 only 14–17 percent of recipients were black, far below the proportion of their need" (Gordon 1994, 275–77).

Over subsequent decades, the profile of welfare recipients changed. Never married, divorced, and separated female-headed families consumed a considerable part of the AFDC caseload (Besharov 1996; Cammisa 1998, 16).[8] This changing demographic led to increased public disdain for welfare, a perception that retained historic distinctions of widows as deserving, and unmarried and minority welfare mothers as undeserving, of public assistance. Growing public resentment resulted in critiques of the current system and more restrictive welfare policies.

The Personal Responsibility and Work Opportunity Reconciliation Act of 1996

More restrictive practices materialized in the form of the 1996 Personal Responsibility and Work Opportunity Reconciliation Act. Characterized by strict work requirements and sanctions, PRWORA's centerpiece was the block grant known as Temporary Assistance to Needy Families, which repealed individual entitlement and replaced AFDC. PRWORA also prominently linked marriage and welfare, declaring marriage to be an essential social institution.

The Married Family Ideal Thrives in PRWORA Discussions

As is evident in the discussion that follows, throughout the welfare reform hearings and debates that led to the passage of the 1996 act, witnesses and legislators relied on a married family ideal to evaluate welfare families. Like their predecessors who advocated for mothers' pensions and Aid to Dependent Children, those who testified in the 1996 welfare reform discussions used depictions of welfare families and perceptions of ideal families to warrant policies designed to enforce marriage.

Throughout the hearings and debates, witnesses and legislators demonstrated a preference for the traditional nuclear family, or what Representative Amo Houghton (R-N.Y.) referred to as a "normal sort of classic family" (House Committee on Ways and Means 1995a, 234–35). Those who testified justified their predilection for this family ideal on the basis of (1) empirical data and (2) personal preference.

First, some empirical evidence suggests that intact families are beneficial to children, families, and society. For example, data indicate that children in single-parent families (especially those families on welfare) fare worse than children in intact nuclear families. Clearly delineating the value of the intact family, Dr. Nicholas Zill, vice president and director of Child and Family Studies for Westat, Incorporated, in Maryland, asserted:

What the findings of these studies consistently show is that in our society the best thing for a child's well-being is to be raised by both biological parents, who live together in a reasonably harmonious—but not necessarily a perfectly fulfilling—marriage. Growing up in a single-parent family, a stepfamily and, indeed, virtually any family type other than an intact two-parent family is associated with poorer health, lower achievement and an increased incidence of conduct and emotional problems in children. (House Committee on Ways and Means 1996b, 46)

Single-parent families tend to be less economically stable than their married counterparts. "Child poverty rates for white households with a male parent present in 1992 were 10.3 percent compared with 45.9 percent for those with a female head; comparable figures for black families were 19.4 percent and 67.1 percent" (Weaver 2001, 11). According to a February 2003 National Conference of State Legislatures brief, "about 6 percent of children in married-couple families were poor in 1999 compared to more than 35 percent in single-mother families" (Jarchow, p. 2). "In 2001, 81 percent of nonpoor families with children were headed by married couples" as compared to "only 40 percent among poor fmailies with children" (Haskens, Ron and Isabel Sawhill, 2033. Work and Marriage: The Way to End Poverty and Welfare. Brookings Instition, Welfare Reform and Beyond Brief #28 Available online at http://www.brookings.edu/).

Moreover, as both primary caregivers and primary breadwinners, single parents face a number of barriers to success in the paid labor market. Single-parent families experience these challenges to varying degrees, but the challenges for single mothers on welfare, especially those referred to as the hard to employ, are pronounced. Such challenges include personal and family issues (e.g., mental or physical health problems), human capital deficits (e.g., limited work experience, low levels of education), and logistical obstacles (e.g., transportation difficulties, lack of quality child care) (Pavetti 2002, 135–42).[9] Clearly then, there are some real-world indicators that warrant legislator discussion of single-parent families.

Second, in addition to empirical evidence, legislators and witnesses also demonstrated a normative preference for the intact family. In a telling statement, Representative Sander Levin (D-Mich.) remarked, "[M]aybe I am old fashioned. I think there is a strong, preference for a two-parent family" (House Committee on Ways and Means 1996b,73–80). Representative and House Democratic Leader Richard A. Gephardt (Mo.) agreed: "All of us believe strongly that if there are two parents available that there is a better chance that children will get a proper start and will be dealt with properly (House Committee on Ways and Means 1995a, 37). Observing the historical role of the traditional family, Charles Murray of the American Enterprise Institute, claimed: "Throughout human history, a single woman with a small child has not been a viable economic unit; neither have the single woman and child been a legitimate social unit" (House Committee on Ways and Means 1994b, p. 847; Senate Committee on Finance 1994b, 181). Elaborating on the importance of intact families, Senator Dan Coats (R-Ind.) explained: "[F]amilies are the seedbed of all our skills and attitudes. They teach us our view of work and the importance of moral truths...During countless eras when no other organized unit of society even functioned, the family was the institution that made survival of the cultural, political, economic, and social order possible" (Senate Committee on Labor and Human Resources 1995a, 3; *Cong. Rec.* 1996, S8513).

Boston University Professor Glenn C. Loury explained the benefits of marriage on controlling the negative impulses of men, even as he defended men's roles as economic providers and normative heads of household:

In a recent essay in *Policy Review* anthropologist David Murray...stresses the universal recognition of marriage, and child bearing within marriage, as a means of domesticating—one could also say of civilizing—young males. "Neighborhoods without fathers, are seedbeds for predators" writes Murray.... As [George] Gilder has recently written, "Unless they [teenaged boys] are tamed by marriage and the provider role, they become enemies of civilization. Males rule, whether through economic power as in civilized society, or through violent coercion by the male gangs in the inner city.... Thus, it is crucial to consider the impact of the welfare state on the socialization of young men." (House Committee on Ways and Means 1995b, 146)

In other words, marriage performs a socializing role for both the husband and the children. According to these passages, intact families are the crucible of American civilization: Families safeguard core values by transmitting them to their children, a process that ensures a thriving and productive citizenship. Such statements, then, support heterosexual, monogamous, nuclear-family unions as the ultimate relationship standard to which American citizens should strive. Furthermore, these empirical measures and personal preferences validate marriage and engender support for marriage as a reform strategy.

LEGISLATOR CONSTRUCTIONS OF WELFARE FAMILIES

With an intact family ideal as a frame of reference, legislators and witnesses discussed families on welfare. As Doctor Joe S. McIlhaney, president of the Medical Institute for Sexual Health in Austin, Texas, suggested, representatives and witnesses frequently compare and contrast the intact ideal family with single-parent welfare families. McIlhaney argued:

[There are] two communities in our society. First, the community of two people who love each other, live together for life, have children, and offer those children greater opportunities. The second community is of single parents, often forced to live in poverty with diminished hopes for their children and with all the diseases we have been talking about. (House Committee on Ways and Means 1996b, 67)

Many representatives compared the ideal families to what they refer to as broken or dysfunctional families. Representative Marge Roukema (R-N.J.), for example, claimed that the welfare system "promotes unhealthy, unproductive, dysfunctional families that sentence children to a lifetime of economic, social, and emotional deprivation" (*Cong. Rec.* 1995, H3374).

Importantly, those who testified about the harmful consequences of single-parent families advanced causal arguments, beginning with the assumption that out-of-wedlock births result in welfare dependence. In a March 1996 hearing entitled "Causes of Poverty with a Focus on Out-Of-Wedlock Births," Chairman E. Clay Shaw connected unwed motherhood with welfare receipt: "Out-of-wedlock birth is the driving force behind surging welfare caseloads and long-term dependence" (House Committee on Ways and Means 1996b, 2). Later in the legislative process, Senator Trent Lott (R-Miss.) concisely concluded: "There is already a national consensus that illegitimacy is the key factor that drives the growth of welfare. It is the single most powerful force pushing women and children into poverty" (*Cong. Rec.* 1995, S12794).

Many witnesses and legislators contended that out-of-wedlock births and single-parent families harm society because they result in a variety of social pathologies, including welfare dependence, crime, drugs, moral degeneracy, and disease. Heidi H. Stirrup, Director of Government Relations for the Christian Coalition in Washington, D.C., testified, for example, that "few will dispute the fact that there is a moral and social decline in America today, beginning with the decay of the very basic unit of our society—the family." Stirrup concluded that "illegitimacy" is "the single most important social problem today largely because it contributes to many other social problems such as crime, drugs, poverty, illiteracy, welfare and homelessness" (Senate Committee on Finance 1996a, 106, 204). Charles Murray argued: "My proposition is that illegitimacy is the single most important social problem of our time—more important than crime, drugs, poverty, illiteracy, welfare or homelessness because it drives everything else" (House Committee on Ways and Means 1994b, 846; see also Senate Committee on Finance 1995i, 97). Similarly Robert Rector, of the Heritage Foundation, claimed that "illegitimacy...is a powerful factor contributing to almost all other current social problems" (House Committee on Economic and Educational Opportunities 1995a, 23). Andrea Sheldon, director of government affairs at the Traditional Values Coalition, argued, "The collapse of the family is the most important issue facing American society because it is the root cause of a multitude of other social and economic problems" (House Committee on Ways and Means 1996b, 101). Peter J. Ferrara, of the National Center for Policy Analysis, emphasized that the "collapse of work and family has bred urban decay, crime, drug addiction and numerous other social afflictions. This social tragedy is the direct result of our current welfare system" (House Committee on Ways and Means 1995c, 854; Senate Committee on Finance 1995g, 45).

Echoing witness testimony, Senator Charles E. Grassley (R-Iowa) observed: "There are really a lot of negative consequences to out-of-wedlock births, on the child, on the family, on society as a whole. All of these are very dramatic, in the sense that so many social and pathological problems can be traced back to that sort of a situation" (Senate Committee on Finance 1995a, 30). Grassley concluded that attention to out-of-wedlock births must be central to welfare reform efforts: "Another issue that must be addressed in real welfare reform is the serious rise in out-of-wedlock births, which I believe is welfare enemy No. 1" (Senate Committee on Governmental Affairs 1995, 36; Senate Committee on Finance 1994a, 37). Representative Shaw (R-Fla.) asserted: "The one thing that unifies I think this Congress is illegitimacy is really tearing up society...and it is really creating havoc from an economic standpoint, from a standpoint of lawlessness" (House Committee on Ways and Means 1994a, 396). Later, Representative James Talent (R-Mo.) argued that out-of-wedlock births are "one of the biggest threats to American life and our lifestyle, to continued decency and prosperity in this country" (House Committee on Ways and Means 1994a, 546). Finally, Senator Phil Gramm (R-Tex.) warned:

Under the current trend, illegitimacy could be the norm and not the exception in America by the turn of the century. I think anybody who is not frightened by this prospect fails to understand that no great civilization has ever risen in history that was not built on strong families. No civilization has ever survived the destruction of its families, and I do not believe America is going to be the first. (*Cong. Rec.* 1995, 12690)

These passages, which target all single-parent families as threats to the social order and fundamental values, blur the distinction between welfare families and all American families, many of whom do not conform to the intact family model.[10] Further, the unmistakable similarity among these passages underscores the Republican party's efforts to create a unified coalition of support. The sheer volume of testimony creates the perception that out-of-wedlock births cause welfare dependency, even though such a perception is not entirely accurate, as is evident in chapter 6.

Although participants in the hearings and debates were mindful of the consequences of single-parent families on society, they were particularly concerned with how single-parent families affect children in terms of health, education, relationships, and self-sufficiency. For example, Nancy Ebb, senior staff attorney for the Children's Defense Fund, reported that "AFDC children are three times more likely than non-poor children to be in poor health. Nearly one-third more suffer from delays in growth of development, a 'significant' emotional or behavioral problem, or a learning disability" (House Committee on Ways and Means 1993a, 85). Speaking on behalf of the American Academy of Pediatrics, Jack P. Shonkoff, M.D., declared: "Low-income children have poorer health than other children. For example, they have a higher incidence of low birth weight, asthma, infectious diseases, suicide, homicide and drug abuse. They have lower immunization rates and poorer nutrition" (House Committee on Ways and Means 1995c, 1046). Senator Charles E. Grassley (R-Iowa) pointed out in both the hearings and debates: "Recent studies have shown, however, that children born outside marriage are 2 to 3 times more likely to have emotional or behavioral problems than those in intact families. They have higher risks of child abuse and neglect, poor performance in school, having children of their own as teenagers, having their own marriages end in divorce and six times greater risk of being poor" (Senate Finance Committee 1994a, 37; Senate Committee on Governmental Affairs 1995, 36; *Cong. Rec.* 1995, S13509). Later in the debates, Senator Spencer Abraham (R-Mich.) reported:

We now know that the children who never know their fathers fare far worse in crucial aspects of life than do children who grow up with both parents. For example, children of single parents are twice as likely to drop out of high school, 2 1/2 times as likely to become teen mothers, and 1.4 times as likely to be idle, out of school and out of work, as children who grew up with both parents. (*Cong. Rec.* 1995, S11818)

Most legislators are gravely concerned because they believe that the current welfare system undermines the family by discouraging marriage, encouraging women to leave their husbands, impairing the ability of men to provide for their families, and substituting governmental supervision for parental responsibility. For example, Representative Y. Tim Hutchinson (R-Ark.) argued, "The system has undermined...the very foundation of civil society, that is the family" (House Committee on Ways and Means 1994a, 554, 555). Others noted that welfare threatens marriage by making separation and divorce financially attractive. Representative Sheila Jackson-Lee (D-Tex.) asserted, "[W]e would like to reaffirm marriage or relationships so that the male would not have to leave the home in order to receive some sort of help for his family" (House Committee on Ways and Means 1995b, 658). Representative David McIntosh (R-Ind.) contended that the "welfare system...creates incentives for women to leave their husbands in order to receive benefits, it penalizes families that stick together, and it ultimately undermines the family as an institution in our society" (*Cong. Rec.* 1995, H3687). Senator Barbara Mikulski (D-Md.) expressed that she is "concerned that the very nature of welfare rules themselves works against men and that essentially the message to women in many instances is that you will do better if the man leaves the house than if he stays in the house." Consequently, Mikulski, as well as other witnesses and legislators, warned that the welfare system is "emasculating" men by supporting the "dismissal of men as having an important role...in the family," characterizing men as "simply a revenue stream in loafers," and usurping the role of father as husband and breadwinner (Senate Committee on Labor and Human Resources 1995a, 12, 160, 161).[11] Later in the debates, Representative Charlie Norwood (R-Ga.) inquired:

Could the welfare system be any more destructive to the family than it is? It has made fathers trivial.... Fathers have been replaced by the Federal Government through the welfare system.... [A]n entire generation of young people are being born today without fathers. Why do children need fathers in today's America? The food on their table comes from food stamps. The roof over their head comes from public housing. When you need a doctor, there's always Medicaid. And of course the clothes on their backs come by way of a welfare check. We are replacing the financial importance of fathers with the power of the Federal Government to take from one man's labor and give to others. But what of the moral importance of fathers? That role has simply been abandoned by the welfare system. (*Cong. Rec.* 1995, H3716)

Comments like these suggest that the welfare system forces men from their homes and takes away their primary role as family breadwinner. As a result, many legislators fear that the welfare system encourages illegitimacy and single-mother homes.

As is evident in the preceding discussion, legislator and witness perceptions of families are based on empirical evidence, anecdotal stories, and the sense that the traditional family is a normative imperative. These perceptions are accurate to the extent that they reflect the lived experiences and challenges some single-parent families face. However, they also distort reality by focusing on marital status as the primary factor in the success or failure of families, despite evidence that, as this chapter and chapter 6 will later discuss, contradicts this assumption. Furthermore, the passages encourage legislators to consider marriage as a reform strategy to the exclusion of other options.

Legislating the Traditional Family Ideal

Many factors such as partisan politics, public opinion, and special interest groups exert influence on legislation. As this chapter demonstrates, however, witness and legislator perceptions of welfare families and ideal families clearly correspond to the resulting legislation, highlighting the significance of historical ideology and linguistic frames in shaping policy outcomes.

Framing the welfare hearings and debates through the lens of a family-wage model suggests a narrative in which two-parent families are the best family form. Senator Bob Dole (R-Kans.) acknowledged as much, "So today we begin to write a new story...a story about an America that recognizes that the family is the most important unit in our society" (*Cong. Rec.* 1995, S13801).

Not surprisingly, many of the proposals that witnesses and legislators advanced were designed to encourage nuclear families by promoting marriage, or "marriagefare" and "wedfare" (*Cong. Rec.* 1995, S11754; House Committee on Ways and Means 1995a, 611). President Clinton's 1994 Work and Responsibility Act asserted that "Public policy ought to promote the establishment of two-parent families...living together within marriage" (House Committee on Ways and Means 1994a, 257). Many proposals offer benefits and economic incentives to couples who marry. "Public Housing for Intact Families" of Section 1204, proposed housing modifications to give "preference to any family that includes 2 individuals who are legally married to each other" (*Cong. Rec.* 1995, S12720). Senator Thomas Daschle (D-S.Dak.) favored a Republican bill designed to end the tax disincentives to marriage, often referred to as a marriage penalty: "Today, if a welfare recipient is married, that person is ineligible for the full benefits created through the welfare system. That is wrong. So we eliminate the penalty for married welfare recipients" (*Cong. Rec.* 1995, S11800–S11801). Other proposals offer men financial incentives to marry the mother of their children. For example, Clinton's 1994 Work and Responsibility Act offers fathers an opportunity for child-support forgiveness. "Under the proposal, families who unite or reunite in marriage can have their arrearages suspended or forgiven if the family income is less than twice the Federal Poverty guideline" (House Committee on Ways and Means 1994a, 257–58).

Still other proposals include penalties and sanctions for those considering divorce. For example, one part of Section 1207, entitled "Set-Aside for

States with Approved Family Reconciliation Plans," makes divorce diffi-cult. The amendment states that "a State must have in effect laws requir-ing that prior to a final dissolution of marriage of a couple who have one or more children under 12 years, the couple shall be required to…partici-pate in counseling programs…that include discussion of the psychologi-cal and economic impact of the divorce on the couple, the children of the couple, and society" (*Cong. Rec.* 1995, S12716, S12722). Relying on the intact family standard, this and other proposals aim to discourage "union dissolution."

PRWORA affirms the marriage emphasis of these proposals. As quoted in the epigraph to this paper, the act begins not by addressing poverty reduction, but by affirming marriage as "the foundation of a successful society" (*PRWORA of 1996*, 2110). PRWORA also allocates money to states for abstinence education. The law specifies that the purpose of such edu-cation is to teach people "that a mutually faithful monogamous relation-ship in context of marriage is the expected standard of human sexual activity," and that "sexual activity outside of the context of marriage is likely to have harmful psychological and physical effects," as well as "harmful consequences for the child, the child's parents, and society" (2354). As in discussions surrounding mothers' pensions and ADC legis-lation, discussions surrounding the 1996 reforms are fraught with racial, class, and gender issues.

Racial Characterizations of Welfare Mothers and Fathers

Those who testified in the hearings and debates typically character-ized welfare families as African American, a historically consistent and powerful linkage of minorities to undeserving welfare status. Noting this connection and its mediated roots, Representative Ford (D-Tenn.) commented, "In all of the television shows that we have seen, we have projected African-Americans to be the cheats on welfare" (House Com-mittee on Ways and Means 1995c, 985). Rarely are these images con-tested.[12]

Witnesses and legislators disproportionately linked African American and Hispanic families to the chronic poverty, out-of-wedlock births, and undesirable behaviors associated with welfare families. For example, Murray pointed out: "The 1991 story for blacks is that illegitimacy has now reached 68 percent of births to black women…[and] the values of unsocialized male adolescents [have been] made norms—physical vio-lence, immediate gratification, and predatory sex. This is the culture now taking over the black inner city" (Senate Committee on Finance 1994b, 179–80). Later in the hearing process, Representative Philip Crane (R-Ill.) remarked:

[B]ack in the midtwenties in New York, 85 percent of black families were still together and they looked after their children. And today they are projecting that by the year 2000 in our major cities, 85 percent of black children are going to be illegitimates if these trends aren't reversed. You bring a child up in a handicapped circumstance like that with no future and the deterioration of our educational system where he is illiterate, he has nothing to look forward to, and he has the enticement of gangs and drugs and so forth. (House Committee on Ways and Means 1995a, 328)

These passages, typical of many others, powerfully relegate problems associated with illegitimacy and poverty to minority groups, principally African Americans.[13]

Constructions of welfare mothers as predominantly mothers of minority groups (principally African American) also facilitate extended conversations in the hearings about how to ease restrictions on interracial adoptions. During the hearings, Dr. Carol Statuto Bevan, vice president for research and public policy at the National Council for Adoption, suggested, "[T]ransracial adoption should be promoted when a same-race adoption is not immediately available" (House Committee on Ways and Means and House Committee on Economic and Educational Opportunities 1995, 103). Michael D. Tanner, director of health and welfare studies at the Cato Institute in Washington, D.C., urged legislators to eliminate "barriers to transracial adoptions" (Senate Committee on Finance 1995b, 6). One of the amendments to H.R. 4 in Title II, Child Protection Block Grant Program, "SEC. 430. Removal of Barriers to Interethnic Adoption," purports "to decrease the length of time that children wait to be adopted and to prevent discrimination in the placement of children on the basis of race, color, or national origin" (*Cong. Rec.* 1995, H3458). Speaking on behalf this amendment, Senator John McCain (R-Ariz.) noted, "Sound research has found that interracial adoptions do not hurt the children or deprive them of their culture" (*Cong. Rec.* 1995, S13777). Kentucky Representative Jim Bunning (R) explained:

This is not an indictment of the black community. Black Americans have a long tradition of "taking care of their own" through informal adoption, kinship care, and other arrangements that are not made public and do not show up in official counts. But, given all that the black community has done, and given 20 years of Federal money going for minority recruitment, we still have a large number of black children with no place to call home. (*Cong. Rec.* 1995, H3526)

Indeed, depictions of minority welfare recipients as more likely to be abusive, unskilled, and uneducated, legislator preference for two-parent families, and research about the effects of welfare families on children foster consideration of these interracial adoption proposals.

The focus on black welfare recipients is especially interesting given empirical evidence available to legislators. Although data show that black women are disproportionately represented on the welfare rolls relative to their population and are more likely to rely on welfare for long-term spells, it is also true that black welfare recipients represent a smaller percentage of total welfare recipients and the poor than whites (Bane and Ellwood 1994, 45–49; Gilens 1999, 102; Weaver 2000, 20–21). In addition, "[T]he impact of race per se is quite modest [on welfare receipt duration] after controlling for other factors" (Bane and Ellwood 1994, 45), a fact that would argue against singling out race as an issue. According to Gilens, "racial stereotypes play a central role in generating opposition to welfare in America" and "racial stereotypes constitute an obstacle to public support for anti-poverty programs" (1999, 3).[14] Gilens further explained that according to public opinion polls, although most people are supportive of programs to help the poor, most people also believe that the majority of the poor are undeserving of aid, a fact Gilens attributed to racial stereotyping (11–30). Still other scholars have argued convincingly that predominant descriptions of welfare mothers as black underscores a historical devaluation of the caregiving work of women and of women of color in particular (Orloff 2001, 149).

Affirming the Traditional Nuclear Family

The hearings, debates, proposals, and resulting 1996 act also affirm traditional gender norms of men as breadwinners and women as caretakers. Much of the testimony in the hearings and debates reaffirms a man's role as provider for his family. For example, Stephen H. Martin (R), senator of the Commonwealth of Virginia and chair of the Task Force on Empowerment, Opportunity, and Urban Poverty for the American Legislative Exchange Council, observed: "Work is essential to achieve financial security and move upward, but having a job provides a person more than just a paycheck. It gives him a sense of purpose and responsibility. It makes him a role model for his family and compels him to contribute in their enhancement and their success" (House Committee on Ways and Means 1995b, 336). During one hearing, "Contract with America—Overview," Representative Crane (R-Ill.) feared "the destruction of so many of the traditional values upon which this Republic was founded." Describing those values in terms of the typical American, Crane asserted that "your basic American" is "a God-fearing person.... [H]e believes in family and traditional values.... [H]e believes in the work ethic and finally when the country goes to war, he is trying to jump in front of you in the line to enlist" (House Committee on Ways and Means 1995a, 18). Later in the debates, Senator Jon Kyl (R-Ariz.) invoked the words of Teddy Roosevelt, saying,

"The first requirement of a good citizen in this Republic of course is that he shall be able and willing to pull his own weight" (*Cong. Rec.* 1996, S8513). The gendered "he" pronouns are striking in volumes of testimony in which "she" is the standard pronoun used to refer to welfare recipients. Implicitly depicting work, family support, and patriotism as masculine traits, these passages seem to affirm a family-wage model with the man as breadwinner and head of household.

Other examples of how legislation codifies fathers as financial providers are found in strict child-support provisions. Indeed, PRWORA includes some of the toughest child-support enforcement measures in history. PRWORA requires states to operate a child-support enforcement program and the Act indicates that children are eligible to use a paternity-establishment system until they are 18 years of age, after which they have no claim on their father's finances (2245). If fathers were perceived as providing important benefits beyond financial support, the legislation presumably would have supported paternity identification after children attained adulthood. PRWORA sanctions on men are also largely financial, threatening to impose liens on property, withhold wages, or revoke professional licenses (2205–6, 2209–14, 2224, 2225, 2251). Remedies such as child-support enforcement, wage withholding, and paternity identification may seem somewhat progressive because they acknowledge male responsibility, but the remedies still

reflect the domination of and are derivative and dependent upon the traditional male-headed family model. State-established fatherhood is offered as the panacea for the economic needs of children. Even more disturbing on a symbolic as well as a policy level is the fact that the fatherhood solution is presented as foundational. Fathers are essential to the resolution of problems encompassed by and extending beyond child poverty. Fathers are economic providers and disciplinarians in patriarchal nuclear families—it is to a semblance of this institution that we must revert. (Fineman 1995, 113)

Because welfare legislation is directed at forcibly garnishing the earnings and assets of fathers in support of their children, it reinforces stereotypical gender norms of husbands and fathers as economic providers.

Even as the legislation affirms a men's breadwinner status, it also highlights women's primary caregiver status. Indeed, the very labels legislators use to discuss welfare problems such as "out-of-wedlock births" and "never-married mothers," call attention to women (i.e., as childbearers and mothers). If legislators had used other names for "out-of-wedlock childbirth," such as premarital sexual intercourse, they might have reframed the discussion on both women's and men's marital choices and reproductive actions. Similarly, legislative use of the term "illegitimacy" to describe children of unmarried mothers calls attention to women's marital choices, suggesting that "the marital status of the child's mother has implications for the quality of the child" (Fineman 1995, 122).

Like the language used to characterize welfare problems, much of the evidence furnished in support of proposals and legislation focuses exclusively on women. Typical chart titles reflecting this emphasis include "Marriage and Divorce Rates Among Women, 1920 to 1991," "Fertility Rates for Women Ages 15 to 44, All Women and Unmarried Women 1940 to 1991," "Fertility Rates among Teenage Women Total and Unmarried, 1940 to 1991," and "Increases in Number of Poor Divorced and Never-Married Female-Headed Families" (House Committee on Ways and Means 1993a, 38, 39, 40, 48).[15] Noticeably absent from the hearings, debates, and resulting legislation are data detailing the sexual habits, fertility rates, and marital status of men or the effect of men's reproductive choices on the well-being of their children. This persistent focus on women seems to justify such policies as family caps that condition aid on women's sexual behavior. As June M. Axinn and Amy E. Hirsch observed: "Current welfare reform ties income transfers to women's sexual reproductive behavior but fails to include similar sanctions against men. For example, a father's failure to pay child support does not result in denial of eligibility for or penalties attached to unemployment compensation, SSI, or Social Security" (1993, 571).[16]

Furthermore, PRWORA's promotion of the twin goals of work and marriage exposes a historical tension between welfare recipients as caregivers and as breadwinners. The hearing and debates resolved this tension in favor of women as caretakers. Representative Ed Pastor (D-Ariz.) expressed this assessment well when he remarked: "Mothers on welfare have a unique responsibility of having two jobs. First, as a parent. Second, as a principal wage earner" (House Committee on Ways and Means 1994a, 571). To that end, the discussions and legislation surrounding this tension reflected the prioritization of women as mothers first. For example, Senator Dianne Feinstein (D-Calif.) explained: "While work requirements are appropriate for many people, mothers are the most important influence in a young child's life. Work requirements should be compatible with raising a family and guiding young children. I believe a 20-hour work week requirement for mothers with young children...is reasonable" (*Cong. Rec.* 1995, S19166). Later in the debates, Representative Nancy L. Johnson (R-Conn.) affirmed the role of women as mothers when she proposed that welfare mothers could "work for half a day in new day care centers...as skilled master teachers. Let welfare mothers, who are good care providers, be the soldiers in those day care centers and then in the afternoon go to education and training centers while other welfare recipients staff the day care centers. It will cut the cost of day care and it will allow the money to be used powerfully in the transition period" (*Cong. Rec.* 1996, H7797).

PRWORA itself validates women's primary responsibilities as caregivers through legislation that exempts welfare mothers who have children under the age of 6 from full-time work requirements and exempts women with small children from working altogether if they cannot find satisfactory child care. Prioritizing a mother's primary responsibility to young children, PRWORA encourage states "to assign the highest priority to requiring adults in 2-parent families and adults in single-parent families that include older preschool or school-age children to be engaged in work activities" (*PRWORA of 1996*, 2134). Moreover, PRWORA's mandating of second-chance homes for some mothers (and not fathers) to learn parenting skills, among other requirements, also fuels the perception that women are primarily responsible for child care. As a result, although the legislation claims to enforce work and personal responsibility, it encourages mothers on welfare to take part-time, low-wage jobs, as well as encourages women to rely on the financial contributions of others (e.g., a partner, family, friends). Even though these strategies seemingly respect the importance of motherhood, they are also likely detrimental to women's long-term self-sufficiency and independence.

WHY MARRIAGE?: A SNAPSHOT OF FAMILY STRUCTURES IN THE UNITED STATES

As has been shown, throughout the legislative process, witnesses and legislators related stories about families on welfare and evaluated those welfare families in terms of an ideal nuclear family. Witness and legislator testimony about families is consistent with the resulting legislation. However, PRWORA's emphasis on marriage, in conjunction with congressional discussions about promoting marriage in the Act's reauthorization proposals, may be surprising given available data on American family structures.

Changing Family Demographics

Nationally, marriage and divorce rates, although leveling off over the past decade, provide strong evidence that the nuclear family of parents living with their biological children is not the predominant family form today. In general, the number of married couples living with their children has declined during the past decades. The headline on the front page of a May 15, 2001, *New York Times* article highlights the changing family demographic: "For First Time, Nuclear Families Drop Below 25% of Households" (Schmitt 2001).[17] According to 2000 U.S. Census Bureau data, in 1990, 38 percent of white married couples lived with their own children; by 1999, that percentage had fallen to 36.2 percent. In 1990, 26.4 percent of black families comprised married adults with their own children; by 1999, that number had fallen to 23.3 percent. By type of family, the census data also indicate that female-headed families living with their own children under age 18 fell slightly from 63 percent in 1980 to 61 percent in 1999; married-couple households living with their own children also declined, from 51 percent to 46 percent, during the same period. Charles Murray added that the white marriage ratio dropped by one-quarter during the last half of the twentieth century, from 72 to 54 percent, whereas the black marriage ratio dropped from 66 to 32 percent during the same period (2001, 147). Even as marriage ratios declined, divorce rates climbed. The divorce rate doubled from 1960 to 1980, and today, 40 out of every 100 marriages end in divorce (Horn and Sawhill 2001, 421). Such statistics demonstrate that although married-couple households are still present, a variety of other family structures also exist in significant numbers (Coontz 2000, x; Dornbusch and Strober 1998, 4–6; Stacey 1996).

Changes in marriage patterns also indicate that many children are likely to live at least part of their lives in a single-parent family. According to Horn and Sawhill, "By some estimates, 60 percent of children born in the 1990s will spend a significant portion of their childhood in a home without their father" (2001, 421).[18] More recently, it was estimated that "one of three children in the U.S. is born to unmarried parents" (McClanahan, Garfinkel, and Mincy 2002, 152; Fragile Families Research Brief 2002).

Marriage and divorce statistics among lower-income families are especially striking according to data from the Fragile Families Study, one of the largest studies of low-income families to date, and the Three-City Study, an ongoing research project involving low-income families in Boston, Chicago, and San Antonio. Information from these studies indicates a high prevalence of cohabitation and high marriage-failure rates among the few unmarried parents who eventually marry. Specifically, Andrew Cherlin and Paula Fomby found that although there was a modest 4 percent increase in the number of children living with two adults within one year, the percentage occurred more through cohabitation than through marriage. Moreover, "virtually all of the increase involved a mother and a man who was not the child's biological father." In addition, "42 percent of the mothers who were cohabiting at the first interview had ended the relationship by the second interview [and] 18 percent of the mothers who were married at the first interview had separated by the second interview" (2002, 1–3; Kotlowitz 2002). According to a June 2002 Fragile Families Research Brief on "The Living Arrangements of New Unmarried Mothers," 34 percent of the mothers live in a nuclear household (defined as a mother, father, and child living together), 33 percent live with other adults, 17 percent live alone, and 15 percent live with a partner and another adult. These data suggest that the nuclear family is not necessarily the primary or dominant family form.

Although a variety of family structures exist, especially in the very families that the 1996 act and subsequent proposals purport to address, legislators continue to privilege marriage as a primary reform objective. Based on evidence that nuclear families are better for children than are other types of families, this marriage promotion might still be considered sound public policy were it not for several additional factors. As elaborated on in chapter 6, considerable policy research and public opinion polls cast doubt on the feasibility and desirability of marriage as a reform strategy.

LEGISLATING FAMILIES: IMPLICATIONS AND ALTERNATIVES

Legislators and other proponents of the traditional nuclear family have a historical presumption, in that legal, social, economic, and religious mandates favor intact families. Empirical data also justify arguments about the benefits of some two-parent families (in which children live with both of their biological parents) on children and society. Nevertheless, it is a reality that a significant number of American families do not conform to the traditional intact family ideal and that other family forms do exist. Thus, although there are many complex factors contributing to the legislation's focus on marriage, this chapter suggests that discursive frames and ideological commitments to a family-wage model play an important role in public policy discussions, with at least three important implications.

The first implication of this chapter is that reforms based largely on ideological commitments and partial discursive frames may be ill equipped to deal with the realities of many impoverished American families. Indeed, the 1996 Personal Responsibility and Work Opportunity Reconciliation Act promotes a family structure that is arguably no longer dominant in American society. As is noted in *The Moral Construction of Poverty: Welfare Reform in America:* "While policies, as interpreted and applied, are often diverse, contradictory and ambiguous, their *names* ... are something different. A policy's name allows us to ignore inconsistencies and ambiguities; the name reassures us that there is agreement on the dominant ideology and that change has come about; the name masks hesitations and contradictory actions that minimize or cancel accomplishment" (Handler and Hasenfeld 1991, 41, emphasis in original). Similarly, labels emergent in the hearings and debates, such as "American family," "intact family," "traditional family," "welfare family," and "dysfunctional family" insinuate agreement about what constitutes *the* American family, a status to which all Americans should aspire. By constructing this image of the ideal family and by implementing policies to encourage the formation of this ideal, PRWORA essentially codifies mainstream middle-class

American values about family into a national policy that does not neces-sarily reflect the realities of many Americans. For example, traditional models demonstrate a "lack of relevance to the lives of most immigrants, Mexican Americans, African Americans, rural families, and the urban poor" (Coontz 1995, 12).[19]

As a result, a second, and related, implication of this chapter is that PRWORA stratifies and cleaves society along racial, gender, and class lines. Witnesses and legislators have testified that the legislation enacted is likely to impact members of minority groups more harshly. Senator Carol Moseley-Braun (D-Ill.) expressed this concern in one welfare reform hear-ing, noting that the welfare reform bill would have a disparate impact in terms of race and geography (Senate Committee on Finance 1996a, 120). Capitalizing on her remark, Senator Daniel Patrick Moynihan (D-N.Y.) emphasized, "Finally, could I just put the administration on notice that Senator Carol Moseley-Braun (D-Ill.) has said that that disparity of impact between black children and white children, twice as many black children as white children, may very well give rise to a civil rights cause of action" (Senate Committee on Finance 1996a, 95). U.S. Health and Human Ser-vices Secretary Shalala also admitted that the 1996 legislation proposals would disproportionately affect African Americans: "[B]ecause of what we know about African-American families, their educational levels, their lack of access to jobs,... more of the families affected would be African-American families" (Senate Committee on Finance 1996a, 61).

More recently, during an August 1, 2002, Brookings Institution Welfare Reform and Beyond forum, Ronald B. Mincy, professor of social policy and social work at Columbia University, expressed concern that some pro-posals could have "differential effects on black and non-black families." Citing one example, Mincy argued convincingly that some policies, like increased child support, affect black mothers and "non-black" mothers very differently. Increasing child support for "non-black mothers," he observed, may improve the likelihood that the parents will marry, but increasing child support for black mothers encourages black mothers to retain their independence and refrain from marriage. Although Mincy believes that marriage is "better for children," he also cautioned: "We have had in this country a hundred years of very different family forma-tion patterns by race and ethnicity and as we move into this arena of using welfare policy to influence family formation, we have to respect those dif-ferences by race and ethnicity. Otherwise what we're going to do is try to put a one size fits all policy that in fact doesn't affect all children in the same way." These observations urge legislators and welfare reform experts to avoid solutions that are based on "typical welfare recipient" cat-egories without giving considerable attention to a complex of factors, including race, ethnicity, and class.

Another way in which the congressional proceedings fueled divisiveness was by regulating the sexual reproductive behavior of lower-income, unmarried women. Family cap experiments penalize mothers on welfare for bearing children while on welfare. Funds for abstinence programs that include a ban on contraceptive education—funds that are extended in the GOP House bill passed on February 13, 2003—prevent these same women from learning about how to manage their sexual and reproductive health. More important, access to contraceptive information is available for many other women who are married or who have economic means. The underlying subtext of these policies appears to be that lower-income women should marry or remain abstinent. Because welfare reforms do not similarly penalize men of any class for their reproductive behavior and because the welfare reforms do not similarly penalize women in traditional family structures or who are of sufficient financial means, the reforms exhibit both a sex and class double standard.

The welfare reform hearings, debates, and resulting legislation may further fuel divisiveness along racial, class, and ethnic lines by linking welfare to lower-income minority women as well as to major social pathologies, including crime, drug abuse, and violence. These links, whether explicit or implicit, may encourage legislators to view welfare recipients, especially minority recipients, with suspicion. Stigmatizing adults and children on welfare is harmful and counterproductive. Work promotion strategies predicated on employers hiring welfare recipients, for example, are doomed to failure if welfare recipients are systematically linked to social ills. Employers may believe that investing in welfare recipients is not worth the effort; the perceived risks may outweigh the perceived benefits.

Stigmatizing recipients also encourages public disdain for dependence, privatizes social responsibility, and places many women in a double bind. Because many of women's historical responsibilities as caretakers and nurturers require some level of dependence, such activities are at further risk of being devalued. With the passage of PRWORA, "Caregiving has been shifted to an even more marginal status within the U.S. policy regime, as claims based on the status of family caregiver have been eliminated" (Orloff 2001, 141). Such a shift has profound implications for women, because women, in their roles of wives, mothers, and daughters, have largely borne the responsibility of dependence.

The presence of children creates dependency not only because the children are themselves dependent, but also because the person who assumes primary care for them becomes dependent on social and other institutions for accommodations so that such care can be delivered.... Typically it is women who bear the costs of the expectations associated with such intimate relations in our society. Women are not compensated for bearing these costs, and in the make-believe world of abstract legal equality they are, in fact, penalized. (Fineman 1995, 25–26)

Promotion of a two-parent family-wage model to care for such dependents, as in the case of welfare reforms, results in the privatization of dependency. In nuclear families, the reality is that either both parents work and are able to afford child care for their dependent children, or one parent works (typically the male) while the other stays home to care for the children. Social responsibility for dependency is thus privatized, both for two-parent families and for single-parent families of sufficient economic means. But many families of any form (married, divorced, separated, never-married) with children must often rely on some form of public assistance to make ends meet. Like their predecessors who relied on mothers' pensions or ADC, many mothers frequently find themselves in a double bind. As Sanford Schram summarized: "The trap of welfare receipt is the double bind of work and family commitments for single mothers who are damned for taking welfare while trying to fulfill their roles as good mothers and are equally damned when they go to work if their children end up neglected" (2000, 25; see also Coley, Chase-Lansdale, and Li-Grining 2001; Edin and Lein 1997; Handler and Hasenfeld 1991, 22).

A third and final implication of this chapter is that ideological commitments to a married family ideal discourage policy makers from seeking and considering solutions that might improve the social structures and family support systems in which different family models might thrive.[20] However desirable the traditional nuclear family might be to some advocates and however ingrained the idea of intact families is in American culture, aspiring to or enforcing the ideal may dissuade policy makers from examining the benefits of a wide range of healthy family forms or from seeking solutions that address the material realities of many families who do not conform to the ideal. A number of social science scholars have pointed to effective welfare reform strategies, such as earnings supplements, increased wages, and child-care and health-care subsidies, all of which would assist single-parent and low-income families in escaping poverty.[21] Still others urge a reconsideration of how we, as a society, value the work of caring and nurturing (Hartmann and Hsiao-ye Yi 2001, 175; Tronto 2001, 72). "True reform," explained Fineman, "would embrace the notion that everyone in society—both those welfare recipients who are currently labeled dependent and the members of other, more fortunate classes who receive their subsidies through the tax system or social security—is the recipient of government support in some form" (2001, 37).[22] These strategies, however, are all predicated on recognition of single-parent (and other nontraditional) families as legitimate (or at least

inevitable) family forms, of caretaking as valuable work worthy of support, and of dependency as an inevitable and even desirable component of
a healthy society. Unfortunately, current policy discussions are unlikely to
recognize such realities, because "[r]omanticizing 'traditional' families
and gender roles will not produce the changes in job structures, work policies, child care, medical practice, educational preparation, political discourse, and gender inequities that would permit families to develop moral
and ethical systems relevant to [today's] realities" (Coontz 1995, 14).

NOTES

1. See, for example, Condit's (1990) study of the abortion debate, Duffy's (1997)
fantasy theme analysis of the Iowa riverboat gambling controversy, and Hogan
and Dorsey's (1991) study of nuclear freeze debates.

2. In practice, the pensions were below or at subsistence level, forcing many
women to combine work with their pensions to earn a living wage. In other words,
and despite some reformers' intentions, mothers' pensions did not provide
women with sufficient means to remain home and care for their children (Coll
1971, 79; Katz 1996, 133).

3. Gordon pointed out that, "Many working class, immigrant, and minority
women participated in these social reform campaigns, but the national leadership
was dominated by privileged white Protestant women, whose bonds and affinities
were so strong that they formed a close comradeship and even, however inadver-
tently, made it difficult for women from different backgrounds to participate"
(1994, 71). Gordon also indicated that many individuals in the United States questioned the viability of the family-wage structure. Due to the strong middle-class
women's movement and the relatively weaker voices of working and poor women
in national politics, however, the concerns regarding the family-wage system did
not exert much influence (57–60).

4. Consult also Axinn and Levin 1997, 133–35, 144–45; Goodwin 1997, 160–69,
185–88; Gordon 1994, 111–43.

5. By 1934, for example, at least 110,000 families of the nation's 1.4 million
female-headed households received mothers' aid (Abramovitz 1996, 315; Brown
1940, 330; Coll 1971, 80; Gordon 1994, 284–85).

6. AFDC, in turn, was most recently replaced by the TANF block grant as part
of PRWORA.

7. See also Axinn and Levin 1997, 195; Handler and Hasenfeld 1991, 104; and
Piven and Cloward 1971, 111–14.

8. Gordon cautioned against using the term "female-headed" because it is too
easily confused with "single motherhood." In addition, the term implies that
households have heads, "normatively male." "Thus, . . . today 'female-headed
household' is used without a common opposite phrase; we do not normally call a
two-parent household either male-headed (or 'double-headed'). Both the terms
female-headed and single motherhood also obscure the many diverse reasons why
women are single mothers, including among others, the choice to remain unmarried, spousal death, divorce, separation" (1994, 18). Despite this important objec-

tion, I use the term female-headed because it is the term used in the congressional deliberation and supporting evidence

9. For two comprehensive accounts of the current difficulties and challenges associated with welfare families, consult the essays in *Welfare Reform and Beyond: The Future of the Safety Net,* edited by Sawhill, Weaver, Haskins, and Kane (2002c), and *The New World of Welfare,* edited by Rebecca Blank and Ron Haskins (2001).

10. The predominance of these negative depictions led one of the sole dis-senters, Kate Michelman, of the National Abortion Rights Action League, to com-ment: "I am just amazed, as I listen to this discussion and the discussions in the past days, that all the ills of society are being blamed on the welfare system, and that women, of course, and their behavior is primarily responsible for the failure of families to be whole and well" (House Committee on Ways and Means 1995c, 868).

11. Other related comments include those of Eloise Anderson, director of Cali-fornia's Department of Social Services, who noted that welfare "marginalize[s] poor men. It makes men at the low-income level redundant.... I have watched far too many women 'marry' the State through the AFDC program. The State makes a poor husband, and a worse father" (House Committee on Ways and Means 1995a, 655, 657); David Burgess, of the Texas Fathers Alliance and American Fathers Coalition, explained that welfare policies "drive men away from their families and away from their children" (House Committee on Ways and Means 1995c, 1245); Michael J. Horowitz, of the Manhattan Institute, claimed: "What the government has really done is to substitute the bureaucratic state for the male.... [T]hese crazy incentives of a system...have made males irrelevant,...have feminized poverty and masculinized irresponsibility" (House Committee on Ways and Means 1994b, 1123); Donald M. Fraser, mayor of Minneapolis and first vice president of the National League of Cities, stated: "I don't want to sound too traditional here, but it has been a primary role for men to help support a family. But welfare has inter-vened now" (House Select Committee on Hunger Domestic Task Force 1992b, 19); Delaware Governor Thomas R. Carper explained: "When a gal gets pregnant, she marries the welfare office, not the guy who has fathered the child" (House Com-mittee on Ways and Means 1995b, 17); Laurie A. Casey, of the Children's Rights Council, explained: "Men are not deserting their families. Men do not abandon their children. Men are being forced out of their homes" (House Committee on Ways and Means 1993c, 157); Senator Lauch Faircloth (R-N.C.) observed: "Welfare has transformed the low-income working husband from a necessary breadwinner into a financial handicap" (*Cong. Rec.* 1995, S11783); Representative Hutchinson (R-Ark.) lamented: "The low-income working husband is no longer the chief breadwinner, but instead a net economic handicap" (House Committee on Ways and Means 1995b, 536).

12. A few individuals did protest the connections they saw legislators making among race, class, and welfare. See, for example, the comments of Representative Major R. Owens (D-N.Y.) (*Cong. Rec.* 1995, H3400, H3404), Dr. Ronald Walters, chair of the Department of Political Science at Howard University, (House Com-mittee on Government Operations, 1994, 83), and Illinois Senator Carol Moseley-Braun (D) (Senate Committee on Finance 1995i, 90).

13. See also the comments of Rep. John C. Danforth, Senate Committee on Finance 1994b, 72; and New York Rep. Floyd Flake, House Committee on Ways and Means 1994a, 569.

14. In an earlier study, Gilens concluded that public "racial attitudes are the single most important influence on whites' welfare views," and that these "negative views of black welfare mothers are more politically potent, generating greater opposition to welfare than comparable views of white mothers" (1996, 53).

15. In another hearing, Ruth Ellen Wasem, of Congressional Research Service, supplied additional graphs that focused on women's marital status, fertility, and childbearing behaviors. Dr. Nicholas Zill linked women's marital status with their child's seatbelt use, school performance, and mental health (House Committee on Ways and Means 1996b, 47–48).

16. Axinn and Hirsch acknowledged that a portion of a father's unemployment benefits may be intercepted to pay child support, but the amount deducted is based on what the father owes and the father does not suffer additional sanctions (1993, 571).

17. The author of this article, Eric Schmitt, explained that this change "results from a number of factors, like many men and women delaying both marriage and having children, more couples living longer after their adult children leave home and the number of single-parent families growing much faster than the number of married couples" (2001, A1).

18. Sara McLanahan and Irwin Garfinkel found similar results, noting, "Half of all children born in the 1980's will live with a single mother before reaching the age of 18. Half of these children will be poor" (1994, A27). Also consult Theda Skocpol and William Julius Wilson, who estimated, "One in two children will grow up at least part of the time in a single-parent family" (1994, A21; Popenoe 1996, 2–3).

19. For additional material on this point, consult Allen 2000; Carothers 1998, 316; and Greene 1995.

20. Naples (1997, 937) made a similar argument. See also Axinn and Hirsch (1993).

21. For a review of proposed strategies, consult Sawhill, Weaver, Haskins, and Kane, 2002c; and Hirschmann and Liebert 2001, 111–82.

22. Fineman's views echo those of social activist and feminist Crystal Eathman who remarked in 1920 "It seems that the only way we can keep mothers free, at least in a capitalist society, is by the establishment of a principle that the occupation of raising children is peculiarly and directly a service to society, and that the mother upon whom the necessity and privilege of performing this service naturaly falls is entitled to an adequate economic reward from the political government." "Now We Can Begin" speech reprinted in *Man Cannot Speak for Her.* Vol II compiled by Karlyn Kohrs Cambell. Praeger: New York © 1989, p. 539.

Part III

The Rhetorical Force of Depiction in American Welfare Policy

In Search of an Exigence to Warrant Reform: Public Opinion, Policy Research, and Anecdotal Evidence

> Now unfortunately, there is a lot of misinformation out there. The rhetoric is often times far from the reality. We've all heard of endless anecdotal situations. You can almost prove anything with an anecdote, but all of the anecdotes in the world lying out there [don't] add up to statistics which do give us some indication of what's really going on. But, rhetoric can be very distorting.... And this entire hearing is assigned to strip away the rhetoric and to get away from the anecdotal analysis, if you will, of policy by metaphor, and get right to the specifics.
>
> Congressman Bill Emerson (R-Mo.), House Select Committee on Hunger, Domestic Task Force 1992a, 3–4

As Congressman Emerson (R-Mo.) implied early in the welfare reform hearings process, policy-making, at its best, evokes an image of rational decision making in which legislators review empirical data, hear expert witness testimony, discuss alternatives, and implement policies based on sound evidence. In the public policy-making arena, in which legislators and witnesses argue in favor of the effectiveness of one policy alternative over another, one might also expect to encounter a record of hearings and debates wherein legislators' comments reinforce statistical evidence, public opinion, and witness testimony. A discursive examination of the congressional hearings and debates on welfare, however, suggests that some forms of evidence, such as public opinion and policy research, played a surprisingly limited role in warranting policy changes in the 1996 PRWORA and subsequent reauthorization proposals.

During the legislative hearings and debates surrounding PRWORA and its reauthorization, legislators had access to many forms of data, including stories about welfare recipients and their families, public opinion polls, and policy research.[1] Chapters 4 and 5 discuss the role of these narratives in detail. Specifically, chapter 4 demonstrates how the rhetorical appeal of some depictions warrants the exclusion of certain forms of evidence, such as welfare recipient testimony. Chapter 5 shows the influence of histori- cally rooted ideologies, such as the preference for nuclear families and the family-wage model, on the deliberations, policy proposals, and enacted legislation. Building on the arguments of preceding chapters, this chapter examines the extent to which the depictions used to justify legislation reflect policy research and public opinion polls.

Interestingly, a review of polling data and policy research available to legislators reveals that considerable evidence does not fully support, and in some cases contradicts, stories about welfare recipients and their fami- lies. Nevertheless, legislators continued to privilege the evidentiary value of these stories to warrant policy change. Consequently, this chapter sug- gests that public opinion and policy research have limited rhetorical force in guiding welfare policy change. In contrast, this chapter further argues that anecdotal evidence has significant rhetorical appeal. Indeed, the power of anecdotes to vivify complex social problems ensures that anec- dotes will continue to play a vital role in social policy deliberations and outcomes. In making this argument, this chapter begins by reviewing rel- evant literature on public opinion polls and policy research, providing examples of the role of polling data and policy research on the 1996 act and reauthorization proposals. The chapter proceeds with an examination of witness and legislator testimony about policy research and anecdotal evidence as warrants for policy change. The chapter concludes with a dis- cussion of rhetorical and policy implications.

THE ROLE OF PUBLIC OPINION POLLS AND POLICY RESEARCH IN WELFARE REFORM

To warrant policy reforms, legislators may draw on a variety of resources. Public opinion polls and policy research are perhaps some of the most obvious resources to which legislators turn.[2] The extent to which public opinion and research play a role in politics is a contested issue. Nevertheless, most scholars and many legislators agree that public opin- ion and policy research should play a vital role in the policy-making pro- cess. The intent of the following discussion, then, is not to provide a comprehensive comparison of public opinion polls and policy research with resulting legislation. Such a task is beyond the scope of this study. Rather, the intention is to provide a few examples to illustrate the limited rhetorical force of public opinion and policy research as compared with anecdotal evidence in guiding welfare reform deliberations.

Public Opinion

Measures of public opinion (e.g., public opinion polls) have generated a great deal of discussion among scholars from a variety of disciplines. Several of these scholars have argued that opinion polls continue to play important and vital roles in the democratic process at the state and federal levels (Heith 2000; Norrander and Wilcox 1999; Shaw 2000). Such views have led to a popular assumption that "policy change directly reflects changes in public opinion on substantive issues. If the public increases its support for elements associated with specific approaches to welfare reform...for example...parties and politicians may feel compelled to adapt their position to make them closer to those of the public" (Weaver 2000, 169). Supported in part by a National Science Foundation grant, James A. Stimson, Michael B. MacKuen, and Robert S. Erickson concluded that public opinion polls play a role in legislative decision making at the federal level. The authors found that House members are responsive to public opinion and that there is a "clear and strong relationship between public opinion and Senate policymaking"(1995, 553–55). Although communication scholar J. Michael Hogan cautioned scholars against conflating public opinion with poll data, he nevertheless observed that the idea of polls representing public opinion has "cultural legitimacy." According to Hogan, "Polls continue to shape both the agenda and the outcomes of public debate," in part, due to the efforts of the Gallup Poll's founder, George Gallup, who "redefined public opinion as that which the polls measured" (1997, 161, 173).

Other scholars have doubted the strong or direct influence of opinion polls on the policy-making process. Political science professor Alan D. Monroe, for example, noted a decline in the consistency between public opinion and public policy between 1980 and 1993 (1998, 7). More recently, in *Politicians Don't Pander,* Lawrence R. Jacobs and Robert Shapiro claimed, "[T]he influence of public opinion on government policy is *less* than it has been in the past and certainly less than commonly assumed by political pundits and some scholars" (2000, xvi, emphasis in original).

Although scholars may disagree on the nature and function of public opinion research, most agree with Jacobs and Shapiro that "creating the expectation that substantial government responsiveness to public opinion is appropriate and necessary" is critical to our democratic health (338). In addition, most scholars, including Susan Herbst, have concluded that the relative power of opinion polls to guide important decisions related to public policy and elections is a complex and understudied issue that requires further attention (1993, 158–59). In fact, Herbst urged scholars to explore the degree to which politicians use (or ignore) polling data, suggesting that one fruitful line of inquiry would be conducting discursive analyses of such texts as congressional hearings, news articles, and speeches (171). Indeed, one objective of this chapter is to explore the role of public opinion in policy deliberations through a rhetorical analysis of the hearings and debates surrounding the passage of PRWORA in 1996.

Public Opinion and PRWORA: An "Unfinished Agenda"

Simply stated, in recent welfare reform deliberations, polling data did not appear to inform legislator decisions, at least not explicitly. Although it is difficult to know the extent to which policy makers were aware of public opinion during the hearings and debates, it is apparent that legislators did not directly rely on public opinion to warrant specific policy decisions. Admittedly, as they testified, legislators invoked the supposed preferences of the American people. For example, chair of the Subcommittee on Human Resources E. Clay Shaw (R-Fla.) asserted: "The American people know our current system is broken. They want it fixed" (House Committee on Ways and Means 1995b, 7). Tennessee Representative Harold Ford (D) explained, "[T]he vast majority of the American people and even the welfare population itself would like to be connected and go to work and be placed in a job" (House Committee on Ways and Means 1994b, 1147). Aside from a few vague references to "what the American people want," however, throughout the four years of policy deliberations leading to the passage of PRWORA, legislators did not extensively discuss public opinion surveys. Such ambiguous references to American views in the absence of public opinion polling data certainly call into question a common assumption that public opinion exerts a direct influence on legislative outcomes.

Allowing that legislators were aware of public opinion, however, the fact still remains that PRWORA does not fully reflect public views as expressed in the polls. The legislators' persistent focus on out-of-wedlock births as one of the most important welfare problems does not mirror polling data. According to polls, respondents do not believe that out-of-wedlock births and welfare receipt are even correlated. For example, an August 1995 NBC/*Wall Street Journal* poll reported that only 20 percent of respondents believed that reducing out-of-wedlock births was the most important goal for reforming welfare (Weaver 2000, 176).

Polling data also show a discrepancy between public views on some welfare issues and the enacted reforms, indicating that the public does not necessarily support PRWORA's more stringent reforms. For example, PRWORA contains provisions for stricter work requirements, improved child-care support, and time limits, all of which the public supports in general. Polls also demonstrate, however, that Americans favor more flexibility in work requirement exemptions, increased social support services, and increased welfare spending than are included in PRWORA. A

November 30, 1993, *U.S. News and World Report* poll reported that 71 percent of respondents favored work requirement exemptions for single parents with drug and alcohol problems, 63 percent desired exemptions for families that "the government cannot find a job and provide child care for," and 60 percent said families should be exempt from work requirements if they "cannot find a job where jobs are hard to find." In addition, a January 24, 1997, Associated Press poll noted that 57 percent of respondents said women with children younger than age one should be exempt from work requirements, and 40 percent said women with children younger than three ought to be exempt from work requirements (Gilens 1999, 186). PRWORA's work requirements are arguably more severe than what these polls suggest are supported by the American public. For example, although states cannot terminate assistance to single parents who fail to meet work requirements if child care is unavailable, unsuitable, or unaffordable, states do have the choice of exempting from work mothers with children under twelve months (*PRWORA of 1996*, 2131, 2133; *Cong. Rec.* 1995, S12433).[3] By 2000, 22 states had extended work requirements to parents with children less than one year old (Gais and Weaver 2002, 34).

Public opinion polls also suggest the American public is willing to spend more money on social services than what PRWORA allocates. According to several polls, 96 percent of Americans believe the government should provide job training, education, and child care for poor people in preparation for employment (NBC/*Wall Street Journal* poll, April 1995; The Joint Center for Political and Economic Studies poll, July 1992; CBS/*New York Times* poll, August 1996). Although a 1994 November Harris poll noted that only 28 percent of those surveyed would be willing to pay higher taxes to support welfare, a variety of other polls have indicated that a majority of Americans would be willing to pay higher taxes to reduce poverty; reduce homelessness; provide job training, education, and public service jobs to welfare recipients; and feed and provide medical care for poor children.[4] As of March 1994, although only 37 percent of the public believed that the government was spending too little or about the right amount on welfare, 82 percent believed that the government was spending too little or about the right amount on assistance to the poor (Weaver, Shapiro, and Jacobs 1995, 619). PRWORA is arguably weaker on social service supports and spending for the poor than what polls suggest the public desires. According to an August 22, 1996, *New York Times* article by Francis X. Clines, many groups, such as the Children's Defense Fund, National Organization of Women, and Feminist Majority, were outraged by PRWORA's weak social support provision (A1).

Although polls demonstrate that most Americans favor the idea of time limits, polls also report that the majority of Americans believe the government ought to provide assistance to those welfare recipients who demonstrate a commitment to work. For example, a December 1994 CBS/*New York Times* poll found that 75 percent of the respondents believed that welfare recipients should receive assistance as long as they work for benefits, even after those recipients reach their time limit. A Henry J. Kaiser Foundation/Harvard School of Public Health poll during the same period indicated that 62 percent of respondents suggested that welfare parents, after reaching their time limits, should do community service in exchange for benefits; an additional 27 percent said that those parents should be guaranteed jobs after being cut off of welfare. Even in cases in which recipients refuse to work, most Americans do not endorse terminating benefits entirely (Weaver 2000, 183). For example, a January 24, 1997, Associated Press poll reported that 61 percent of respondents said the government should provide sufficient aid (e.g., food and shelter) to families, even when a recipient with a young child at home refused or could not work; only 39 percent advocated cutting off benefits entirely (Gilens 1999, 186). In other words, although most Americans express strong support for public policies that foster work, most are also unwilling to endorse policies lacking in entitlement language or significant safety nets. The removal of entitlement language from PRWORA, as well as the fact that by 2001, in 36 states "a family loses their entire welfare benefit if the adult fails to comply with the work requirement," reflect a more stringent approach than what is expressed in polls (Sawhill, Weaver, and Kane 2002, 4).

Polling data clearly point to some discrepancies between PRWORA and public opinion views. Offering some compelling reasons for this discrepancy, political science scholars R. Kent Weaver, Robert Y. Shapiro, and Lawrence R. Jacobs explained, "Examining trends in public opinion toward particular proposed welfare reform proposals currently being debated is hampered by the paucity thus far of identically worded survey questions repeated over time" (1995, 608). The problem with different question wrding is that, in general, the public responds more favorably to questions when the plight of poor children, rather than that of welfare recipients, is emphasized. For example, many polls demonstrate that American citizens are strongly committed to assisting poor people. When asked whether government spending should be increased, decreased, or remain the same for assistance to poor people, a 1994 General Social Survey revealed that 59 percent of the respondents desired to increase assistance. When surveyed about spending on welfare, however, almost two-thirds of respondents in 1995 polls said they thought too much was being spent on welfare (Weaver 2000, 172). Similarly, in an April 1985 *Los Angeles Times* poll, surveying the attitudes of poor and nonpoor people about welfare, respondents overwhelmingly disagreed with the statement that "Most poor people are lazy" and "Most poor people prefer to stay on welfare." Furthermore, 78 percent of poor and 71 percent of nonpoor respondents indicated, "Most poor people would rather earn their own living" (Gilens 1999, 39, 56). When people were asked to assess the character of welfare recipients, however, the results were strikingly different. A December 1994 *Time*/CNN poll reported that 66 percent of those surveyed believed that welfare recipients were taking advantage of the system, whereas only 34 percent believed that people receiving welfare were truly in need of help. A January 1995 ABC News poll showed that 59 percent of respondents believed most able-bodied welfare recipients preferred to "stay at home and collect benefits" even though they could work, and only 41 percent believed that "Most able-bodied people on welfare wanted to work but could not because of circumstances" (Gilens 1999, 62). The difference in public opinion about aid to the poor versus aid to welfare recipients clearly demonstrates the impact of question wording on responses—even as it affirms the public's historical distinction between the worthy (poor) and unworthy (welfare recipients).

Weaver related that a second problem in analyzing public opinion with regard to welfare "is that it may not be clear what the public means by the terms when responding to questions, because surveys do not identify specific programs" (2000, 172). Consequently, it is difficult to assess whether the public is responding to questions about welfare by associating welfare with TANF or by associating welfare with any combination of public assistance programs, such as food stamps, Head Start, and Medicaid. Moreover, questions typically worded in a dichotomous and simplistic manner do not fully account for the complexity in the public's thinking about welfare issues (172). Martin Gilens elaborated, in his analysis of public opinion polls, that Americans' attitudes toward welfare are more complex and that their support of PRWORA is much more qualified than what might be expected (1999, 184, 189).

A third problem in assessing public opinion is accounting for the phenomenon of priming. Weaver explained that during the hearings and debates leading to PRWORA's passage, "[B]oth the Clinton administration and Republicans invested heavily in trying to influence how the public sees welfare and in trying to associate the other party with unpopular positions" (2000, 171). Jacobs and Shapiro made a similar point, arguing that policy makers used public opinion to find out how they could "prime" public opinion favorably to justify their own political agenda (2000, 129–30). This priming, which largely concerned "the evils of the system," accounted for growing public resentment of the welfare system prior to PRWORA's passage, as well as for the prominence of the issue on the public's agenda (Weaver 2000, 171). To the extent that public discontent pushed welfare onto the reform agenda, polling data influenced legislative deliberations. Because priming likely influenced public opposition and because public opinion appears not to have offered legislators much guidance with regard to specific policy alternatives, the rhetorical force of opinion poll data on legislative outcomes is mitigated considerably.

Consequently, Martin Gilens argued that the "1996 welfare reforms represented a small step toward bringing antipoverty policy more into line with public desires. But those reforms responded primarily to Americans' cynicism toward welfare recipients and their desire to cut welfare benefits to the undeserving. Only token efforts were made in the 1996 legislation to satisfy the positive desires of the American public to *increase* spending for the deserving poor" (1999, 216). In this sense, PRWORA represents a "half-finished agenda," in that it does not fully represent public opinion. Jacobs and Shapiro agreed, claiming, "Clinton and his advisers focused on Americans' opposition to 'welfare' reform but apparently did not seriously explore the public's continuing support for government 'assistance for the poor'" (2000, 282).

Policy Research

A second source of information that policy makers may use to warrant welfare reforms is data from policy research, often presented in the form of expert testimony. Policy research, according to Allen Schick, "refers to the systematic inquiry, typically using the tools of analysis, into the objectives and effects of government programs." Policy research "strives for objectivity. It is careful about the methods used and emphasizes the systematic collection and interpretation of data" (1991, 100). Many scholars have acknowledged the benefits of policy research to the welfare policy-making process.[5] In his book, *Ending Welfare As We Know It*, Brookings Institution senior fellow R. Kent Weaver related, "Several studies have concluded that policy research, especially evaluation research on work-to-welfare experiments, played an unusually strong part in shaping" the Family Support Act of 1988 (2000, 144; see also, Danziger 2001, 144–47).[6] Judith M. Gueron, a witness in the welfare hearings and president of Manpower Research Demonstration Corporation, added: "Over the past 20 years, policy researchers have built a solid foundation of high-quality studies on the effectiveness of various welfare reform approaches. This knowledge base has proven the envy of other fields" (2001, 182). Gueron further contended that this field-tested information, designed to answer questions posed by policy makers and program operators, has played a "significant role in shaping social policy and program practice" (165). In *Social Science and Policymaking*, David L. Featherman (Director and Senior Research Scientist) and Maris A. Vinovski, (Senior Research Scientist) at Michigan's Institute for Social Research, concurred, emphasizing that the quality of social science research has improved considerably over the past 50 years in tandem with a growing federal need for policy research. With this massive growth in research studies, however, the relevance of the social sciences to policy making "has become of late more diffused and ambiguous as policy-making and administration have become more decentralized and fractured and as trust in government has waned" (2001, 1, 70).

To assist in understanding the multiple functions that research may perform, Weaver argued that policy research provides legislators with three important kinds of information: factual (What is happening?), explanatory (What accounts for trends and patterns in factual data?), and prescriptive (What can be done?) (2000, 136–37).[7] Weaver also acknowledged that policy makers use this information to varying degrees and in several ways. For instance, information may be used to produce a consensus about which approach should be pursued, thereby serving what Weaver termed a "technocratic function." Policy makers may also use research as a "fire alarm," signaling that an issue is a high priority and should be placed on the legislative agenda. A third way legislators use policy research is as a "circuit breaker" to reject proposals that are high risk. Finally, policy makers may use information simply as "ammunition," selecting data that reinforce their arguments while "rejecting and even casting doubt on research that questions those preferences" (136–39). As is evident in the following section, this framework is useful in providing insight into the role that policy research played in forming recent welfare reform proposals and legislation.

Policy Research Plays a Limited Role in Guiding Reform Decisions

Clearly, as explained in previous chapters, representations of welfare recipients and their families do reflect some empirical data. Nevertheless, a considerable portion of policy research appears to have played a surprisingly limited role, especially with regard to the enacted proposals. A brief examination of three aspects of the welfare debate—legislator discussions surrounding welfare fraud, out-of-wedlock births, and marriage—exemplifies how policy research lacks rhetorical force in the recent welfare reform decision-making process.

Welfare Fraud

As chapter 4 evinces, legislators and witnesses frequently accuse welfare recipients of fraudulent behavior. One form of fraud that receives considerable attention is food stamp fraud. Appropriations for the food stamp program (FSP) expired on September 30, 2002, at the same time as the Temporary Assistance for Needy Families (TANF) block grant. Michael Wiseman, professor of public policy and economics at George Washington University, explained the significance of this expiration: "The

1996 legislation that created TANF included food stamp provisions, and the close connections between TANF and the FSP mean that the welfare reform reauthorization debate involves both" (2002, 173).

Defining food stamp trafficking, assistant secretary for Food and Consumer Services Ellen Haas testified, "Trafficking occurs when a person approaches a recipient and offers to buy his or her food stamps—usually at 50 or 60 percent discount" (Senate Committee on Agriculture, Nutrition, and Forestry 1994, 53). Throughout the hearings and debates, legislators and witnesses focused their attention on fraud committed by welfare recipients relying on mediated anecdotal evidence for support. Representative Philip Crane (R-Ill.) narrated:

On "60 Minutes" some years ago, they had a report where a darkened car was going down the streets of New York City. Maybe you saw that. They had a hidden camera in the back seat and they pull[ed] up to a prostitute at the corner and asked her how much she charges, and she said $100. And they said, what if we pay you in food stamps. And she promptly said, $200. And they went on a little further and here was a dope trafficker, and I forget what the measurement was of whatever drug he was selling, but the thing was that he knew immediately that whatever the going price was, if you paid in food stamps, it was double just like with the prostitute.... And then they showed a couple of crooked grocery stores where the prostitute could come in and make the transaction turning in the food stamps and the grocer would give her $150 in cash and he pocketed 50 bucks in cash, too. (House Committee on Ways and Means 1995a, 588)

Senator Jesse Helms (R-N.C.) added:

[T]he *Los Angeles Times* reported [that] welfare recipients falsified and inflated claims for emergency assistance, once again taking advantage of an already much abused and mismanaged Food Stamp Program.... In fact, the February, 1994, edition of *Reader's Digest* contains an article entitled "The Food Stamp Racket" which reports that of the $24 billion taxpayers fork over for food stamps, nearly $2 billion is lost to fraud, waste and abuse. (Senate Committee on Agriculture, Nutrition, and Forestry 1994, 5)[8]

Legislators seemed to rely on this anecdotal evidence throughout the congressional procedings. For example, in one hearing, Governor George Pataki (R-NY) reported: "I...have heard the anecdotal reports of the use of food stamps as a type of currency for every other commodity but food that we would like to see....It is a very real problem" (House Committee on Ways and Means, 12 January 1995, 588). Influenced by stories of food stamp trafficking in the hearings, Representative Frank Riggs (R-CA) commented in the debates: "There are stories that are renowned and quite legion about food stamp recipients exchanging their food stamps for all sorts of different items...Liquor or drugs, obviously items that go far beyond the basic food supplies or foodstuffs that the food stamps are intended to provide" ("Report on Resolution Providing for Further Consideration of H.R. 4," Congressional Record, 21 March 1995, H3413). All of these examples lend credence to stereotypical depictions of welfare recipients as drug users and criminals even as they support the belief that welfare recipient fraud is a major welfare problem.

Indeed, the focus of the hearings and debates was frequently on fraud by welfare recipients, but a closer examination of aforementioned and other passages also reveals that vendors, retailers, as well as the government, are culpable for fraud and costly mistakes. For example, according to the *Reader's Digest* article cited by Senator Helms (R-N.C.), "Mistakes are rife. In 1992, $1.7 billion worth of food stamps were overpaid or sent to ineligible people." Based on Food and Nutrition Service investigations, Ellen Haas claimed that store vendors, not welfare recipients, are largely responsible for food stamp trafficking (Senate Committee on Agriculture, Nutrition, and Forestry 1994, 33, 53). Senator Bob Dole (R-Kans.) reported, "[M]ost beneficiaries and providers do not abuse them [welfare programs]" (13, 14). Roland W. Burris, Illinois attorney general, informed Congress of the following: "Our investigation uncovered two distinct groups involved in the fraud. First, we caught the WIC [Women, Infants, and Children] vendors who were exchanging food instruments for cash.... The second group found to be implicated ... was health clinic employees" (Senate Committee on Agriculture, Nutrition, and Forestry 1994, 16). Responding to this testimony, Wisconsin Representative Russell Feingold observed, "You stated that the vendors were the number one problem. I think that is going to be of interest to many Americans who may assume that it is the recipients who are the real troublemakers" (Senate Committee on Agriculture, Nutrition, and Forestry 1994, 22). These findings indicate that when fraud occurs, the offenders are often not welfare recipients. Such evidence provides legislators with reasons for not heavily targeting fraud and abuse in welfare reform efforts.

Although evidence demonstrates fraud on the part of recipients, vendors, and the government, PRWORA provisions focus on fraud on the part of welfare recipients. PRWORA requires states to establish and enforce "standards and procedures to ensure against program fraud and abuse" (*PRWORA of 1996*, 2115, 2138, 2139). Some adults are required to register for work or participate in work or training programs as a condition of food stamp eligibility. Recipients who do not meet these requirements may be sanctioned. As a result of the 1996 act, states are also required to "reduce (or, at state option, eliminate) the food stamp grant when a TANF sanction is imposed" (Bloom and Winstead 2002, 50).[9] Notably, the enforcement of sanctions on states that commit errors in distributing food stamps is not proportional to the enforcement of sanctions on welfare recipients. According to Michael Wiseman: "States can be charged for the benefit cost of error rates in excess of national averages. In practice such penalties are often waived; when enforced, states pay by investing the fine in programs to improve performance" (2002, 174). Although some welfare recipients do commit fraud, Wiseman suggested that the stringent eligibility assessment and recertification procedures characteristic of the 1996 reforms may be counterproductive (178). For example, constructions of welfare recipients as fraudulent seem to exert considerable persuasive force, informing legislation that focuses attention on ensuring benefit accuracy rather than on "helping people buy food," the ostensible purpose of the food stamp program (174).

A Focus on Out-of-Wedlock Births

The force of anecdotal evidence in the hearings and debates is also evident in the extensive discussions surrounding out-of-wedlock births. In fact, PRWORA states, "It is the sense of the Congress that prevention of out-of-wedlock pregnancy and reduction in out-of-wedlock birth are very important Government interests" (2112). Evidence presented in the hearings, however, is ambiguous with regard to the relationship between out-of-wedlock births and welfare receipt and does not provide policy makers with clear guidance in crafting policy alternatives. Many witnesses and legislators presented data indicating that out-of-wedlock births are not pertinent to welfare reform discussions.[10] Quoting testimony from James Q. Wilson, Senator Daniel Patrick Moynihan (D-N.Y.) concluded: "We are told that ending AFDC will reduce illegitimacy, but we do not know that. It is at best, an informed guess" (Senate Committee on Finance 1995i, 2). In one illustrative hearing, whose title periemeit a cause-effect unic— "Causes of Poverty, with a Focus on Out-of-Wedlock Births,"—Representative Sander Levin (D-Mich.) asked a panel of welfare scholars, "Do any of you know the percentage of children born out of wedlock in this country that are born to women on welfare?" (House Committee on Ways and Means 1996b, 82). After four years of welfare hearings, invited guests could not provide conclusive data to answer this question.

Some evidence presented in the hearings indicates that out-of-wedlock births affect individuals of high socioeconomic standing more so than welfare recipients. For example, Robert M. Greenstein, executive director for the Center on Budget and Policy Priorities, noted that out-of-wedlock births, although heavier among low-income women, "are actually rising at a faster rate among non-poor women than among poor women" (Senate Committee on Finance 1995b, 47). Based on his research, Frank Furstenberg, sociology professor at the University of Pennsylvania, emphasized, "No link has been established between these trends [decline in marriage and nonmarital childbearing] and public welfare policies or the generosity of family support systems cross-nationally" (House Committee on Ways and Means 1996b, 73). These studies imply that focusing on the relationship between welfare and out-of-wedlock childbearing is not central to welfare reform discussions.

There were other expert witnesses who testified that welfare and out-of-wedlock births are not related. For example, Sister Mary Rose McGeady, president of Covenant House in New York, argued:

The point I wish to make is that while the welfare reform debate has focused national attention on illegitimate births in the United States, in fact, two-thirds of these single women having "illegitimate" children are not below the poverty line, not high school dropouts, not teenagers, and not on welfare. . . . [O]ur experience is that there is no correlation between dependence on public assistance by single mothers and the out-of-wedlock birth rate in this country. (House Committee on Ways and Means 1996b, 108)

Drawing on witness testimony, Representative Barbara Kennelly (D-Calif.) forcefully contended:

When you take the time to look more closely, you learn some startling facts. As several of our witnesses today will tell us, many of the myths and stereotypes that seem to drive much of public policymaking today are misleading. . . . What are the facts? . . . [M]any single women giving birth are not poor. . . . [W]elfare programs are not among the primary reasons for the rising number of out-of-wedlock births. (House Committee on Ways and Means 1996b, 7)

Chair of the Subcommittee on Human Resources Harold E. Ford (D-Tenn.) noted that out-of-wedlock childbearing has erroneously become a welfare issue and that out-of-wedlock childbearing is a phenomenon that affects all socioeconomic classes.

Others who testified, however, provided compelling evidence that welfare receipt and out-of-wedlock births are intimately connected. For instance, in one hearing, Representative James Talent (R-Mo.) referenced several studies of welfare and illegitimacy, the majority of which show a correlation between welfare and illegitimacy (House Committee on Ways and Means 1994a, 548–50). Later in the debates, Senator Lauch Faircloth (R-N.C.) requested: "I ask unanimous consent a list prepared by the Heritage Foundation of 19 recent academic studies on the link between welfare benefits and out-of-wedlock births be printed in the RECORD" (*Cong. Rec.* 1995, S13527). This list of studies represents a select set conducted largely by conservative groups and institutions.

Other witnesses and legislators offered their firm opinion about the cause-and-effect relationship between welfare and out-of-wedlock births. Cathy Young, vice president of the Women's Freedom Network in Washington, D.C., testified: "There is much debate about whether welfare causes young women to have children out of wedlock. I think we can all

agree that in its present form it certainly enables them to bear children neither they nor the men in their lives expect to support" (House Committee
on Ways and Means 1995c, 1237). Kate Walsh O'Beirne, vice president of
government relations at the Heritage Foundation, observed, "[T]he family
has collapsed, illegitimacy has skyrocketed, and crime has escalated in
direct proportion with welfare spending" (House Committee on Ways
and Means 1995a, 371). Representative Tom DeLay (R-Tex.) explained: "It
is sort of like trying to define obscenity. We can't define it, but we can sure
recognize it when we see it. And most studies and statistics show that illegitimacy goes up as welfare is imposed upon this country.... In light of
those statistics, we should be doing everything possible to discourage out-
of-wedlock births" (House Committee on Ways and Means 1994a, 447). In
contrast to the research mentioned earlier, this information provides legislators with reasons to curb out-of-wedlock births as a strategy for reducing welfare dependence.

In the end, those who testified presented conflicting evidence on the
relationship between out-of-wedlock births and welfare. Whether the
relationship is causal or correlational is unclear. What is clear, however, is
that those who believe an important relationship exists used the few existing studies that support their view as ammunition to influence the legislation, even as they seemingly ignored contradictory results. As Weaver
surmised, "[T]o many policymakers (especially conservatives), research
suggesting that welfare did not increase illegitimacy ... was irrelevant in
the sense that even if these arguments were correct, it was still wrong for
the welfare system to send a signal of approval or to provide an incentive
for behavior that was morally wrong" (2000, 151). Not surprisingly, then,
PRWORA contains provisions designed to reduce unwed motherhood
and, thereby, reduce welfare dependence. For example, PRWORA reads
that states must provide evidence of how they are going to "prevent and
reduce the incidence of out-of-wedlock pregnancies" (*PRWORA of 1996*,
2113–14). To achieve significant reductions, the act gives states a "[b]onus
to reward decrease in illegitimacy," as long as abortion rates do not
increase (2118; *Cong. Rec.* 1995, S12431).

A Focus on Marriage

As chapter 5 demonstrates, throughout the hearings and debates, legislators compared intact families with single-parent families and argued
that single-parenthood is the cause of numerous social ills (e.g., crime,
drugs, moral decay). As a result, legislators advocated proposals designed
to strengthen families by promoting marriage and discouraging divorce.
Many scholars, however, would challenge legislators' reasoning when it
comes to comparing single-parent families on welfare and intact, ideal
two-parent families and to assuming that single-parent families cause

social problems. Law professor Martha Fineman, for example, argued that contrasting single-parent families and stable two-parent families "disingenuously compares idealized nuclear families with those of single mothers already in trouble" (1995, 104; Sidel 1998, 33–57; Stacey 1994, 55–59). Fineman also contended that the focus on single parents is based on a faulty causal argument that single-motherhood results in poverty and other social problems. According to Fineman, "In political and professional discourse, single-mother status is defined as one of the primary predictors of poverty—predictor often being translated into cause" (1995, 106). Offering further evidence to debunk the causal arguments, McLanahan and Garfinkel wrote:

As compared with children from the same social class who live with both parents, children of single mothers are twice as likely to drop out of high school and to become single parents themselves and half again as likely to have trouble finding and keeping a steady job. But this does not mean that single motherhood is the major cause of these social problems. For example, the dropout rate for the country as a whole is about 19 percent; for children in two-parent families, it is 13 percent. Thus, dropout rates would still be unacceptably high even if there were not single-mother families. (1994 A27; Chase-Lansdale, et al. 2002)

In addition, considerable research exists to challenge the assumption that marriage promotion is desirable and feasible. Even among scholars who grant that two-parent families are best for children, there is substantial agreement that this fact holds true only when the children are raised by their married, biological parents who maintain a low-conflict relationship (Jarchow 2003; Parke 2003). In fact, evidence supports the proposition that children of unwed mothers fare similarly to children of divorced, widowed, and separated mothers. "People who assail unwed mothers would never dream of using the same language about mothers who are divorced or widowed. But in terms of social problems, there is little distinction. In a comparison of children whose mothers have the same educational background, children of divorced parents do just about as poorly as children of unmarried parents" (McLanahan and Garfinkel 1994, A27; Parke 2003). Public policy professor Andrew Cherlin concurred, based on evidence from the Three-City Study. At a June 12, 2002, Science and Public Policy Briefing, Cherlin reported that the well-being of children in single-parent families is no greater than the well-being of children in stepfamilies. According to Horn and Sawhill, the difference cannot be explained by income differences; instead, stepfamilies that "have household incomes nearly equivalent to continuously married households, offer children few of the benefits of an intact, two-parent household" (2001, 427). Even testimony in the 1996 hearings from Dr. Nicholas Zill conceded a similar point: "Growing up in a single-parent family, a stepfamily and, indeed, virtually any family type other than an intact two-parent family is associated with poorer health, lower achievement and an increased incidence of conduct and emotional problems in children" (House Committee on Ways and Means 1996b, 46). Given the increasing percentages of children who are growing up in single-parent and stepfamilies, this evidence casts doubt on the effectiveness of national policies that promote marriage, in general, in order to produce the benefits associated with intact families.[11]

There is additional evidence that marriage promotion may not be sound public policy. Some leading social policy scholars believe that marriage-promotion strategies may actually be harmful to children. For example, evidence points to the number of family transitions a child experiences as being a greater predictor of high-risk behaviors, such as teen pregnancy, than time spent in a single-parent family (Cherlin and Fomby 2002, 6). Consequently, children of women who are married and stay married and children of single parents who remain single may actually "do better" than children of single parents who remarry. In fact, according to Jeanne Brooks-Gunn (2002), senior research affiliate for the Joint Center for Poverty Research at Northwestern University, cohabiting families most closely resemble married families rather than single-parent families. Based on evidence from the Fragile Families Study, there are many situations in which the biological mothers and fathers simply shouldn't live together. Citing examples of such instances from the Fragile Families data, McLanahan, Garfinkel, and Mincy noted, "[A]pproximately 38 percent of unwed fathers have been incarcerated, which suggests that a substantial proportion of these men have had lifestyles that are potentially harmful to children" (2002, 154).[12]

Several social scientists have also argued that some data (e.g. stable or declining rates for divorce and teenage pregnancy, an increase in employment and higher earnings for single mothers, and a decline in welfare payments for lower-income families) present a strong case against the focus on marriage (Sawhill, Weaver, and Kane 2002, 8–19; Sawhill 2002, 160). Evidence further suggests that marriage is not even the most common route off welfare. Data from the *Green Book*,[13] prepared for the use of members of the Committee on Ways and Means, the House committee of jurisdiction over welfare, indicates that "46 percent of exits from the AFDC program occur because of work," whereas only "11 percent exit AFDC because of marriage, remarriage, or reconciliation" (*Green Book*, 1994, 450). In *Welfare Realities: From Rhetoric to Reform*, Mary Jo Bane and David Ellwood estimated that approximately 40 percent of women leave welfare for work, whereas only 29.4 percent leave for marriage (1994, 57, 59; see also Haskens and Sawhill 2003).[14] These statistics imply that marriage may not be as effective in reducing welfare dependence as other strategies.

Moreover, no research exists on whether programs to promote and strengthen marriages actually exert a positive effect on increasing marriage rates. In addition, although several programs have shown promise in reducing marital disruption, these programs deal with middle-income families, not low-income or welfare-dependent families (Wilcox 2002). A June 2002 research brief from the Welfare Reform and Family Formation Project reported that existing research attends only superficially to the effect of reforms on family formation and that there still exists a "lack of evidence concerning how TANF has influenced family formation thus far" (Fein, London, Mauldon 2002, 2, 4). A September 2003 Center on Budget and Policy Priorities paper charges that "committing such a substantal amount of federal funding" to "narrow, untested marriage promotion programs" as is the case in recent House and Senate bills is "unwarrented" (Parroh, Sharon and Shawn Fremstad, "The Senate Finance Committee's TANF Reauthorization Bill" 9/22/03 available on-line at http://www. centeronbudget.org). Indeed, it would seem that there is no evidence suggesting that governments can be successful in encouraging marriage for low-income populations. The absence of research on the potential effectiveness of government supported marriage programs is compelling evidence for legislators exercising caution in promoting marriage.

Despite all of these facts, policy makers passed legislation and are considering reauthorization proposals that promote marriage, policies that are in line with the family-wage model. There is significant evidence that legislators were aware of much of this empirical data. For instance, some legislators were exposed to data indicating that traditional families represented a relatively small percentage of all family types: the "nuclear family, with Dad as the breadwinner and Mom staying home is no longer the norm; approximately 10 percent of families fit into this category. This certainly should not be the norm for divorced or unwed families" (House Committee on Ways and Means 1995c, 1500). University of Michigan social work and public policy professor Sheldon Danziger also challenged the focus of welfare reform hearings on unmarried mothers, testifying that "[t]he decline in the numbers of two-parent families is a problem that affects society at large. This is not just a welfare issue" (Senate Committee on Finance 1996a, 112).

If it can be assumed that poverty reduction is one goal of welfare reform, legislators heard evidence in the hearings and debates that might more appropriately refocus discussion on two-parent families. In one hearing, Representative Fred Grandy (R-Iowa) and Thomas Gabe, congressional research services specialist, presented charts and graphs rationalizing the focus on single-parent families (House Committee on Ways and Means 1993a, 47). Indeed, the graphs did demonstrate that a significant number of single-parent families are living in poverty. Perhaps more interesting for the purposes of this discussion, however, is that the graphs also showed that in 1989, there were nearly a million and a half more two-parent families in poverty than female-headed families. This evidence does point to a correlation among single-parent families, welfare receipt, and poverty; yet, the research also indicates that not all single-parent families are poor and that many more two-parent families experience poverty. In other words, the evidence presented in the hearings does not justify the almost exclusive focus on single-parent families and implies that family structure may not be as central to welfare reform policies as some would like to believe.

During reauthorization hearings, legislators continued to promote marriage, even in the face of strong counterevidence in the 2000 *Green Book*, which reports in a section entitled "Implications for TANF":

Findings presented in this appendix indicate that ending dependence on government benefits through job preparation, work, and marriage—the second objective of TANF—may be an elusive goal. Available evaluations generally show that welfare initiatives have little or no impact on marriage....Programs that increase incomes instead have been found to reduce dependence on welfare.... Evaluations indicate that, at least in the short run, many TANF recipients will be unable to escape poverty through work unless taxpayers provide an earnings supplement of some kind. (1410–11)

In this quote, contrary to the emphases on family structure and marriage promotion present in both the 1996 act and subsequent proposals, research available to legislators indicates that marriage promotion is unlikely to work. On the contrary, increased income and work supplements show promise as poverty-reduction strategies. In the end, despite significant research demonstrating that many Americans do not live in traditional nuclear families (see chapter 5), that there are potential negative consequences to marriage promotion, and that federal reforms are unlikely to result in measurable increases in marriage rates, legislators still prioritize marriage as a primary solution to welfare.

Because policy research seems to have had such a limited force in warranting welfare reforms, many scholars have condemned PRWORA for ignoring such data at worst or selectively using the data at best. For example, "Previous efforts to reform welfare have been cautious, incremental, and knowledge-based, as officials balanced their fears of hurting vulnerable people and burdening budgets against their desire to move the system in new directions. In contrast, the legislation signed in 1996 was a radical leap into the unknown" (Gueron 2001, 172). Sheldon Danziger concurred: "Social scientists have conducted hundreds of empirical studies related to various aspects of welfare policies in the thirty-five years since the War on Poverty was declared. Major findings of this research and their policy implications were virtually ignored, however, in the welfare reform debates leading up to President Clinton's signing of the Personal Responsibility and Work Opportunity Reconciliation Act of 1996" (2001, 137). Welfare scholar William Julius Wilson, author of *When Work Disappears: The World of the New Urban Poor,* also indicted legislators for their failure to consider the full range of empirical literature available during the policy-making process.

> Although it is reasonable to argue that policymakers are not aware of a good deal of empirical research on the effects of welfare, the General Accounting Office (GAO), an investigative arm of Congress, released a study in early 1987 reporting that there was no conclusive evidence to support the prevailing common beliefs that welfare discourages individuals from working, breaks up two-parent families, or affects the childbearing rates of unmarried women, even young unmarried women.... Although these conclusions should come as no surprise to poverty researchers familiar with the empirical literature, they should have generated a stir among members of Congress. (1996, 163–64)

Wilson further asserted that legislators ignored social science studies and instead based welfare policy on the highly publicized, but not scientifically grounded, studies of such conservative scholars as Charles Murray and Lawrence Mead (164).

Taking a more moderate approach, Weaver found that "[p]oliticians neither ignored nor relied completely on policy research about problems and programs, instead they weighed the research against other types of knowledge and electoral and coalitional considerations" (2000, 168). Indeed, in some cases, research did not exist on the issues that policy makers were discussing; in other instances, research did not illuminate clear solutions to the problems that policy makers had identified.

Examining the functions of policy research in light of Weaver's framework provides insight into how legislators used evidence throughout their deliberations. Because most research did not produce a consensus on the courses of action that policy makers should pursue, it seems apparent that legislators did not use research in a technocratic function. Nor did the policy research perform a circuit breaker function, because legislators clearly advocated such proposals as marriage promotion in the face of considerable research that questioned this approach. As a result, and in the face of what they perceived to be relatively ambiguous or incomplete data, policy makers largely used social science evidence to perform fire alarm and ammunition functions. That is, they used factual evidence, such as growing caseloads and out-of-wedlock birthrates in the early 1990s, to justify the importance of addressing welfare reform at the federal level. In addition, they used evidence, such as the importance of two-parent families, as ammunition for supporting their preferences for marriage as a solution to the welfare problem (Weaver 2000, 160–62,167–68).

Policy by Anecdote or by Scientific Method: Legislator and Witness Perspectives

As this chapter evinces, policy research and polling data exerted an arguably weak force in the welfare deliberations, to the extent that legislators relied on this information partially at best and ignored critical evidence at worst. In any case, legislators made only vague references to public opinion and cited policy research sparingly to warrant specific reforms. Such a conclusion is especially surprising because many legislators and witnesses who testified indicated a strong desire to base policy on evidence gained through systematic social science methods.

Those who testified frequently suggested that successful and effective policies must be rooted in facts, statistics, and research. In a typical statement, executive director for the Center on Budget and Policy Priorities Robert Greenstein asserted, "[I]f welfare reform is to be effective over the long term, policymakers will need to distinguish between proposals that have a basis in research findings and those rooted in strong beliefs, but not backed by evidence at this point" (Senate Committee on Finance 1994b, 47). Early in the hearing process, Congressman Emerson (R-Mo.) urged policy makers to attend to statistical evidence in a passage that bears repeating:

Now unfortunately, there is a lot of misinformation out there. The rhetoric is often times far from the reality. We've all heard of endless anecdotal situations. You can almost prove anything with an anecdote, but all of the anecdotes in the world lying out there [don't] add up to statistics which do give us some indication of what's really going on. But, rhetoric can be very distorting.... And this entire hearing is assigned to strip away the rhetoric and to get away from the anecdotal analysis, if you will, of policy by metaphor, and get right to the specifics. (House Select Committee on Hunger Domestic Task Force 1992a, 3–4)

Throughout the hearings, faith in the power of objectivity and science to guide policy decisions resulted in numerous requests for accurate data. For example, Robert Matsui (D-Calif.), chair of the Subcommittee on Human Resources, charged:

See, I think one of the problems is that you are relying on information in a very anecdotal way, and so you may hit, you may miss, and it may be relevant, and it may not be relevant.... And so it would be my hope that over time you are going to come up with something more than just this anecdotal information.... But, you know, I will tell you how anecdotal this is. You get a GAO report that says about 10 million are taking it [the EITC credit]. You say 14. And then Mr. Primus' own Blue Book it says 13 million—I mean, Green Book, excuse me, Green Book says 13. And, again, you know, what is the difference between 10, 13, and 14 million? Well, it is. It is a big difference. (House Committee on Ways and Means 1993c, 47)

Precisely because he was concerned about inaccurate anecdotal evidence, Matsui urged witnesses to present information grounded in something other than anecdotal stories.

Going further, congressional leaders frequently disparaged nonscientific evidence (e.g., anecdotes, personal opinion) as a basis for policy making because they believed that such evidence is an unreliable source of data that leads to biased decisions. As Representative Kennelly (D-Conn.) explained: "[W]hat gets us off the track is when we start getting into these anecdotal situations" (*Cong. Rec.* 1996, H7790). In particular, legislators faulted nonempirical evidence with being ideological, stereotypical, and fictitious in such a way as to cloud important issues. For instance, referring to comments made by James Q. Wilson, Senator Moynihan (D-N.Y.) stated, "The debate that has begun about welfare reform is, in large measure, based on untested assumptions, ideological posturing, and perverse priorities" (Senate Committee on Finance 1995c, 24). Senator Byron L. Dorgan (D-N.Dak.) agreed, "In public debate we all too often use stereotypes" (*Cong. Rec.* 1995, S12759).

According to those who testified, untested assumptions based on nonscientific evidence influences policy debates and legislation, resulting in potentially harmful consequences. Ronald Walters, chair of the Howard University Department of Political Science, urged: "I think, again, we have to get down to facts and not ideology. If we let the ideology rule our approach to this, we are really going to come out at a dead end, in terms of public policy. We cannot make good public policy from mythology" (House Committee on Government Operations 1994, 124, 65). Professor Bill E. Lawson of the University of Delaware Department of Philosophy warned, "Unwarranted assumptions regarding race, class and gender," which legislators adopt as "basic assumptions," have "made their way into and often frame the public policy debate about welfare reform" (House Committee on Government Operations 1994, 90, 91). In another hearing Illinois Senator Carol Moseley-Braun (D) expressed concern that racially motivated stereotypes were guiding deliberations at the expense of scientific evidence:

If the Senate is going to make headway on a bipartisan package everyone in this body must acknowledge the facts and not give in to the rhetoric. The current welfare debate is being framed by misperceptions and prejudices.... I believe that we in this body must move away from arguments that are racially inflammatory. Theories linking poverty, class, and genetics have been around a long time and scientific data has [sic] proved time and time again that there is not any one factor that is responsible. These arguments are also irrelevant to this debate. The real problems that cause bloated welfare rolls: growing poverty, the lack of jobs in poor communities, and the lack of health care and child care should be the issues at the forefront of the welfare debate. (Senate Committee on Finance 1995i, 90)

Later in the debates, Moseley-Braun continued: "So we are experimenting here based on stereotypes. We talked about the stereotype of the undeserving, freeloading poor for so long that many of my colleagues, I think, are frankly determined not to let those misperceptions stand in the way of their policymaking" (*Cong. Rec.* 1995, S19095). These statements suggest that nonscientific information necessarily results in a sort of uninformed, visceral construction of policy with an implicit contrast to desirable policy grounded in rational, deliberative thought.

Because legislators and witnesses only partially consider, and in some cases ignore, available policy research and public opinion when crafting welfare legislation, and because they also disparage anecdotes, it is reasonable to question what forms of evidence legislators do use to rationalize policy change. Turning to the legislators' words in the PRWORA hearings and debates that led to PRWORA, it is apparent that the main exigency for the types and extent of reform frequently derives from legislators' perceptions and experiences expressed in the form of depictions or anecdotes. Thus, although congressional leaders acknowledged the limitations of anecdotal evidence, they, as well as the witnesses they invited, tended to rely disproportionately on anecdotal information to justify policy change.

Several exchanges in the hearings illuminate why representatives rely on anecdotal evidence in spite of misgivings. In one hearing, welfare recipient Lukisha Jackson, an honor student at the University of Maryland at College Park, testified, based on her personal experience, about why teenagers have children. In discussing the importance of her testimony, Representative Benjamin Cardin (D-Md.) observed: "Ms. Jackson, we hear statistics and it is hard to put a face on the problem, and your presence here today is extremely helpful to us in the work that we have to do" (House Committee on Ways and Means 1994b, 829). Depictions, according to some representatives, personify problems in tangible ways that empirical data cannot.

Another important conversation that occurred in a hearing about the "Administration's Views on Welfare Reform" provides insight into legislator and witness reliance on anecdotal information. In his testimony, Senator Moynihan (D-N.Y.) quoted sociologist Peter Rossi as saying, "If there is any empirical law that is emerging from the past decade of widespread evaluation research activities, it is that the expected value for any measured effect of a social change program is zero." Chair of the Committee on Finance Bob Packwood interpreted Moynihan's statement as meaning, "there is no conceivable way we can know what we are doing." Moynihan responded, "Well, it means that when you measure it, it turns out you do not find out much." Packwood surmised, "In that case, you have got to fall back on philosophy." "You do," Moynihan concurred. "Because you cannot measure," Packwood concluded (Senate Committee on Finance 1995c, 25). In other words, anecdotes assumed a prominent place in the hearing and debate process precisely because legislators believed that social programs are difficult to measure and existing measurements are not always meaningful.

Examples from several other hearings suggest that legislators rely on anecdotes because they cannot provide any other form of evidence. In a May 23, 1996, hearing, for example, several witnesses debated the value of work, noting that working mothers transmit the work ethic to their children. In support of this proposition, those who testified supplied anecdotal evidence. Ed Schilling, director of the Fond Du Lac County Department of Social Services in Wisconsin, explained, "I have no statistical evidence...but anecdotally, the strongest evidence I have is the talking of the parents who have gotten a job" (House Committee on Ways and Means 1996c, 105). Narrating a similar story, Vermont Governor Howard Dean noted:

[T]he person who tells the best story I ever heard...is the President of the United States when he...went to a school and...explained his welfare program. And the teacher turned to one of the kids and said, well, what does welfare reform mean to you? And he said, welfare reform means to me, teacher, that when somebody asks me what my mother does, I say she works in the library not she is on welfare. That changes the whole dynamic of what kids think about parents and what kids think about themselves and what parents think about themselves. (House Committee on Ways and Means 1995a, 586)[15]

When asked whether she agrees that working mothers are better able to raise their children, Mary Jo Bane, assistant secretary for children and families of the U.S. Department of Health and Human Services, replied: "That has been my experience....Some of the most heartening conversations I had as a Commissioner...are with welfare recipients who have been able to move off of welfare into the work force; to hear them talk about the pride their children are taking in the fact that they are working is very inspiring" (House Committee on Ways and Means 1996c, 38). In the absence of policy research, those who testified resorted to personal experiences and anecdotes to support their positions.

In another typical example, Congressman Emerson (R-Mo.) explicitly stated that he was troubled by the preponderance of anecdotal evidence: "And something that has always kind of bothered me—I would just like your reaction to this—is that so many of the things we talk about in this subject arena are anecdotal." Following this comment, witness Sabra Burdick, director of Maine's Bureau of Income Maintenance, responded to a question from Emerson, saying, "I don't know if I can answer that question other than anecdotally." Emerson conceded: "Well, sometimes that's the only thing we have to go with" (House Select Committee on Hunger Domestic Task Force 1992b, 12–13). In fact, Emerson himself occasionally resorted to anecdotal evidence to support his claims. In one hearing, Emerson narrated: "Well, there is a lady, I usually rail against anecdotes, but let me tell you, about a lady named Maria Rodriguez" (House Select Committee on Hunger, Domestic Task Force 1992a, 30). These legislators and witnesses relied on anecdotes because they believed those anecdotes were the best or only forms of evidence available.

Many other witnesses and legislators arrived at similar conclusions. For example, in a welfare hearing on preventing teenage pregnancy, the conversation turned to the relationship between welfare benefits and out-of-wedlock childbearing. Patricia Funderburk Ware, director of the office of adolescent pregnancy programs of the Department of Health and Human Services, remarked to Christopher Shays (R-Conn.): "You said yourself that people do not talk honestly. Part of the reason we cannot talk honestly is because we do not have the studies that show one thing or the other. So I have my anecdotal story and you have yours. And we do not have any other way to base our decisions." In an implicit affirmation of this fact, Mr. Shays matter-of-factly stated that he "will just respond to the anecdotal evidence" with his own personal experience—yet another anecdote to counter a previous anecdote (House Committee on Government Reform and Oversight 1996, 70). Even as legislators and witnesses discouraged anecdotal evidence and warned against mischaracterization, they frequently resorted to stories as a primary means of explaining concepts and backing claims. In a telling comment, Representative Talent (R-Mo.) remarked in one of the last welfare debates, on July 17, 1996: "As my colleagues know, I could talk about statistics.... But I would rather talk about a story" (*Cong. Rec.* 1996, H7758). Not surprisingly, the content of the hearings and debates became a string of depictions in the form of anecdotes, analogies, metaphors, and stories, all of which have assumed a novel-like quality.[16] The late Senator Paul Wellstone (D-Minn.) was so frustrated by the use of anecdotes that, during the debates, he remarked: "I have heard my colleagues come to the floor and give examples. Are we going to now govern by anecdote?" (*Cong. Rec.* 1995, S11749).

RHETORICAL AND PUBLIC POLICY IMPLICATIONS

In his study of American views on welfare reform, Martin Gilens demonstrated that the public's perceptions "are influenced more by vivid examples than by statistical information, even if the evidentiary value of the statistical information is far higher" (1999, 206). Similarly, as this chapter on welfare reform suggests, social policy deliberations are often anecdotal in nature because the depictions vivify problems that are difficult to quantify. Although they warn against the dangers inherent in basing public policy on anecdotes and encourage reliance on social science data, legislators prefer the anecdotes because they are concrete and lack ambiguity. Legislators continue to rely on the anecdotes, despite discrepancies between those characterizations and public opinion polls and policy research. Thus, this case study suggests that when policy research and legislator perceptions conflict, policy makers rely on anecdotal evidence to guide policy-making decisions. Moreover, this chapter casts doubt on the many studies that privilege the rhetorical force of scientifically based information on the legislative process.

Welfare reform scholar Sheldon Danziger hinted at a second implication of this study when he wrote: "[W]ith the exception of the Family Support Act," welfare reform research tends "to be one cycle behind welfare reform policy and to have . . . little impact on policy outcomes. Instead, policies, once they have been implemented, have influenced the nature of subsequent welfare reform research" (2001, 25–26). Political scientist Murray Edelman (1988) observed a similar phenomenon in *Constructing the Political Spectacle.* Edelman commented on the complex linguistic construction of leaders, institutions, policy stances, and social problems and the ways in which political language reinforces dominant ideologies and existing power relationships, thereby partially shaping the reality to which political language responds. Drawing on the work of Edelman, Sanford Schram drew a similarly sobering conclusion. Believing that the very language we use to describe problems "helps construct what is taken to be real, natural, and true," Schram noted that "welfare policy discourse helps construct the ostensibly pregiven problems it is supposed to address" (1995, xxiv). If Danziger, Edelman, and Schram are correct, then the power of anecdotes concerning welfare recipients and their families extends beyond influencing public policy. These anecdotes may, in fact, drive the methodology and research design of the very social science studies that policy makers use to support and rationalize stereotypical welfare depictions and to warrant legislation. Indeed, as Danziger observed, "[W]elfare reform research is once again following policy as numerous studies are analyzing the effects of PRWORA" (2001, 152). In other words, the anecdotes that informed the legislation now appear to be guiding evaluation of the act. As a result, "[T]he research agenda shifted to the evaluation of policies that were being implemented rather than focusing on alternative policies that might be implemented" (151). Under such circumstances, welfare policy may prove ineffectual in achieving legislators' stated goals of poverty reduction, independence, and self-sufficiency. On the contrary, and far more cynically, welfare policy may continue to promote the very maladies it seeks to remedy, such as dependence and poverty.

Finally, this chapter evidences the important role that rhetorical scholars may continue to play in policy analysis. The knowledge-making power of depictive rhetoric (e.g., metaphor, anecdotes, and stories) is perhaps most contested in the sciences because, as feminist theorist Nancy Leys Stepan explained, science "has traditionally enjoyed" an "intellectually priviliged status as the repository of nonmetaphorical, empirical, politically neutral, universal knowledge" (1993, 359). As a science in its ideal form, however, public policy making shares a similar prestige.

Nevertheless, many scholars have concurred that policy making frequently occurs in the absence of empirically verifiable data. Consequently, public policy scholars and analysts have questioned prevailing rationalist models of policy making (Majone 1990, 157; Reich 1990, 7–10; White 1994, 506–7). Scholars critical of such rationalist paradigms have attended to the role of language, specifically that of metaphor and narrative in policy analysis (Fischer and Forester 1993, 5; Graham 1986, 303; Roe 1994; Stark 1992, 515; Throgmorton 1993, 117; Williams and Matheny 1995; Yanow 1993, 56). As political scientist Sanford Schram explained, "There is an increasing recognition that the postmodern interest in the political implications of linguistic practices, such as metaphor and symbolism, has direct relevance for studying and making of public policy" (1993, 249).[17] Concurrent with an increasing attention to the role of language in policy studies are calls by communication scholars to use communication research as a vehicle for influencing public policy. For instance, noting that communication scholars have had little to say to public policy makers, David Docherty, David Morrison, and Michael Tracey urged communication scholars to become involved in policy making, examine policy debates, and, in general, investigate the relationship between an "institutionally based articulation of particular symbol systems and the formation of public consciousness" (1993, 233, 237; see also Mueller 1995, 459; Noam 1993, 199–200). Understanding how policy develops from public discussion is a crucial step in being able to influence policy making.

This chapter's analysis of the congressional hearings and debates suggests that, at least in the case of welfare reform, policy research played a minor role in policy formation. By analyzing the patterns of depictive rhetoric used in the hearings and debates in light of welfare's historical context, as discussed in previous chapters, this chapter shows how anecdotal information continues to shape perceptions of welfare and warrant policy actions. As a result, this chapter underscores a significant opportunity for rhetorical scholars to draw on a variety of rhetorical theories, principles, and methods to provide a deeper understanding of the social construction of public policy and the policy formation process.

NOTES

1. R. Kent Weaver argued: "Research findings were reported in congressional hearings, in the news and opinion pages of newspapers, and in publications that cater to policymakers. Those for whom welfare issues were less important and who were least involved in shaping policy presumably paid little attention, but it would be difficult to argue that information was not easily accessible to those most involved" (2000, 160).

2. Weaver suggested that interest groups are also an obvious source of information. In his *Ending Welfare As We Know It*, however, Weaver noted, "Policymaking concerning low-income families is usually one of the areas where group analysis is seen as least helpful." In fact, Weaver contended that interest groups did not drive the welfare reform process and ultimately had an "ambiguous impact on the politics of welfare reform from 1992 to 1996" (2000, 196, 218, 220).

3. PRWORA asserts that a single parent with a child under the age of six meets work participation requirements if she works at least 20 hours per week (*PRWORA of 1996*, 2132).

4. Marist Institute poll, February 1991; *CBS News* poll, January 1992; *Gallup* poll, August 1992; *NBC News* poll, January 1995, *Times Mirror* poll, March 1994; CBS/*New York Times* poll, April 1995; NBC/*Wall Street Journal* poll, June 1994; *Time*/CNN poll, October 1989 (Weaver, Shapiro, and Jacobs 1995, 606–27).

5. Other scholars have been skeptical of policy research and questioned both the reliability of social science data and the extent to which data ought to influence policy making. For instance, some scholars, such as Sanford Schram, contended that social science research is "impoverished" and unable to provide a coherent basis for rational policy making (1995, xxvi). In his book *Welfare in America: How Social Science Fails the Poor,* William M. Epstein critiqued the social science research, program design, and evaluations that have formed the basis of welfare reform policies.

6. Although Weaver observed that many scholars believe that policy research played an important role in the passage of the Family Support Act, he also argued that even in this case, "the effect of policy research was strongly constrained as to how much and under what conditions it was felt" (2000, 144).

7. Through an examination of the 1971 congressional debates on National Health Insurance, Kristine Davis explored the various functions of legislative hearings (fact-finding, justifying committee positions, propagandizing, record-building, problem-solving) and concluded that record-building (amassing materials for members' later use) was the predominant function of legislative hearings (1981 102–4).

8. These articles are appended to the Senate Committee on Agriculture, Nutrition, and Forestry 1994, hearing.

9. Prior to the 1996 act, when family benefits were cut, the effect of the sanction could be tempered by an increase in food stamp allowances. The 1996 act, however, prohibits states from increasing food stamp benefits to offset the hardships of a sanction (Bloom and Winstead 2002, 50).

10. Executive director for the Center on Budget and Policy Priorities Robert Greenstein admitted, "[W]elfare is not a primary cause of out-of-wedlock childbearing" (Senate Committee on Finance 1995b, 50).

11. For an alternative view, consult Haskins and Primus 2002, 68–69.

12. For an opposing view, consult "Dispelling Myths about Unmarried Fathers," a May 2000 Fragile Families Research Brief.

13. "The *Green Book* is compiled by the staff of the Committee on Ways and Means of the U.S. House of Representatives from many sources and it provides program descriptions and historical data on a wide variety of social and economic topics, including Social Security, employment, earnings, welfare, child support, health insurance, the elderly, families with children, poverty, and taxation. It has become a standard reference work for those interested in the direction of social policy in the United States" (House Committee on Ways and Means 2000). The 1994, 1996, 1998, and 2000 editions are available (http://aspe.hhs.gov/2000gb).

14. Using a hierarchical classification system, Bane and Ellwood presented evidence showing that 29.4 percent of all endings to welfare are attributable to the head of a female household becoming a wife, and 25 percent could be traced to an increase in earnings (1994, 57). The authors acknowledged that different classification systems yield different results. Consequently, "If we had to pick a single number for the significance of work exits, we'd probably pick one closer to the 40 percent who had moderate earnings in their first year of welfare than the 25 percent we find using our hierarchical classification system" (59).

15. Representative Jack Kingston (R-Ga.) made a similar statement: "I heard President Clinton say one of the best things about people getting off of welfare is when the 12-year-old child at school…is asked 'What does your Momma do?' instead of saying 'She is on welfare,' They can say, 'She works'" (*Cong. Rec.* 1996, H7749).

16. Robert B. Asen's (2002) rhetorical analysis of hearings, debates, and speeches surrounding three major welfare legislative acts, including the 1981 Omnibus Budget Reconciliation Act (OBRA), the 1988 Family Support Act (FSA), and the 1996 Personal Responsibility and Work Opportunity Reconciliation Act (PRWORA), supports the narrativity of welfare reform hearings.

17. See also Edelman 1988; Forester 1993; Garvin and Eyles 1997; Kaplan 1993; Nimmo and Combs 1990; and Schram and Neisser 1997.

Chapter 7

American Welfare Policy and the Ineluctable Appeal of Language: Conclusion and Implications

> The discursive practices embedded in any particular policy work to prefigure our understandings of policy problems. The use of symbols, metaphors, and other figurative practices promotes the narrative implied by the policy. Symbols, metaphors, and so on narrate a particular understanding of a problem and reinforce the idea that it is an accurate depiction. They "naturalize" that depiction by making it seem to be the only "real" way to understand the problem, and not just one of many ways to understand it.
>
> Sanford F. Schram 1995, 125

As this epigraph contends, the depictions inherent in the welfare reform deliberations shape our collective understanding of the root causes of welfare dependency, the goals of welfare reform, and the best methods for achieving welfare reform. Welfare reform proceedings, like many social policy deliberations, are frequently anecdotal in nature because the depictions vivify problems that are difficult to quantify. Although they warn against the dangers inherent in basing public policy on depictions, legislators often prefer the depictions as warrants for policy action. Legislators continue to rely on the depictions, despite discrepancies between those characterizations and policy research. Thus, this book suggests that when social science, public opinion, and legislator perceptions of welfare problem conflict, policy makers rely on narrative depictions. Indeed, such depictions appear to be extremely powerful and influential in guiding public policy-making decisions.

Depictions emergent in the hearings and debates are not always fully supported by policy research, but this does not mean that the depictions are false or untrue. Borrowing from communication theorist Kenneth

Burke, these depictions are "faithful *reflections* of reality" even as they represent selections and deflections of that reality (1969, 59). In other words, the depictions accurately reflect the lived experiences of some welfare recipients, select the experiences of others as normative and ideal, while simultaneously deflecting the lived experiences of others. Although depictions are real to the extent that they do represent the lived experiences of some recipients on welfare, they also suggest a description of the most typical welfare recipient. One example,[1] in addition to those supplied in previous chapters, is helpful in making this point.

As explained in chapters 4 and 5, many legislators associate welfare recipients with bearing multiple children, often to gain higher welfare payments. Interestingly, many of the former welfare recipients who testified in the hearings have more than two children. Moreover, many of the stories told about welfare recipients are of sexually promiscuous women who have three or more children.[2] The very presence of these witnesses and stories lends credence to dominant perceptions of the welfare population as being characterized by large families. So powerful, in fact, are these characterizations that preventing out-of-wedlock births, especially among women already on welfare, becomes a centerpiece of welfare reform legislation. In addition, many measures at both the state[3] and federal levels attempt to control the reproductive choices of welfare mothers. PRWORA, for example, allows states to pursue family cap policies through waivers.

According to statistics, however, the average welfare family includes two or fewer children, approximating the national average.[4] In addition, citing a press release signed by 79 scholars who are "well-known for their research on poverty, labor markets, and family structures," social policy scholar Mimi Abramovitz explained that there is little evidence supporting the notion that welfare payments have any impact on a mother's decision to bear children (1996, 364–65). Such information correlates with findings discussed in chapter 5, which cast doubt on a direct link between out-of-wedlock childbearing and welfare payments.

Nevertheless, representations of welfare recipients as bearing multiple children can be considered accurate because they do describe the characteristics of some welfare recipients. However, in many cases, the witnesses who testified and the stories that emerged in the hearings and debates ceased to become descriptions of a select handful of recipients and instead became descriptions of the welfare population as a whole. In other words, the accounts of instances began to take on qualities of representative anecdotes. The paradox, to paraphrase Burke, is that the stories, in their selectivity, are necessarily reductive even as in their reflection they appear to offer sufficient scope (Burke 1969, 59).

The representativeness of the "typical welfare recipient" construct is tempting because it allows legislators to categorize welfare recipients neatly into misfortunate, feckless, or young frameworks. Most welfare experts, however, caution against talking about a typical welfare recipient, arguing that the welfare population is much too diverse, heterogeneous, and dynamic to capture in a few categories. For example, Mary Jo Bane and David Ellwood, authors of *Welfare Realities* and both appointed by the Clinton administration to assist in its welfare proposal, reported that "both liberals and conservatives" are guilty of "overly simplistic stereo-typing" when it comes to describing the welfare population (1994, 60).

Despite the vibrant diversity of the welfare population, the consistency and volume of repetitive categories of welfare families emergent in the hearings and debates encourages legislators to judge those categories as being coherent and representative of all welfare families. The link among historical values of work and family, the depictions of welfare recipients and families emergent in the hearings, and the corresponding legislation underscore the significance of repetitive depictions and ideology in shaping policy change. Consequently, this book makes at least three important rhetorical contributions with regard to depiction, argument, and narrative.

DEPICTION IN PUBLIC ARGUMENT

First, this book illustrates a process currently overlooked in studies of public moral argument and policy making—the role of depictions in policy formation. By providing a comprehensive analysis of the role and functions of depiction in public decision making, this book contributes to a clearer understanding of depictions in public moral argument. This study further demonstrates that depictions function in many of the same ways that communication scholar Michael Osborn (1986) predicted. That is, representations of welfare recipients and their families function to present reality to audiences, intensify feelings, build identification, sustain and implement action, and reaffirm identity.

As Osborn explained, repetitive presentations ultimately function as "culturetypes," or repetitive symbols that reinforce an audience's adherence to a core set of values. "The importance of such symbols is that they show us what we already know and accept...[and] they imply shared evaluative outlooks.... Most often, stereotypes [culturetypes] are accepted without question and without awareness of their service as anchors of the social order" (1986, 82–83). In the case of welfare reform, the depictions confirm our faith in time-honored and cherished values of hard work, self-help, family (nuclear), and faith (in God) as keys to success. The recurrence and volume of similar depictions of welfare recipients and their families create a discursive reality of the welfare system for congressional representatives. These depictions are successful to the extent that they correspond with policy makers' preexisting notions and that policy makers believe the representations fairly typify the characteristics, attitudes, and behaviors of most welfare recipients.

According to Osborn, in addition to presenting reality vividly to audiences, depictions perform a second major function—they intensify an audience's reactions to a subject matter. "Depiction also intensifies by reducing vast numbers of a subject to a few synecdochal [sic] instances or examples for which it is possible to develop human recognition" (86–87). This case study of welfare reform deliberation and legislation provides one concrete instance of how depictions intensify audience's reactions to discourse. Reducing the millions of welfare recipients to just a few character motives, values, and behaviors, the depictions provide legislators with a working understanding of the typical welfare recipient. This representative anecdote becomes the paradigmatic form upon which public policy is based. Political scientists W. Lance Bennett and Murray Edelman referred to this process as "selective documentation," arguing that these "formula stories" are appealing because they are easily recognized by listeners and because they reduce complex problems into clear, accessible explanations (1985, 161–63).

The third and fourth functions of depictions, according to Osborn, are to facilitate identification and implement action. "Certain presentations become authorized as legitimate group perspectives. Intensified feeling must be converted into group emotion: we discover together that we share feelings. In that discovery we affirm our identification in a community" (Osborn 1986, 89). One way in which identification is heightened, according to Osborn, is through the use of "culturetypal" narratives:

Culturetypes, we have observed, often derive their power from fantasies and folk tales in which they are embedded, fiction which often passes for history. To the extent that they compress and resonate stories that explain the origins and purposes of a society, culturetypes may come to function as implicit myths. As expressions of *mythos,* they may constitute a source of proof in rhetoric that rivals *logos, ethos,* and *pathos.* (90)

Stories of American citizens who overcome adversity through hard work and personal responsibility are archetypal in nature and have attained a mythical status. In accordance with Osborn, those who testified "scan the past for graphic lessons that can influence and lend urgency to present decisions. Often these examples will be drawn from myths accepted as serious interpretations of reality. The designs themselves will be offered as ways to actuate the promise of culturetypes" (93). In the case of welfare reform deliberations, representatives and witnesses frequently invoked lessons and stories from America's past (e.g., Horatio Alger) in recounting their rise to fortune through an adherence to cherished American ideals. Representations of individuals who overcame adversity during the Great Depression through hard work, parents who proudly refused public assistance and eventually succeeded, and welfare recipients who became congressional leaders in spite of their poor upbringings help sustain the faith in a rugged individualism, pull-yourself-up-by-the-bootstraps mentality. Conversely, stories of young minority women who, as a result of generous welfare policies, gave birth to multiple children, purchased nonnutritious foodstuffs with public assistance, and abused their children serve as evidence that current policies are antithetical to core American values.

As evidenced by legislators frequently invoking depictions to warrant proposals, these stories do constitute a source of proof that rivals other forms of evidence. Moreover, this proof appears quite rational. As stock stories, the narratives embedded in the hearings and debates reinforce the values, morals, and beliefs of the normative order; many of the depictions, for example, reaffirm faith in the American dream. Bennett and Edelman explained that when the stories "evoke familiar beliefs and values, the psychological inclination is to regard selected documentary detail as 'facts' that authenticate the story. In this fashion, fragments of real-life situations become perceived as wholes, while the excluded aspects of situations are neglected, rationalized away, or dismissed" (1985, 166). Similarly, select depictions of welfare recipients and accounts of success become representative wholes that guide policy outcomes. Together, these depictions rationalize welfare legislation designed to preserve ideals of work, marriage, personal responsibility, and religion.

A fifth and final function of depiction, according to Osborn, is to reaffirm community identity. "Such rhetoric awakens these moral markers...and coronates them as basic premises that ought to govern moral reasoning. Thus the effect if not the duty of reaffirmative rhetoric is to strengthen the grounding of those enthymemes vital to social judgment and deliberation" (1986, 95). One example is illustrative. Depictions of welfare recipients and their families powerfully strengthen commitment to such values as marriage and two-parent families. So strong is legislator faith in two-parent families and childbearing in the context of marriage that this commitment becomes a central tenet of public policy. In spite of considerable research that casts doubt on the desirability and feasibility of marriage as a welfare reform strategy, legislators elevate marriage as a basic premise that continues to guide reform efforts in the context of a public moral argument.

Clearly, the five functions of depiction seem to evolve in a circular pattern, from presentation, intensification, identification, implementation, and reaffirmation, feeding back into presentation. But the purpose of this book is not to suggest that policy makers and citizens are at the mercy of the logic inherent in the stories they tell. Rather, the object is to learn to use depictive forms consciously and purposefully, recognizing how they function and to what end. These strategies are discussed in the final section of this chapter.

THE FUNCTION OF NARRATIVE IN PUBLIC POLICY FORMATION

A second main contribution of this study is its advancement of narrative theory as outlined by rhetorical theorist Walter Fisher (1984; 1985; 1995). Implying that audiences have the power to interpret and assess narratives, Fisher's narrative paradigm endows audiences with significant control in the creation of meaning. Fisher's insistence upon audiences' ability to judge a text critically based on its narrative rationality, however, discounts the power of discourse to shape and position audiences' understanding of their world in particular ways. The analysis of welfare legislation in this book challenges Fisher's faith in the democratic and participatory functions of narrativity in public discourse in two ways.

First, in contrast to Fisher's theory of narrative rationality as a judgment that the audience brings to a text, this case study of welfare reform suggests that the narratives formed within the hearings and debates are constitutive in nature and position legislators to act in particular ways (Charland 1987). For instance, the Republicans, as the majority party, are able to invite witnesses who support their positions and can structure the order and format of panels to highlight favorable testimony. Consequently, Republican staff can arrange a group of texts with a fairly controlled metanarrative. This crafted narrative, in turn, positions legislators to act in roles that are politically beneficial. Dominant narratives of the feckless and young welfare recipients invite legislators to act as guardians of fundamental values and the traditional family, protectors of American society, discipliners of recalcitrant youth, punishers of undeserving welfare recipients, supporters of the truly needy, and faithful stewards of a righteous plan. Because they can be manipulated artfully to position policy makers in politically self-serving roles, legislative hearings and debates are not just exploratory or informative, but also constitutive.

Second, far from being "inimical to elitist politics," narratives, as this book suggests, actually foster elitist argument and delegitimate particular public voices. As detailed in chapter 4, rather than bypassing elite audiences, as Fisher would hope, narrative public moral argument privileges the interpretations of a select group of legislators who have considerable freedom to invite witnesses and structure the hearings in support of their political agendas. Moreover, representations of welfare recipients as largely uneducated, unskilled, immoral, criminal, and abusive create an image of welfare recipients as incapable of speaking wisely about their own experiences. As a result, these depictions and narratives ultimately justify the almost complete exclusion of welfare recipients from the hearings and debates.[5]

Of course, some legislators and witnesses are concerned with the lack of welfare recipient testimony. For example, according to Representative Bernard Sanders (I-Vt.): "[U]nfortunately, in the U.S. Congress, poor people very often do not have the opportunity to come forward and make their point.... [They have] ideas that we should be hearing a lot more of" (House Committee on Government Operations 1994, 57). Welfare recipient Sherry Honkala also spoke of the need for "consulting with actual real welfare recipients, not ones that are pulled from...the Republican party or from the Democratic party but real welfare recipients.... I am kind of scared because the upcoming hearings on that kind of stuff I don't think there will be much actual real welfare recipients' participation in the testimony" (House Committee on Economic and Educational Opportunities 1995a, 77).

Despite such opposition, legislators largely ignore welfare recipient testimony in the hearings, even joking about its irrelevance. In one hearing, the late Senator Paul Wellstone (D-Minn.) spoke about the plight of welfare recipients, noting that "there are all of these cultural stereotypes, and these mothers and children do not exactly have the money to get on NBC and CBS and ABC and run ads, taking on some of these myths." Wellstone suggested: "I really think we ought to have a hearing where we have many more of these mothers here, testifying. I must say that their voice has been absent in what has been going on here, in the House of Representatives and the U.S. Senate." Senator Nancy L. Kassebaum (R-Kans.), chair of the House Committee on Labor and Human Resources, responded: "Well, we have a former welfare recipient who will testify later this morning." Wellstone retorted: "One. We do, and I thank you. One. But I think we need to have a hearing, I am not trying to get into a big, acrimonious debate. I am just saying that I think it would be an important foundation for good public policy if we devoted one morning to a hearing where we just had the mothers come in and talk about their experiences with welfare and talk about what they think would constitute good reform." Capitalizing on a previous joke, Kassebaum replied: "Well, we will do our best. Maybe we can balance it with the angry men." Senator Christopher Dodd (D-Conn.) chimed in: "Why don't we just do husbands and wives? [Laughter]" (Senate Committee on Labor and Human Resources 1995a, 31–32, 33). Legislators and witnesses have so discredited the opinion of welfare recipients through rhetorical depictions of welfare recipients that the very idea of an entire panel of recipients testifying about reform is quickly dismissed. Kassebaum and Dodd trivialized the idea, using the suggestion as an opportunity for levity. Even Kassebaum's response to Wellstone suggests that one welfare recipient's testimony is adequate to represent an entire population. In the end, it seems that welfare recipient views are perceived as immaterial to the public policy process.

The few welfare recipient stories included in the hearings are largely those of the misfortunate welfare recipient, the individual who conformed to the family and work ethics and eventually succeeded. The people who testified were typically *former* welfare recipients, individuals who succeeded through their own efforts with limited (if any) public assistance. Although these former welfare recipients sometimes challenged unfavorable constructions of recipients, they almost never disputed the underlying values of hard work, independence, and family that form the context of welfare deliberations. As a result, their stories often reinforce the authority of elites. For instance, former welfare recipient Gladys Marisette, of Topeka, Kansas, criticized: "We hear too often the stories of how billions of tax dollars are being wasted fraudulently by numerous welfare recipients.... [I]t is a very sad display of the picture that has been painted regarding such a wonderful cause" (Senate Committee on Labor and Human Resources 1995a, 49–50). At the same time, Marisette credited her success, in part, to her own "perseverance," or hard work. Former welfare recipient Pam Harris White stated that hard work and skills training enabled her to escape poverty and welfare dependence. As a result: "Today I am gainfully employed as a property manager and I am totally independent of welfare. I want to add with pride that all of my children are doing well.... [T]hey are all drug free [and]...have never been involved in criminal activity and I am not a grandmother." Harris White added that because "poor motivation" and a "lack of values" lead to teenage pregnancy and welfare dependence, welfare reform should be time limited to encourage people to develop good habits (House Committee on Ways and Means 1995b, 179). Rather than challenging the historical and ideological hegemony that marginalizes welfare recipients, these recipients proudly demonstrate how enacting fundamental values and beliefs in their own lives leads to success.

Likewise, the testimony of welfare recipient Walt Myers, of Saegertown, Pennsylvania, illustrates how recipient testimony reinforces dominant ideologies. Drawing on his unusual experience[6] as a welfare recipient, Myers addressed how his adherence to mainstream middle-class American values of marriage and hard work did not yield financial success.

This led me to write a letter to Mr. Perot. I acknowledged that he was an intelligent man because he is a millionaire. I asked him how the welfare people go about getting jobs when our mills are gone. I said, humorously, that I was an avid hunter and occasional fisherman. All the time I hunted, I did not see a job go by that I might shoot, nor while I fished I did not see one that I might snag. (House Committee on Ways and Means 1995c, 1299)

Of importance is Myers's linking of intelligence to wealth. According to Myers, Perot's millionaire status is clear evidence of his intelligence and his ability to offer solutions to Myers's dilemma. This type of statement reinforces the perception that government legislators and welfare scholars, as educated and wealthy individuals, are in a better position to evaluate the welfare situation than are the poor welfare recipients themselves.

It is not surprising that welfare recipient discourse does not challenge, but rather reinforces, dominant welfare theories. According to communication theorist Raymie McKerrow: "Those who are dominated also participate in the social structure and are affected by—and affect—the orders of discourse by which their actions are moderated." McKerrow further argued that the possibilities for marginalized individuals to challenge dominant discourse "are muted by the fact that the subject already is interpellated with the dominant ideology. Actions oriented toward change will tend to be conducive to power maintenance rather than to its removal" (1989, 93–94). Similarly, this analysis of welfare reform legislation finds that dominant ideological influences, combined with the nature of the hearings as highly controlled conversations with carefully selected witnesses, mitigate possibilities for counterhegemonic discourse.

Thus, although Fisher claimed that "[t]he sort of hierarchy condemned by the narrative praxis is the sort that is marked by the will to power, the kind of system in which elites struggle to dominate and to use the people for their own ends," this study suggests otherwise (1984, 9). Contrary to Fisher's assertions that through narrative discourse "'people' do judge the stories that are told for and about them" (9), an analysis of the congressional hearings and debates that led to the passage of the 1996 Personal Responsibility and Work Opportunity Reconciliation Act points to the power of some depictions to facilitate elite discourse, discourage the participation of alternative public viewpoints, and reinforce dominant ideologies.

CONTEXT AND THE CREATION OF PRESENCE IN LEGISLATIVE HEARINGS AND DEBATES

A third major benefit of this study is its contribution to rhetorical argument theory. In one of the most comprehensive studies of argumentation, the *New Rhetoric: A Treatise on Argumentation,* Chaim Perelman and L. Olbrechts-Tyteca (1971) argued that an essential component to successful argumentation is presence, or the process by which rhetors enhance the primacy and immediacy of certain elements of the speech to their audiences. According to Perelman and Olbrechts-Tyteca individual rhetors can accomplish presence through data selection and arrangement, through data interpretation, and through stylistic figures.

Building on the concept of presence, this case study demonstrates how presence can be achieved with multiple rhetors (e.g., legislators and witnesses who testify) and in multiple texts (e.g., the entire series of hearings and debates from the 102nd, 103rd, and 104th Congresses). Furthermore, this book also show how the historical context of welfare reform in America lends presence to certain values that inform the contemporary hearings and debates, predisposing legislators and witnesses to interpret information in particular ways.

In addition, the Republican's ability to craft a metanarrative about welfare through witness selection and panel structuring lends presence to ideas favorable to the Republican platform. These contexts frame the legislative dialogue and serve as the scene upon which all legislators test, debate, and refine their ideas. Importantly, these contexts do not value all ideas equally. For instance, the historical context affirms the policy arguments that are consistent with the values and assumptions of that context. Context can be used to inform the political process by creating presence:

When an account fashions the "facts" of a situation around *a priori* assumptions, history seems clear and undeniable because the analytical perspective has made it so. And so the vicious cycle continues: stereotypical narratives selectively exclude inconsistent or contradictory information, leaving the psychological impression that one is experiencing reality-driven objectivity. The irony of this sort of "narrative objectivity" is that, while an individual or a group may feel ever more convinced of the truth of a vision, the collectivity of individuals or groups may generate any number of opposing objective visions. When confronted with each other, these opposing objective visions have little basis for reconciliation, with the result that power, domination, or varieties of dehumanizing "tolerance" become the human relations strategies of last resort. (Bennett and Edelman 1985, 162)

During welfare reform proceedings, the context crafted by Republican staff creates the appearance of a clear set of facts about welfare. These facts are informed by historical welfare experiences, depictions, public opinion, and policy research. Within this context, policy makers, regardless of political affiliation, demonstrate remarkable agreement over the set of values (work, marriage, individual responsibility, Judeo-Christian ideals) that should inform policy making, the characterizations of welfare recipients and their families, and the proposals that will resolve welfare problems. One explanation for such agreement is that the contextual field in which the legislators debate welfare reform does not permit significant variance in opinion. Consequently, this book posits that what appears to be more influential in guiding public-policy decisions is not the quality of the deliberative logic but rather the conceptual background upon which policy makers test their arguments.

An examination of arguments that appear to counter the dominant viewpoints in the hearings and debates provides an excellent example of how context creates presence. According to Perelman and Olbrechts-Tyteca, "A tendentious argument, deliberately put forward on behalf of a party it is one's interest or duty to favor, will have to be completed by the adverse argument in order to reach a balance in the appraisal of the known elements. The judge will not make a decision before he has heard both parties" (1971, 119). The dominant arguments and testimonials in the debates were often countered with adverse or opposing viewpoints. Indeed, in the hearings, two witnesses did attempt to challenge the racial, ethnic, and class biases that informed depictions of welfare recipients. Sonia M. Pérez, director of the Poverty Project at the National Council of La Raza, and Katherine McFate, associate director of research for social policy at the Joint Center for Political and Economic Studies, both argued that the welfare reform discussions and proposals were replete with racist tendencies.[7]

Pérez stated that the hearings were discriminatory because they did not represent the voices or unique experiences of Latinas. "One of the most troubling aspects of the welfare reform debate that began over a year ago," she explained, "is that it has been separated from the larger issue of poverty. Instead, the focus has been on the amount of federal funding spent on AFDC and on the behavior of poor women, and has rarely included the factors that lead poor and/or unemployed families to use AFDC" (House Committee on Ways and Means 1995c, 1103). In a similar vein, McFate argued that the Republican proposals, namely those associated with the Contract with America, disproportionately targeted low-income African American families:

The majority of AFDC recipients in the United States are not black, but the groups targeted by the Contract's welfare reform proposals are disproportionately black. The Contract targets three groups of current welfare recipients for exclusion, the children of unmarried teenage mothers, the children of unmarried mothers regardless of their age for whom paternity has not been established, and families who have accumulated 5 years of AFDC support. About half of black AFDC mothers have never married, compared to 31 percent of whites and 14 percent of Hispanics.... Because black families are more likely to be in this system longer, they are also more likely to hit the limit and be pushed off. Remember that long-term AFDC recipients are the least experienced, the least educated part of the welfare population, and they have very low basic skills.... If a 5-year time limit had been put in place 5 years ago, about 54 percent of the current black AFDC families would have exhausted their eligibility for support. (House Committee on Ways and Means 1995c, 1091)

Both of these women charged that the welfare policies discriminate against African Americans and Latinas. These opposing arguments, which are well reasoned and logically presented, failed to ignite a significant response from representatives. In addition, because they represent some of the only challenges to prevailing perceptions of welfare recipients and their families, these and the few other countertestimonials also failed to provide a formidable balance against the weight of dominant testimony.

This failure is possible because the context of the hearings powerfully gave presence to the values of work, family, and personal responsibility, while detracting focus from issues of structural inequities, discrimination, and prejudicial policies. Within this context, the depictions of Pérez, McFate, and others serve primarily as illustrations, not examples. This distinction is a subtle but important one: "While an example must be beyond question, an illustration need not be, as adherence to the rule does not depend on it" (Perelman and Olbrechts-Tyteca 1971, 357). In addition:

Because an illustration seeks to increase presence by making an abstract rule concrete by means of a particular case, there is a tendency to see an illustration as a "vivid picture of an abstract matter." But unlike an analogy, an illustration does not lead to replacement of the abstract by the concrete, or to the transposition of structure into another sphere. It really *is* a particular case, it corroborates the rule, it can even, as in proverbs actually serve to state the rule.... Very often, the purpose of an illustration is to promote understanding of the rule, by means of an unquestionable instance of its application. (360)

As illustrations, the depictions of welfare recipients and their families presuppose an existing rule established by the historical welfare context. As such, the depictions serve merely to corroborate what history has already demonstrated to be true—that values of work, family, and individual responsibility lead to success and that welfare recipients, by virtue of their dependence on public assistance, must not be enacting these fundamental cherished values.

Depictions functioning most frequently as illustrations in the hearings and debates explain, in part, the failure of testimony to provide a strong opposing viewpoint. "The inadequate illustration does not play the same role as the invalidating case, because the rule is not called into question and hence the inadequate statement of the illustration reflects on the person using it, testifying to his misunderstanding or misinterpretation of the rule" (Perelman and Olbrechts-Tyteca 1971, 361). Communication theorist Raymie McKerrow likewise stated: "[P]ower, exercised in terms of law and sovereign right, transforms...or naturalizes the social relation: it becomes the norm, and discourse related to its maintenance is 'normal.' Challenges are therefore abnormal and irrational by definition" (1989, 99). The alternative illustrations provided by Pérez, McFate, and others who have attacked policy proposals do not challenge the validity of the underlying rule.

On the contrary, both Pérez and McFate endorsed hard work as a key to overcoming adversity and implied that with proper skills, training, and experience individuals can rise out of poverty. Their comments validate monogamous relationships within the context of marriage and a nuclear family. Although their intention may be to charge welfare legislation with racist tendencies, their views do just the opposite. Indeed, their depictions of minority groups seemingly confirm representations of African Americans and Latinas as more uneducated, unskilled, and welfare-dependent than other racial and ethnic groups. By couching their arguments within a particular historical framework, a context that typically associates undeserving welfare status with minority groups, the comments of McFate and Pérez actually reinforce the historical context within which legislators debate and interpret depictions and public policy. Moreover, their criticisms of PRWORA can be dismissed easily and attributed to their misunderstanding of the rule of how adherence to fundamental values yields success.

EFFECTIVE STRATEGIES FOR INFLUENCING PUBLIC POLICY

Finally, this case study suggests implications beneficial to public policy practitioners. Many welfare experts and scholars, such as Judith Gueron (2001), Sheldon Danziger (2001), and Martin Gilens (1999), have expressed concern that current welfare legislation does not reflect policy research or public opinion. This analysis of welfare reform legislation suggests one compelling reason for the failure of social policy to capture thoroughly public viewpoints and research, and that is the power of depictions to shape reality and prescribe courses of action. In the case of the 1996 welfare reforms, what appears to be most important about the depictions is not whether they reflect logical arguments or verifiable evidence (although some do). Instead, the more salient aspect of welfare depictions is whether they establish "verisimilitude, the sense of closeness of the world modeled" in the hearings and debates to "that already experienced by the legislators." According to Osborn, "To the degree that verisimilitude is established, the rhetoric in the one can be transferred and transformed into action in the other" (1986, 86). This case study suggests a coherency among historical representations of welfare, depictions of welfare emergent in the hearings and debates, and legislator perceptions of welfare, all of which are ultimately transformed into policy action.

If, as this case study suggests, representations of welfare recipients ultimately impact public policy decision making, then, on a practical level, public policy practitioners need to learn how to construct rhetorically attractive messages (narratives, arguments, depictions) that influence policy making. This study implies that an understanding of the rules and assumptions that currently guide welfare reform deliberations is a necessary precursor to informed and effective policy making. As political scientist Sanford Schram explained in the epigraph to this chapter, "Highlighting the ways in which discourse helps construct what is taken to be real, natural, and true creates resources for working toward alternative arrangements" (1995, xxiv). Rhetorical-critical methods are especially suited to uncovering the tensions inherent in discourse and revealing how discourse works to sustain, challenge, and reform structural and power relations in various sociohistorical contexts. McKerrow, who referred to this process as "critical rhetoric," outlined a strategy for unmasking the discourse rules and processes that govern who speaks, which topics are appropriate to address, and what counts as authoritative evidence (1989, 93). Using a similar approach, policy advocates can expose how the rules and assumptions that govern social policy making influence legislative outcomes. Adopting a critical approach to the evidence and data that support depictions in legislative hearings and debates prepares legislators, public policy advocates, and citizens to better evaluate the arguments that warrant policy changes.

Once policy advocates understand the complex discursive and social practices that inform current legislation, they can create compelling narratives and depictions to influence policy. For policy makers who desire to perpetuate the status quo, creating powerful depictions means constructing representations that reinforce dominant societal beliefs, complement supposed historical truths, and uphold socially sanctioned values. In other words, as narrative theory suggests, some stories are better than others because they cohere and resonate with their audiences. Policy makers who tell the best stories and who paint a vivid picture of problems and solutions that is consistent with their audiences' experiences are more likely to achieve their desired goals. Ultimately, then, "Rather than asking where to place the strongest arguments in a sequence," policy advocates should consider "how to build powerful, overall impressions by the end of the presentation" (Osborn 1986, 87).

In contrast, policy advocates who wish to counter current welfare reform legislation need to construct alternative rhetorical contexts favorable to their arguments. In Perelman's and Olbrechts-Tyteca's terms, policy advocates interested in producing counterhegemonic discourse must craft depictions that serve as examples for establishing a new set of legislative premises, rather than illustrations for reinforcing existing rules

(1971, 356–61). Those who challenge dominant constructs, beliefs, and attitudes face a difficult task. Historical context and legislative rules that favor the majority party and that allow this party to select witnesses and structure hearings in a way that gives presence to prevailing values and belief systems may mitigate the effects of radical discourse. Nevertheless, several communication theories offer promising methods for constructing effective narratives and depictions that challenge dominant political frames. In an article entitled "'Going Meta': Definition and Political Applications," communication theorist Herbert W. Simons outlined a strategy of "Going Meta," a process by which people critique dominant ideological taken-for-granted frames by engaging in frame-altering responses (1994, 471). Osborn mentioned a similar technique to counter prevailing depictions in the form of innovative presentations. Citing metaphors as one especially potent form of innovative presentation, Osborn argued that the innovative presentation "crosses and disturbs patterns of expectation established by repetitive presentation" (1986, 83). Using these techniques in the public moral argument over welfare, policy advocates may offer self-reflexive narratives and metaphors—new interpretive paradigms— that expose the hidden assumptions currently governing welfare debates and suggest alternative premises to guide deliberations.

Maurice Charland's theory of constitutive rhetoric also implies auspicious possibilities for constructing discourse that provide policy makers with "new perspectives and motives" for action (1987, 142). One way to influence the policy-making process is to provide "stories that . . . shift and re-work the subject and its motives" (148). In addition to stories, social policy makers may also draw on other rhetorical forms that compete with the persuasive force of depictions. For instance, different aesthetic practices, such as "music, drama, architecture, and fashion," can also "elicit new modes of experience and being" and, therefore, promote changes in social meaning (148). Introducing new stories and aesthetic practices into the legislative arena can position (or constitute) policy makers to think and act in different ways.

Legislators have already demonstrated some willingness to participate in innovative aesthetic practices during the hearings and debates leading to the passage of the 1996 act. For instance, in one welfare hearing, chair of the House Committee on Human Resources and Intergovernmental Relations Christopher Shays (R-Conn.) invited teenagers who were participating in a teenage pregnancy prevention program to sing their theme song. Shays proclaimed: "I would love to end [the hearing] with a nice theme song. . . . I am taking tremendous glee in the fact that I am overruling my staff. I feel like I am exerting myself. You are allowed to clap. You are allowed to do whatever you want" (House Committee on Government Reform and Oversight 1996, 147). Although some may dispute the efficacy of singing songs in Congress, Shays's enthusiasm is indicative of some legislator's interest in alternative forms of testimony. In addition, a March 27, 1995, hearing, entitled "Simulation Hearing on Obtaining Federal and State Assistance," gave legislators first-hand knowledge of the difficulties welfare recipients face in applying for federal programs. During this hearing, legislators formed teams, assumed the role of a typical welfare family, and tried to apply for the federal and state welfare programs for which this fictional family was eligible. Although only three members attended the hearing, this creative role-playing exercise dramatically exposed participants to the complex bureaucracy that governs welfare and the scarce resources available to needy families. By introducing new stories and aesthetic experiences such as these into the legislative arena, policy makers can establish a new framework within which to debate a given social policy, thereby providing a context that gives presence to alternative depictions and alternative solutions.

NOTES

   1. As another example, frequent characterizations embedded in the hearings and debates depict welfare recipients as moving to states with higher welfare payments and with abusing drugs and alcohol. Many legislators accused welfare recipients of committing fraud by claiming benefits in multiple states at the same time or by shopping around to locate a home in a high-paying welfare state. Reflecting the prevalence of this view, Senator Joseph Lieberman (D-Conn.) inquired about the availability of studies that demonstrate whether welfare recipients "shop from jurisdiction to jurisdiction, State to State, to go to States that offer more or have less onerous requirements?" He explained, "[W]hen I was in the State legislature in the 1970s... Connecticut and a lot of other States were passing residency requirements which were based on the presumption that because we had a higher AFDC benefit level that, in fact, we were becoming a magnet for welfare recipients" (Senate Committee on Governmental Affairs 1995, 28). So predominant are these perceptions that PRWORA includes provisions to address migration. For example, PRWORA requires states to indicate whether and how the state intends to treat families who move from one state to another differently from families who currently reside in the state (*PRWORA of 1996*, 2114, 2124). These predominant characterizations are not supported fully by data, however. In an article entitled "Welfare Migration as Policy Rumor: A Statistical Accounting," Sanford F. Schram, Lawrence Nitz, and Gary Krueger provided significant empirical evidence that welfare migration is a relatively insignificant phenomenon (1997, 148–49).
   In addition constructions of welfare recipeints discussed in Chapter 4 revealed a common perception of recipients as drug and alcohol abusers. Mathematica Policy Research senior fellow LaDonna Pavetti concluded that, contrary to popular perceptions of welfare recipients as drug or alcohol dependent, "the most common potential barriers to work are human capital deficits [limited work experience and

education] and transportation issues which affected between one-third and one-half of the recipients.... Alcohol and drug dependence was the least common obstacle, affecting no more than 13 percent of recipients" (2002, 137–38). Indeed, there are likely instances of some welfare recipients migrating to states with higher-paying benefits, and some welfare recipients clearly do abuse alcohol and drugs. The problem is, however, that these characterizations frequently become representative of the welfare population as a whole, thus driving policy outcomes.

2. See chapter 4, note 1.

3. Abramovitz discussed several state plans to control women's reproduction (1996, 364).

4. "Forty-three percent of families receiving AFDC have one child and 30 percent have two" (Abramovitz 1996, 364).

5. Many disabling images that compare welfare recipients to animals, rodents, and insects support the exclusion of welfare recipient testimony from the hearings and debates. The comparisons also suggest that public assistance results in dependence and stifles self-sufficiency. For example, Navada Representative John Ensign (R) commented "Being a veterinarian, I always get back to animal examples. It reminds me almost of what we do to animals when we put them in zoos. They lose the ability to hunt, as people on welfare almost lose the desire, the willingness to go out and work. That is similar to what we are doing with people on welfare" (House Committee on Ways and Means, Subcommittee on Human Resources, 23 May 1996, 101).

Perhaps the animal comparison that received the most public attention occurred in a March 24, 1995 debate. During this debate, Representative Jack Kingston
(R-GA) compared welfare recipients to dolphins:

> [N]ot long ago a fisherman off the coast of Savannah discovered if he sailed his boats to a certian spot each day and fed a school of dolphins that they would start gathering at that spot daily. Next he observed a lot of Yankees heading south on I-95 who had pockets and briefcases and purses full of money. So, being an astute entrepreneur, he then put one and one together and he said, hey tourists, want to see some fish? For 20 bucks I will take you out in my boats. You will see hundreds of them, and for an extra 5 bucks I will throw in a fish head and you too can play Jacques Cousteau, and the tourists just kept pulling off I-95 and jamming the exit. The fisherman was growing rich and the dolphins fat. Then enter Fish and Wildlife. Hold everything, they said, you cannot do this; you are making the fish dependent, you are disturbing their ability to fend for themselves. And they were right. It was not in the best long-term interests of the dolphins. Question: Why do not we elevate people to the same status as dolphins? ("Helping Americans Get Off Welfare," *Congressional Record*, 24 March 1995, H3738)

A few moments later, Florida Representative John L. Mica (R) told virtually the same story, only in his dramatic acount, welfare recipients were cast as alligators:

> Mr. Chairman, I represent Florida where we have many lakes and natural reserves. If you vist these areas, you may see a sign like this that reads, "do not feed the alligators." We post these signs for several reasons. First,

because if left in a natural state, alligators can fend for themsleves. They work, gather food and care for their young. Second, we post these warnings because unnatural feeding and artificial care creates dependency. When dependency sets in, these otherwise able-bodied alligators can no longer survive on their own. Now, I know people are not alligators, but I submit to you that with our current handout, nonwork welfare system, we have upset the natural order. We have failed to understand the simple warning signs. We have created a system of dependency. ("Personal Responsibilty Act of 1995," *Congressional Record*, 24 March 1995, H3766)

Stil later, Wyoming Representative Barbara Cubin (R) offered a third version of essentially the same narrative, except this time, welfare recipients were likened to wolves:

[R]ecently the Federal Government introduced wolves into the State of Wyoming, and they put them in pens and brought elk and venison to them every day. This is what I call the wolf welfare program. The Federal Government introduced them and they have since then provided shelter and they have provided food, they have provided everything that the wolves need for their existence. Guess what? They opened the gate to let the wolves out and now the wolves will not go. They are cutting the fence down to make the wolves go out and the wolves will not go. What has happened with the wolves, just like what happens with human beings, when you take away their incentives, when you take away their freedom, when you take away their dignity, they have to be provided for....Just like any animal in the species, any mammal, when you take away their freedom and their dignity and their ability, they cannot provide for themsleves, and that is what the Democrats' proposal does on welfare. ("Personal Responsibilty Act of 1995," *Congressional Record*, 24 March 1995, H3772)

Representative David C. Funderburk (R-NC) concluded that the welfare system has made "generations of Americans nothing more than animals in the Government barn" ("Personal Responsibilty Act of 1995," *Congressional Record*, 24 March 1995, H3793). Frustrated by these images, Representative Sam Gibbons (D-Fla.) averred in a passage that cannot escape its own literary allusion to "Little Red Riding Hood": "[I]n my 34 years here I thought I had heard it all, but we have a millionaire from Florida comparing children to alligators and we have a gentlewoman in red over here comparing children to wolves. That tops it all" ("Personal Responsibilty Act of 1995," *Congressional Record*, 24 March 1995, H3772).

   6. Notably, Myers is perhaps the only male welfare recipient to testify verbally at the hearings and one of a small handful of male recipients who are even mentioned in the hearings and debates.

   7. Cynthia Newbille, National Black Women's Health Project executive director, made a statement that is subject to a similar analysis (House Committee on Ways and Means 1994a, 646).

References

Abramovitz, Mimi. 1996. *Regulating the Lives of Women: Social Welfare Policy from Colonial Times to the Present.* Boston: South End.

Allen, Walter R. 2000. "African-American Family Life in Societal Context." Pp. 303–18 in *Upon These Shores: Themes in the African-American Experience, 1600 to the Present,* ed. William R. Scott and William G. Shade. New York: Routledge.

Aristotle. 1991. *Art of Rhetoric,* trans. John Henry Freese. Cambridge: Harvard University Press.

Asen, Robert. 2002. "Visions of Poverty: Welfare Policy and Political Imagination." East Lansing: Michigan State University Press.

Axinn, June M., and Amy E. Hirsch. 1993. "Welfare and the 'Reform' of Women." *Families in Society: The Journal of Contemporary Human Services* 74, no. 9 (November): 563–72.

Axinn, June, and Herman Levin. 1997. *Social Welfare: A History of the American Response to Need.* 4th ed. New York: Longman.

Axinn, June, and Mark J. Stern. 2001. *Social Welfare: A History of the American Response to Need.* 5th ed. New York: Allyn and Bacon.

Bane, Mary Jo, and David T. Ellwood. 1994. *Welfare Realities: From Rhetoric to Reform.* Cambridge, Mass.: Harvard University.

Bennett, W. Lance, and Murray Edelman. 1985. "Toward a New Political Narrative." *Journal of Communication* 35 (Autumn): 156–71.

Bennett and Kemp. 2002. Opinion. *New York Times.* 1 August: A24.

Besharov, Douglas J. 1996. "Welfare as We Know It." *Slate,* July 15. Available at, http://slate.msn.com/id/1039.

Billingsley, Andrew and Jeanne M. Giovanni. 1972. *Children of the Storm: Black Children and American Child Welfare.* New York: Harcourt, Brace, Jovanovich.

Bitzer, Lloyd F. 1987. "Rhetorical Public Communication." *Critical Studies in Mass Communication* 4 (December): 425–28.

Black, Edwin. 1970. "The Second Persona." *The Quarterly Journal of Speech* 56 (2): 109–19.

Blank, Rebecca M. 2002. "Welfare and the Economy." pp. 97–103 in *Welfare Reform and Beyond: The Future of the Safety Net,* ed. Isabel V. Sawhill, et al. Washington, D.C.: The Brookings Institution.

Blank, Rebecca, and Ron Haskins, eds. 2001. *The New World of Welfare.* Washington, D.C.: Brookings Institution Press.

Bloom, Dan, and Don Winstead. 2002. "Sanctions and Welfare Reform." pp. 49–56 in *Welfare Reform and Beyond: The Future of the Safety Net,* ed. Isabel V. Sawhill, et al. Washington, D.C.: The Brookings Institution.

Boyer, Paul. 1978. *Urban Masses and Moral Order in America, 1820–1920.* Cambridge: Harvard University Press.

Breckenridge, Sophonisba P. 1927. *Public Welfare Administration in the United States: Select Documents.* Chicago: University of Chicago Press.

Bremner, Robert H., ed. 1971. *Children and Youth in America: A Documentary History, 1866–1932.* Vol. 2. Cambridge, Mass.: Harvard University Press.

———. 1974. *Children and Youth in America: A Documentary History, 1933–1973.* Vol. 3. Cambridge, Mass.: Harvard University Press.

Brooks-Gunn, Jeanne. 2002. "Children and Welfare Reform: Who Benefits and Who Does Not." Paper presented as part of the Federation of Behavioral, Psychological, and Cognitive Sciences and The Foundation for Child Development's Science and Public Policy Briefing on Children and Welfare Reform, The Role of Marriage in Childhood Outcomes, 12 June, Washington, D.C.

Brown, Josephine Chapin. 1940. *Public Relief 1929–1939.* New York: Henry Holt.

Burke, Kenneth. 1969. *A Grammar of Motives.* Berkeley: University of California Press.

Cammisa, Anne Marie. 1998. *From Rhetoric to Reform? Welfare Policy in American Politics.* Dilemmas in American Politics. Boulder, Colo.: Westview.

Carothers, Suzanne C. 1998. "Catching Sense: Learning from Our Mothers to Be Black and Female." pp. 315–27 in *Families in the U.S.: Kinship and Domestic Politics,* ed. Karen V. Hansen and Anita Ilta Garey. Philadelphia: Temple University Press.

Center on Budget and Policy Priorities, 2003. "Poverty Increases and Median Income Declines for Second Consecutive Year" available on-line at http://www.cbpp.org/, 23 September.

Charland, Maurice. 1987. "Constitutive Rhetoric: The Case of the *Peuple Québécois.*" *Quarterly Journal of Speech* 73 (May): 133–50

Chase-Lansdale, P. Lindsay, Rebekah Levine Coley, Brenda J. Lohman, and Laura D. Pittman. 2002. "Welfare Reform: What About the Children?" *Welfare, Children, and Families: A Three-City Study.* Policy Brief 02–1.

Cherlin, Andrew. 2002. "Marriage, Family Formation, and Welfare Reform." Paper presented as part of the Federation of Behavioral, Psychological, and Cognitive Sciences and The Foundation for Child Development's Science and Public Policy Briefing on Children and Welfare Reform, The Role of Marriage in Childhood Outcomes, 12 June, Washington, D.C.

Cherlin, Andrew J., and Paula Fomby. 2002. "A Closer Look at Changes in Children's Living Arrangements in Low-Income Families." *Welfare, Children, and Families: A Three-City Study.* Policy Brief 02–3.

Cloud, Dana L. 1998. "The Rhetoric of <Family Values>: Scapegoating, Utopia, and the Privatization of Social Responsibility." *Western Journal of Communication* 62, no. 4 (Fall): 387–419.

Coalition on Human Needs. 2003. "Senate Finance Committee Approves TANF Reauthorization, retrieved on-line 10/2/03 at http://www.chn/human needs/, 12 September.

Coley, Rebekah Levine, P. Lindsay Chase-Lansdale, and Christine P. Li-Grining. 2001. "Childcare in the Era of Welfare Reform: Quality, Choices, and Preferences." *Welfare, Children, and Families: A Three-City Study.* Policy Brief 01–4.

Coll, Blanche. 1971. *Perspectives in Public Welfare: A History.* Washington, D.C.: U.S. Department of Health, Education, and Welfare.

Condit, Celeste. 1990. *Decoding Abortion Rhetoric: Communicating Social Change.* Urbana: University of Illinois Press.

Congressional Record. 1909. 60th Cong., 2d sess. Vol. 43, pt. 3:2364.

Congressional Record. 1995–96. Washington, D.C.

Coontz, Stephanie. 1995. "The Way We Weren't: The Myth and Reality of the 'Traditional' Family." *National Forum* 75, no. 3 (Summer): 11–14.

———. 2000. *The Way We Never Were: American Families and the Nostalgia Trap.* New York: Basic Books.

Cooper, Cynthia A. 1996. *Violence on Television: Congressional Inquiry, Public Criticism, and Industry Response: A Policy Analysis.* New York: University Press of America.

Corbett, Thomas J. 1995. "Welfare Reform in Wisconsin: The Rhetoric and the Reality." Pp. 19–54 in *The Politics of Welfare Reform,* ed. Donald F. Norris and Lyke Thompson. Thousand Oaks, Calif.: Sage.

Cozic, Charles P., ed. 1997. *Welfare Reform.* At Issue: Opposing Viewpoint Series. San Diego: Greenhaven.

Danziger, Sheldon. 2001. "Welfare Reform Policy from Nixon to Clinton: What Role for Social Science?" Pp. 137–64 in *Social Science and Policymaking: A Search for Relevance in the Twentieth Century,* ed. David L. Featherman and Maris A. Vinovskis. Ann Arbor: University of Michigan Press.

Davies, Gareth, and Martha Derthick. 1997. "Race and Social Welfare Policy: The Social Security Act of 1935." *Political Science Quarterly* 112, no. 2: 217–35.

Davis, Kristine M. 1981. "A Description and Analysis of the Legislative Committee Hearing." *Western Journal of Communication* 45 (Winter): 88–106.

Docherty, David, David Morrison, and Michael Tracey. 1993. "Scholarship As Silence." *Journal of Communication* 43 (Summer): 230–38.

Dolgoff, Ralph, Donald Feldstein, and Louise Skolnik. 1997. *Understanding Social Welfare.* 4th ed. New York: Longman.

Dornbusch, Sanford M., and Myra H. Strober. 1988. *Feminism, Children, and the New Families.* New York: Guilford.

Duffy, Margaret. 1997. "High Stakes: A Fantasy Theme Analysis of the Selling of Riverboat Gambling in Iowa." *Southern Communication Journal* 62 (Winter): 117–32.

Ebenstein, William. 1969. *Great Political Thinkers: Plato to the Present.* 4th ed. New York: Holt, Rinehart, and Winston.

Economic Opportunity Act of 1964. U.S. Public Law 452. 88th Cong., 2d sess., 20 August 1964.

Edelman, Murray. 1977. *Political Language: Words that Succeed and Policies that Fail.* New York: Academic.

———. 1988. *Constructing the Political Spectacle.* Chicago: University of Chicago Press.

Edin, Kathryn, and Laura Lein. 1997. *Making Ends Meet: How Single Mothers Survive Welfare and Low-Wage Work.* New York: Russell Sage Foundation.

Ehrenreich, John H. 1985. *The Altruistic Imagination: A History of Social Work and Social Policy in the United States.* Ithaca, N.Y.: Cornell University Press.

Epstein, William M. 1997. *Welfare in America: How Social Science Fails the Poor.* Madison: University of Wisconsin Press.

Family Support Act of 1988. 1988. U.S. Public Law 485. 100th Cong., 2d sess., 13 Oct.

Featherman, David L., and Maris A. Vinovskis, eds. 2001. *Social Science and Policymaking: A Search for Relevance in the Twentieth Century.* Ann Arbor: University of Michigan Press.

Fein, David J., Rebecca A. London, and Jane Mauldon. 2002. *Welfare Reform and Family Formation: Assessing the Effects.* Bethesda, Md.: Abt Associates, Welfare Reform and Family Formation Project, Brief no. 1.

Fineman, Martha Albertson. 1995. *The Neutered Mother, the Sexual Family, and Other Twentieth Century Tragedies.* New York: Routledge.

———. 2000. "Dependencies." pp. 23–37 in *Women and Welfare: Theory and Practice in the United States and Europe,* ed. Nancy Hirschmann and Ulrike Liebert. New Brunswick, N.J.: Rutgers University Press.

———. 2001. "Dependencies," in *Women and Welfare: Theory and Practice in the United States and Europe,* ed. Nancy Hirschmann and Ulrike Liebert, 23–37. New Brunswick, N.J.: Rutgers University Press.

Fischer, Frank, and John Forester, eds. 1993. *The Argumentative Turn in Policy Analysis and Planning.* Durham, N.C.: Duke University Press.

Fisher, Walter R. 1984. "Narration As a Human Communication Paradigm: The Case of Public Moral Argument." *Communication Monographs* 51 (March): 1–22.

———. 1985. "The Narrative Paradigm: An Elaboration." *Communication Monographs* 52 (December): 347–67.

———. 1987. "Technical Logic, Rhetorical Logic, and Narrative Rationality." *Argumentation* 1, no. 1: 3–21.

———. 1995. "Narration, Knowledge, and the Possibility of Wisdom." pp. 169–92 in *Rethinking Knowledge: Reflections Across the Disciplines,* ed. Robert F. Goodman and Walter R. Fisher. Albany, N.Y.: State University of New York.

Fix, Michael, and Ron Haskins. 2002. "Welfare Benefits for Non-citizens." Pp. 205–12 in *Welfare Reform and Beyond: The Future of the Safety Net,* ed. Isabel V. Sawhill, et al. Washington, D.C.: The Brookings Institution.

Forester, John. 1993. "Learning from Practice Stories: The Priority of Practical Judgment." pp. 186–209 in *The Argumentative Turn in Policy Analysis and Planning,* ed. Frank Fischer and John Forester. Durham, N.C.: Duke University Press.

Foucault, Michel. 1972. *The Archaeology of Knowledge and Discourse on Language.* Translated by A. M. Sheridan Smith. New York: Pantheon.

Fragile Families Research Brief. 2000. "Dispelling Myths About Unmarried Fathers." May, no. 1.

———. 2002. "The Living Arrangements of New Unmarried Mothers." June, no. 7.

Fremstad, Shawn. 2003. "Falling TANF Caseloads Amidst Rising Politics Should Be a Cause of Concern." A Center on Budget and Policy Priorities Brief, available online at http://www.cpbb.org/, 5 September.

Gais, Thomas, and R. Kent Weaver. 2002. "State Policy Choices under Welfare Reform." In *Welfare Reform and Beyond: The Future of the Safety Net,* ed. Sawhill, Isabel V. et al. Washington, D.C.: The Brookings Institution.

Gardetto, Darlaine. 1997. "Hillary Rodham Clinton, Symbolic Gender Politics, and the *New York Times:* January–November 1992." *Political Communication* 14: 225–40.

Garvin, Therese, and John Eyles. 1997. "The Sun Safety Metanarrative: Translating Science into Public Health Discourse." *Policy Sciences* 30: 47–70.

Gilens, Martin. 1996. "'Race Coding' and White Opposition to Welfare." *American Political Science Review* 90, no. 3 (September): 593–604.

———. 1999. *Why Americans Hate Welfare.* Chicago: University of Chicago Press.

Gillespie, Ed, and Bob Schellhas, eds. 1994. *Contract With America: The Bold Plan by Rep. Newt Gingrich, Rep. Dick Armey and the House Republicans to Change the Nation.* New York: Times Books.

Goodwin, Joanne L. 1997. *Gender and the Politics of Welfare Reform: Mother's Pensions in Chicago, 1911–1929.* Chicago: University of Chicago Press.

Gordon, Linda. 1994. *Pitied but Not Entitled: Single Mothers and the History of Welfare, 1890–1935.* New York: Free Press.

Graham, George J., Jr. 1986. "Ethics, Rhetoric, and the Evaluation of Public Policy Consequences." pp. 301–14 in *Policy Analysis: Perspectives, Concepts, and Methods,* ed. William N. Dunn. Greenwich, Conn.: Jai Press.

Greenberg, Mark. 2003. "Most States Far Short of Meeting H.R. 4 Participation Requirements." A Center for Law and Social Policy Brief, 14 May, 1–10.

Greene, Beverly. 1995. African American Families. *National Forum* 75, no. 3 (Summer): 29–32.

Greenstein, Robert. 2003. Remarks presented at the forum "Ending the Safety Net as We Know It?: Assessing the New Federal Block Grant Proposals," co-sponsored by the Brookings Institution Center on Urban and Metropolitan Policy and the Community Service Society of New York. 13 June.

Gring-Pemble, Lisa M. 2001. "'Are We Going to Now Govern by Anecdote?': Rhetorical Constructions of Welfare Recipients in the Congressional Hearings, Debates, and Legislation, 1992–1996." *Quarterly Journal of Speech* (November): 341–65.

———. 2003. Legislating a "Normal, Classic Family": The Rhetorical Construction of Families in American Welfare Policy. Political Communication 20:4, p. 473–98.

Gueron, Judith M. 2001. "Welfare Reform at the State Level: The Role of Social Experiments and Demonstrations." pp. 165–86 in *Social Science and Policymaking: A Search for Relevance in the Twentieth Century,* ed. David L. Featherman and Maris A. Vinovskis. Ann Arbor: University of Michigan Press.

Gutman, Herbert G. 1976. *The Black Family in Slavery and Freedom, 1750–1925.* New York: Pantheon.

Halloran, Michael. 1978. "Doing Public Business in Public." Pp. 118–38 in *Form and Genre: Shaping Rhetorical Action,* ed. Karlyn Kohrs Campbell and Kathleen Hall Jamieson. Falls Church, Va.: Speech Communication Association.

Handler, Joel F., and Yeheskel Hasenfeld. 1991. *The Moral Construction of Poverty: Welfare Reform in America.* Newbury Park, Calif.: Sage.

Harris, John F., and John E. Yang. 1996. "Clinton to Sign Bill Overhauling Welfare." *Washington Post,* 1 August: A1+.

Hartmann, Heidi, and Hsiao-ye-Yi. 2001. "The Rhetoric and Reality of Welfare Reform." pp. 160–76 in *Women and Welfare: Theory and Practice in the United States and Europe,* eds. Nancy Hirschmann and Ulrike Liebert. New Brunswick, N.J.: Rutgers University Press.

Haskins, Ron. 2002. "Ending Entitlements Works for the Poor: A Veteran of the 1996 Welfare Battle Charts Past Successes and Future Challenges." *Philanthropy* (May/June): 15–19.

Haskins, Ron, and Wendell Primus. 2002. "Welfare Reform and Poverty." Pp. 59–70 in *Welfare Reform and Beyond: The Future of the Safety Net,* ed. Isabel V. Sawhill, et al. Washington, D.C.: The Brookings Institution.

Haveman, Robert H. 1995. "The Clinton Alternative to Welfare as We Know It.: Is It Feasible?" In *The Work Alternative: Welfare Reform and the Realities of the Job Market,* ed. Demetra Smith Nightingale and Robert H. Haveman. Washington, D.C.: The Urban Institute Press.

Heith, Diane J. 2000. "The Polls: Polling for a Defense: The White House Public Opinion Apparatus and the Clinton Impeachment." *Presidential Studies Quarterly* 30, no. 4 (December): 783–90.

Herbst, Susan. 1993. *Numbered Voices: How Opinion Polling Has Shaped American Politics.* Chicago: University of Chicago Press.

Hirschmann, Nancy, and Ulrike Liebert, eds. 2001. *Women and Welfare: Theory and Practice in the United States and Europe.* New Brunswick, N.J.: Rutgers University Press.

Hofstadter, Richard. 1965. *Social Darwinism in American Thought.* Boston: Beacon.

Hogan, J. Michael. 1997. "George Gallup and the Rhetoric of Scientific Democracy." *Communication Monographs* 64 (June): 161–79.

Hogan, J. Michael, and Leroy Dorsey. 1991. "Public Opinion and the Nuclear Freeze: The Rhetoric of Popular Sovereignty in Foreign Policy Debate." *Western Journal of Speech Communication* 55 (Fall): 319–38.

Horn, Wade F. 2002. "Family Matters: Wade Horn on Keeping People Married and Getting Fathers Involved." *Philanthropy* (March/April): 10–13.

Horn, Wade, and Isabel Sawhill. 2001. "Fathers, Marriage, and Welfare Reform." pp. 421–41 in *The New World of Welfare,* ed. Rebecca Blank and Ron Haskins. Washington, D.C.: The Brookings Institution.

Hoyt, Charles S. 1877. *Extract From the Tenth Annual Report of the State Board of Charities of the State of New York Relating to the Causes of Pauperism.* Albany, N.Y.: J. B. Parmenter.

Jacobs, Lawrence R., and Robert Shapiro. 2000. *Politicians Don't Pander: Political Manipulation and the Loss of Democratic Responsiveness.* Chicago: University of Chicago Press.

Jarchow, Courtney. 2003. *Strengthening Marriage and Two-Parent Families.* Denver, Colo.: National Conference of State Legislatures Welfare Reform, State Choices on Welfare Series.

Jernegan, Marcus Wilson. 1980. *Laboring and Dependent Classes in Colonial America, 1607–1783.* Westport, Conn.: Greenwood.

Kaplan, Thomas J. 1993. "Reading Policy Narratives: Beginnings, Middles, and Ends." pp. 167–85 in *The Argumentative Turn in Policy Analysis and Planning,* ed. Frank Fischer and John Forester. Durham, N.C.: Duke University Press.

Katz, Michael B. 1993. *Poverty and Policy in American History.* New York: Academic.

———. 1996. *In The Shadow of the Poorhouse: A Social History of Welfare in America.* 10th ed. New York: Basic Books.

Kennedy, George. 1980. *Classical Rhetoric and Its Christian and Secular Tradition from Ancient to Modern Times.* Chapel Hill: University of North Carolina Press.

Kennedy, John F. 1962. *Public Papers of the Presidents of the United States: John F. Kennedy, January 1 to December 31, 1962.* Washington, D.C.: GPO.

Kennedy, Susan Estabrook. 1979. *If All We Did Was to Weep at Home: A History of White Working-Class Women in America.* Bloomington: Indiana University Press.

Kessler-Harris, Alice. 1982. *Out to Work: A History of Wage-Earning Women in the United States.* New York: Oxford University Press.

Klumpp, James F. 1996. "Review of Narrative Policy Analysis: Theory and Practice, by Emery M. Roe." *Quarterly Journal of Speech* 82 (August): 313–314.

Koon, Richard L. 1997. *Welfare Reform: Helping the Least Fortunate become Less Dependent.* New York: Garland.

Kotlowitz, Alex. 2002. It Takes a Wedding. *New York Times,* 13 November.

Lieberman, Robert C. 1995. "Race and the Organization of Welfare Policy." Pp. 156–87 in *Classifying by Race,* ed. Paul E. Peterson. Princeton, N.J.: Princeton University Press.

Majone, Giandomenico. 1990. "Policy Analysis and Public Deliberation." Pp. 157–78 in *The Power of Public Ideas*, ed. Robert B. Reich. Cambridge, Mass.: Harvard University Press.

Matthaei, Julie A. 1982. *An Economic History of Women in America: Women's Work, the Sexual Division of Labor, and the Development of Capitalism.* New York: Schocken.

McKerrow, Raymie E. 1989. "Critical Rhetoric: Theory and Praxis." *Communication Monographs* 56 (June): 91–111.

McLanahan, Sara, and Irwin Garfinkel. 1994. "Welfare Is No Incentive." *New York Times,* 29 July: A27.

McLanahan, Sara, Irwin Garfinkel, and Ronald B. Mincy. 2002. "Fragile Families, Welfare Reform, and Marriage." pp. 152–59 in *Welfare Reform and Beyond: The Future of the Safety Net,* ed. Isabel V. Sawhill, et al. Washington, D.C.: The Brookings Institution.

Miller, M. Linda. 1999. "Public Argument and Legislative Debate in the Rhetorical Construction of Public Policy: The Case of Florida Midwifery Legislation." *Quarterly Journal of Speech* 85 (November): 361–79.

Mincy, Ronald B. Paper presented at "Living On and Off Welfare: Family Experience in Ethnographic Research." A Brookings Institution Welfare Reform and Beyond Forum. August, 2002..

Moffitt, Robert A. 2002. "From Welfare to Work: What the Evidence Shows." pp. 79–86 in *Welfare Reform and Beyond: The Future of the Safety Net,* ed. Sawhill, Isabel V. et al. Washington, D.C.: The Brookings Institution.

Monroe, Alan D. 1998. "Public Opinion and Public Policy, 1980–1993." *Public Opinion Quarterly* 62, no. 6: 6–28.

Mueller, Milton. 1995. "Why Communications Policy Is Passing 'Mass Communication' By: Political Economy as the Missing Link." *Critical Studies in Mass Communication* 12 (December): 455–72.

Murray, Charles. 1984. *Losing Ground: American Social Policy, 1950–1980.* New York: Basic Books.

———. 2001. "Family Formation." Pp. 137–68 in *The New World of Welfare,* ed. Rebecca Blank and Ron Haskins. Washington, D.C.: The Brookings Institution.

Naples, Nancy A. 1997. "The 'New Consensus' on the Gendered 'Social Contract': The 1987–1988 U.S. Congressional Hearings on Welfare Reform." *Signs* 22, no. 4: 907–45.

Neisser, Philip T., and Sanford F. Schram. 1994. "Redoubling Denial: Industrial Welfare Policy Meets Postindustrial Poverty." *Social Text* 41 (Winter): 41–60.

New York. 1914. Report of the New York State Commission on Relief for Widowed Mothers. Albany, N.Y.: J. B. Lyon Company.

The New York Times. 1996. "Text of President Clinton's Announcement on Welfare Legislation," National ed. A24. 1 August.

Nightingale, Demetra Smith, and Robert H. Haveman, eds. 1995. *The Work Alternative: Welfare Reform and the Realities of the Job Market.* Washington, D.C.: The Urban Institute Press.

Nimmo, Dan, and Hames E. Combs. 1990. *Mediated Political Realities.* New York: Longman.

Noam, Eli. 1993. "Reconnecting Communications Studies with Communications Policy." *Journal of Communication* 43 (Summer): 199–206.

Norrander, Barbara, and Clyde Wilcox. 1999. "Public Opinion and Policymaking in the States: The Case of Post-Roe Abortion Policy." *Policy Studies Journal* 27, no. 4: 707–22.

Oleszek, Walter J. 1996. *Congressional Procedures and the Policy Process.* 4th ed. Washington, D.C.: Congressional Quarterly.

Orloff, Ann Shola. 2001. "Ending the Entitlements of Poor Single Mothers: Changing Social Policies, Women's Employment, and Caregiving in the Contemporary United States." pp. 133–59 in *Women and Welfare: Theory and Practice in the United States and Europe,* eds. Nancy Hirschmann and Ulrike Liebert. New Brunswick, N.J.: Rutgers University Press.

Osborn, Michael. 1986. "Rhetorical Depiction." pp. 79–107 in *Form, Genre, and the Study of Political Rhetoric,* eds. Herbert W. Simons and Aram A. Aghazarian. Columbia: University of South Carolina Press.

Parke, Mary. 2003. *Are Married Parents Really Better for Children?: What Research Says about the Effects of Family Structure on Child Well-Being.* Washington, D.C.: Center for Law and Social Policy, Couples and Marriage Series, Brief no. 3.

———. 2003. "Marriage-related Provisions in Recent Welfare Reauthorization Proposals: A Summary." *Center for Law and Social Policy* (June): 1–7.

Patterson, James T. 1994. *America's Struggle Against Poverty, 1900–1994.* Cambridge, Mass.: Harvard University Press.

Pavetti, LaDonna. 2002. "Helping the Hard-to-Employ." Pp. 135–42 in *Welfare Reform and Beyond: The Future of the Safety Net,* eds. Isabel V. Sawhill, et al. Washington, D.C.: The Brookings Institution.

Perelman, Chaim. 1982. *The Realm of Rhetoric.* Trans. William Kuiback. Notre Dame, Ind.: University of Notre Dame Press.

Perelman, Chaim, and L. Obrechts-Tyteca. 1969. *The New Rhetoric: A Treatise on Argumentation.* Translated by John Wilkinson and Purcell Weaver. London: University of Notre Dame Press.

Personal Responsibility and Work Opportunity Reconciliation Act of 1996. U.S. Statutes at Large 110: 2105–2354.

Piven, Frances Fox. 1995. Foreword to *Words of Welfare: The Poverty of Social Science and the Social Science of Poverty,* by Sanford F. Schram. Minneapolis: University of Minnesota Press.

Piven, Frances Fox, and Richard A. Cloward. 1971. *Regulating the Poor: Functions of Public Welfare.* New York: Pantheon.

Pleck, Joseph H. 1998. "American Fathering in Historical Perspective." Pp. 351–61 in *Families in the U.S.: Kinship and Domestic Politics,* ed. Karen V. Hansen and Anita Ilta Garey. Philadelphia: Temple University Press.

Popenoe, David. 1996. *Life without Father.* New York: Free Press.

———. 2002. "New Day Dawning?: In the Struggle over the Family, Foundations Made the Difference." *Philanthropy* (March/April): 14–19.

Quadagno, Jill. 1988. "From Old-Age Assistance to Supplemental Security Income: The Political Economy of Relief in the South, 1935–1972." pp. 235–63 in *The Politics of Social Policy in the United States,* ed. Margaret Weir, Ann Shola Orloff, and Theda Skocpol. Princeton, N.J.: Princeton University Press.

Reich, Robert B., ed. 1990. *The Power of Public Ideas.* Cambridge, Mass.: Harvard University Press.

Roe, Emery M. 1994. *Narrative Policy Analysis: Theory and Practice.* Durham, N.C.: Duke University Press.

Roosevelt, Franklin D. 1938. *The Public Papers and Addresses of Franklin D. Roosevelt.* Vol. 4. New York: Random House.

Sawhill, Isabel. 2002. "What Can Be Done to Reduce Teen Pregnancy and Out-of-Wedlock Births." pp. 160–70 in *Welfare Reform and Beyond: The Future of the Safety Net.* Washington, D.C.: The Brookings Institution.

Sawhill, Isabel, R. Kent Weaver, and Andrea Kane, eds. 2002. "An Overview." pp. 3–8 in *Welfare Reform and Beyond: The Future of the Safety Net.* Washington, D.C.: The Brookings Institution.

Sawhill, Isabel, R. Kent Weaver, Ron Haskins, and Andrea Kane, eds. 2002a. "Problems and Issues for Reauthorization." pp. 20–29 in *Welfare Reform and*

Beyond: The Future of the Safety Net. Washington, D.C.: The Brookings Institution.

———. 2002b. "Results to Date." pp. 9–19 in *Welfare Reform and Beyond: The Future of the Safety Net.* Washington, D.C.: The Brookings Institution.

———. 2002c. *Welfare Reform and Beyond: The Future of the Safety Net.* Washington, D.C.: The Brookings Institution.

Schick, Allen. 1991. "Informed Legislation: Policy Research Versus Ordinary Knowledge," in William Robinson and Clay Wellborn, eds., *Knowledge, Power and Congress* (Congressional Quarterly Press): 99–119.

Schmitt, Eric. 2001. "For First Time, Nuclear Families Drop Below 25% of Households." *New York Times,* 15 May: A1.

Schram, Sanford F. 1993. "Postmodern Policy Analysis: Discourses and Identity in Welfare Policy." *Policy Sciences* 26: 249–70.

———. 1995. *Words of Welfare: The Poverty of Social Science and the Social Science of Poverty.* Minneapolis: University of Minnesota Press.

———. 2000. *After Welfare: The Culture of Postindustrial Social Policy.* New York: New York University Press.

Schram, Sanford F., and Philip T. Neisser, eds. 1997. *Tales of the State: Narrative in Contemporary U.S. Politics and Public Policy.* New York: Rowman and Littlefield.

Schram, Sanford F., Laurence Nitz, and Gary Krueger. 1997. "Welfare Migration as Policy Rumor: A Statistical Accounting." Pp. 139–49 in *Tales of the State: Narrative in Contemporary U.S. Politics and Public Policy*, ed. Sanford F. Schram and Philip T. Neisser. New York: Rowman and Littlefield.

Schuetz, Janice. 1986. "Overlays of Argument in Legislative Process." *Journal of the American Forensic Association* 22 (Spring): 223–34.

Shaw, Greg M. 2000. "The Role of Public Input in State Welfare Policymaking." *Policy Studies Journal* 28, no. 4: 707–20.

Sidel, Ruth. 1998. *Keeping Women and Children Last.* New York: Penguin.

Simons, Herbert W. 1994. "'Going Meta': Definition and Political Applications." *Quarterly Journal of Speech* 80 (November): 468–81.

Skocpol, Theda. 1995. "African Americans in U.S. Social Policy." pp. 129–55 in *Classifying by Race*, ed. Paul E. Peterson. Princeton, N.J.: Princeton University Press.

Skocpol, Theda, and William Julius Wilson. 1994. "Welfare As We Need It." *Washington Post,* 9 February: A21.

Smith, Craig Allen, and Kathy B. Smith. 1990. "The Rhetoric of Political Institutions." pp. 225–54 in *New Directions in Political Communication: A Resource Book*, eds. David L. Swanson and Dan Nimmo. Newbury Park, Calif.: Sage.

Social Security Act of 1935. U.S. Public Law 271. 74th Cong., 2d sess., H.R. 7620.

Stacey, Judith. 1994. "Scents, Scholars, and Stigma: The Revisionist Campaign for Family Values." *Social Text* 40 (Fall): 51–75.

———. 1996. *In the Name of the Family.* Boston: Beacon.

Stark, Andrew. 1992. "Political-Discourse Analysis and the Debate over Canada's Lobbying Legislation." *Canadian Journal of Political Science* 25 (September): 513–34.

Stepan, Nancy Leys. 1993. "Race and Gender: The Role of Analogy in Science," pp. 359–76 in *The "Racial" Economy of Science: Toward a Democratic Future.* Bloomington: Indiana University Press.

Stimson, James A., Michael B. MacKuen, and Robert S. Erickson. 1995. "Dynamic Representation." *American Political Science Review* 89, no. 3 (September): 543–65.

Swanson, David L., and Dan Nimmo, eds. 1990. *New Directions in Political Communication: A Resource Book.* Newbury Park, Calif.: Sage.

Tanner, Michael. 1996. *The End of Welfare: Fighting Poverty in Civil Society.* Washington, D.C.: CATO Institute.

Tentler, Leslie Woodcock. 1982. *Wage-Earning Women: Industrial Work and Family Life in the United States, 1900–1930.* New York: Oxford University Press.

Throgmorton, J. A. 1993. "Survey Research as Rhetorical Trope: Electric Power Planning Arguments in Chicago." Pp. 117–44 in *The Argumentative Turn in Policy Analysis and Planning*, ed. Frank Fischer and John Forester. Durham, N.C.: Duke University Press.

Trattner, Walter I. 1994. *From Poor Law to Welfare State: A History of Social Welfare in America.* 5th edition. New York: Free Press.

Tronto, Joan C. 2001. "Who Cares? Public and Private Caring and the Rethinking of Citizenship." pp. 65–83 in *Women and Welfare: Theory and Practice in the United States and Europe,* eds. Nancy Hirschmann and Ulrike Liebert. New Brunswick, N.J.: Rutgers University Press.

U.S. House. Committee on Agriculture. 1995. Subcommittee on Department Operations, Nutrition, and Foreign Agriculture. *Reforming the Present Welfare System.* 104th Cong., 1st sess. 7–9, 14 February.

———. Committee on Commerce. 1996. *The Personal Responsibility and Work Opportunity Act of 1996.* 104th Cong., 2nd sess. 11 June.

———. Committee on Economic and Educational Opportunities. 1995a. *Contract with America: Hearing on Welfare Reform.* 104th Cong., 1st sess. 18 January.

———. Committee on Economic and Educational Opportunities. 1995b. Subcommittee on Oversight and Investigations. *Simulation Hearing on Obtaining Federal and State Assistance.* 104th Cong., 1st sess. 27 March.

———. Committee on Education and Labor. 1994a. *Hearing on H.R. 4605, Work and Responsibility Act of 1994.* 103rd Cong., 2nd sess. 2 August.

———. Committee on Education and Labor. 1994b. Subcommittee on Human Resources. *Hearing Regarding the Impact of Welfare Reform on Child Care Providers and the Working Poor.* 103rd Cong., 2nd sess. 20 September.

———. Committee on Education and Labor. 1994c. Subcommittee on Human Resources. *Field Hearing on Welfare Reform.* 103rd Cong., 2nd sess. 28 October.

———. Committee on Government Operations. 1994. Subcommittee on Human Resources and Intergovernmental Relations. *Ending Welfare as We Know It: Progress or Paralysis?* 103rd Cong., 2nd sess. 10 March.

———. Committee on Government Reform and Oversight. 1996. Subcommittee on Human Resources and Intergovernmental Relations. *Preventing Teen Pregnancy: Coordinating Community Efforts.* 104th Cong., 2nd sess. 30 April.

————. Committee on Ways and Means. 1962. *Public Welfare Amendments of 1962: Hearing on H.R. 10032*. 87th Cong., 2nd sess. 7, 9, and 13 February.

————. Committee on Ways and Means. 1992. Subcommittee on Human Resources. *Moving Ahead: How America Can Reduce Poverty through Work*. Report prepared by Fred Grandy, Nancy L. Johnson, and E. Clay Shaw. 1–59.

————. Committee on Ways and Means. 1993a. Subcommittee on Human Resources. *Trends in Spending and Caseloads for AFDC and Related Programs*. 103rd Cong., 1st sess. 11 March.

————. Committee on Ways and Means. 1993b. Subcommittee on Human Resources. *Impact of Immigration on Welfare Programs*. 103rd Cong., 1st sess. 15 November.

————. Committee on Ways and Means. 1993c. Subcommittee on Select Revenue Measures and the Subcommittee on Human Resources. *Selected Aspects of Welfare Reform*. 103rd Cong., 1st sess. 30 March.

————. Committee on Ways and Means. 1994. *1994 Green Book*. Washington, D.C.: GPO.

————. Committee on Ways and Means. 1994a. Subcommittee on Human Resources. *Welfare Reform Proposals, Including H.R. 4605, The Work and Responsibility Act of 1994, Part 1*. 103rd Cong., 2nd sess. 14, 26–28 July.

————. Committee on Ways and Means. 1994b. Subcommittee on Human Resources. *Welfare Reform Proposals, Including H.R. 4605, The Work and Responsibility Act of 1994, Part 2*. 103rd Cong., 2nd sess. 29 July, 9, 16 August.

————. Committee on Ways and Means. 1995a. *Contract with America: Overview*. 104th Cong., 1st sess. 5, 10–12 January.

————. Committee on Ways and Means. 1995b. *Contract with America: Welfare Reform, Part 1*. 104th Cong., 1st sess. 13, 20, 23, 27, 30 January.

————. Committee on Ways and Means. 1995c. *Contract with America: Welfare Reform, Part 2*. 104th Cong., 1st sess. 2 February.

————. Committee on Ways and Means. 1995d. Subcommittee on Human Resources. *Child Support Provisions Included in Personal Responsibility Act as Part of the CWA*. 104th Cong., 1st sess. 6 February.

————. Committee on Ways and Means. 1995e. Subcommittee on Human Resources. *Child Support Enforcement and Supplement Security Income*. 104th Cong., 1st sess. 13 June.

————. Committee on Ways and Means. 1995f. Subcommittee on Human Resources. *Welfare Reform Success Stories*. 104th Cong., 1st sess. 6 December.

————. Committee on Ways and Means. 1995g. Subcommittee on Human Resources, Committee on Economic and Educational Opportunities, Subcommittee on Early Childhood, Youth, and Families. *Child Care and Child Welfare*. 104th Cong., 1st. sess. 3 February.

————. Committee on Ways and Means. 1996a. Subcommittee on Human Resources. *National Governors' Association Welfare Reform Proposal*. 104th Cong., 2nd sess. 20 February.

————. Committee on Ways and Means. 1996b. Subcommittee on Human Resources. *Causes of Poverty with a Focus on Out-of-Wedlock Births*. 104th Cong., 2nd sess. 12 March.

———. Committee on Ways and Means. 1996c. Subcommittee on Human Resources. *Welfare Reform.* 104th Cong., 2nd sess. 22, 23 May.

———. Committee on Ways and Means. 2000. *2000 Green Book.* Washington, D.C.: GPO.

———. Committee on Ways and Means. 2002. *Personal Responsibility, Work, and Family Promotion Act.* 107th Cong., 2d sess., H.R. 4737. 16 May.

———. Committee on Ways and Means. 2003. *Personal Responsibility, Work, and Family Promotion Act of 2003.* 108th Cong., 1st sess., H.R. 4. 13 February.

———. Select Committee on Hunger. 1992a. *Beyond Public Assistance: Where Do We Go from Here?* 102nd Cong., 2nd sess. 25 March.

———. Select Committee on Hunger. 1992b. *Rethinking Poverty Policy.* 102nd Cong., 2nd sess. 2 October.

———. Select Committee on Hunger, Domestic Task Force. 1992a. *Federal Policy Perspectives on Welfare Reform: Rhetoric, Reality, and Opportunities.* 102nd Cong., 2nd sess. 9 April.

———. Select Committee on Hunger, Domestic Task Force. 1992b. *State and Local Perspectives on Welfare Reform Rhetoric, Reality, and Opportunities.* 102nd Cong., 2nd sess. 4 June.

U.S. Senate. Committee on Agriculture, Nutrition, and Forestry. 1994. *Fraud in Federal Nutrition Programs.* 103rd Cong., 2nd sess. 2 February.

———. Committee on Appropriations. 1994a. Subcommittee on Labor, Health and Human Services, and Education, and Related Agencies. *Welfare Reform: Special Hearing.* 103rd Cong., 2nd sess. 11 April.

———. Committee on Appropriations. 1994b. Subcommittee on Labor, Health and Human Services, and Education, and Related Agencies. *Welfare Reform: Special Hearing.* 103rd Cong., 2nd sess. 9 December.

———. Committee on Finance. 1992. Subcommittee on Social Security and Family Policy. *Administration's Welfare Reform Proposal.* 102nd Cong., 2nd sess. 4 August.

———. Committee on Finance. 1994a. *Work and Responsibility Act of 1994.* 103rd Cong., 2nd sess. 13 July.

———. Committee on Finance. 1994b. Subcommittee on Social Security and Family Policy. *Welfare Reform.* 103rd Cong., 2nd sess. 18 January, 25 February.

———. Committee on Finance. 1995a. *States' Perspective on Welfare Reform.* 104th Cong., 1st. sess. 8 March.

———. Committee on Finance. 1995b. *Broad Policy Goals of Welfare Reform.* 104th Cong., 1st sess. 9 March.

———. Committee on Finance. 1995c. *Administration's Views on Welfare Reform.* 104th Cong., 1st sess. 10 March.

———. Committee on Finance. 1995d. *Teen Parents and Welfare Reform.* 104th Cong., 1st. sess. 14 March.

———. Committee on Finance. 1995e. *Welfare to Work.* 104th Cong., 1st. sess. 20 March.

———. Committee on Finance. 1995f. *Child Support Enforcement.* 104th Cong., 1st sess. 28 March.

———. Committee on Finance. 1995g. *Welfare Reform: Views of Interested Organizations.* 104th Cong., 1st sess. 29 March.

———. Committee on Finance. 1995h. *Child Welfare Programs*. 104th Cong., 1st sess. 26 April.

———. Committee on Finance. 1995i. *Welfare Reform: Wrap-Up*. 104th Cong., 1st sess. 27 April.

———. Committee on Finance. 1996a. *Governors' Proposals on Welfare and Medicaid*. 104th Cong., 2nd sess. 22, 28, 29 February.

———. Committee on Finance. 1996b. *Welfare and Medicaid Reform*. 104th Cong., 2nd sess. 13, 19 June.

———. Committee on Governmental Affairs. 1995. *Reinventing Government*. 104th Cong., 1st sess. 25 January, 2 February.

———. Committee on Labor and Human Resources. 1995a. *Impact of Welfare Reform on Children and Their Families*. 104th Cong., 1st sess. 28 February, 1 March.

———. Committee on Labor and Human Resources. 1995b. Subcommittee on Children and Families. *Child Care and Development Block Grant: How Is It Working?* 104th Cong., 1st sess. 16 February.

Vobejda, Barbara. 1996. "Clinton Signs Welfare Bill Amid Division." *Washington Post*, 23 August: A1+.

Waller, Margy. 2003a. Remarks made at the Amreican Public Human Services Association Summer Meeting, 21 July.

Waller, Margy. 2003b. Remarks made at a Brookings Institution Welfare Reform and Beyond Forum "Ending the Safety Net as We Know It?: Assessing the New Federal Block Grant Proposals," co-sponsored by the Brookings Institution Center on Urban and Metropolitan Policy and the Community Service Society of New York, 13 June.

Wander, Philip. 1984. "The Third Persona: An Ideological Turn in Rhetorical Theory." *Central States Speech Journal* 35 (Winter): 197–216.

Weaver, R. Kent. 2000. *Ending Welfare As We Know It*. Washington, D.C.: The Brookings Institution.

Weaver, R. Kent, Robert Y. Shapiro, and Lawrence R. Jacobs. 1995. "The Polls—Trends: Welfare." *Public Opinion Quarterly* 59 (Winter): 606–27.

Weiss, Jessica. 2000. *To Have and to Hold: Marriage, the Baby Boom, and Social Change*. Chicago: University of Chicago Press.

White House Working Group on the Family. 2 December 1986. *The Family: Preserving America's Future*. Washington, D.C.: White House Working Group on the Family.

White, Louise. 1994. "Policy Analysis as Discourse." *Journal of Policy Analysis and Management* 13 (Summer): 506–25.

Wilcox, Brian. 2002. "Promoting Marriage in Welfare Reform: What's the Evidence Supporting These Efforts?" Paper presented as part of the Federation of Behavioral, Psychological and Cognitive Sciences and The Foundation for Child Development's Science and Public Policy Briefing on Children and Welfare Reform, The Role of Marriage in Childhood Outcomes, 12 June, Washington, D.C.

Williams, Bruce A., and Albert R. Matheny. 1995. *Democracy, Dialogue, and Environmental Disputes: The Contested Languages of Social Regulations*. New Haven, Conn.: Yale University Press.

Wilson, James Julius. 1987. *The Truly Disadvantaged: The Inner City, The Underclass, and Public Policy.* Chicago: University of Chicago Press.

Wilson, William Julius. 1996. *When Work Disappears: The World of the New Urban Poor.* New York: Vintage.

Wiseman, Michael. 2002. "Food Stamps and Welfare Reform." pp. 173–80 in *Welfare Reform and Beyond: The Future of the Safety Net*, ed. Isabel V. Sawhill, et al. Washington, D.C.: Brookings Institution.

Younow, Dvora. 1993. "The Communication of Policy Meanings: Implementation as Interpretation and Text." *Policy Sciences* 26: 41–61.

Zarefsky, David. 1986. *President Johnson's War on Poverty: Rhetoric and History.* Tuscaloosa: University of Alabama Press.

Index

About the Author

LISA M. GRING-PEMBLE is Assistant Professor of Rhetoric at George Mason University.